GLOBAL STRATEGY

Global Strategy

Air Vice-Marshal
E. J. KINGSTON-McCLOUGHRY
C.B., C.B.E., D.S.O., D.F.C.

Jonathan Cape
THIRTY BEDFORD SQUARE · LONDON

FIRST PUBLISHED 1957

PRINTED IN GREAT BRITAIN IN THE CITY OF OXFORD
AT THE ALDEN PRESS
BOUND BY A. W. BAIN & CO. LTD., LONDON

Contents

I dedicate this book to three very dear friends of
the rising generation — Patricia, Alan and Valerie —
in the hope that an understanding of war may bring
us peace, and that their lives may be less troubled
than our own

Preface

I N 1949 when my book, *War in Three Dimensions*, was published I had completed an attempt at the study of the principles of strategy in modern war. This resulted from an appreciation of the development of air power and its effects during two World Wars. But reflection since has suggested that I only touched upon the fringe of an abstruse though highly important subject. This impression was confirmed by a study of the ramifications of Political Direction and High Command, subsequently published in 1955 under the title of *The Direction of War*. By adopting an inter-Service view of the workings of High Command I was led to an inter-Service view of strategy as such. So far as I am aware no book has been attempted from an inter-Service viewpoint on the problems of strategy in general.

The self-doubts and qualifications that arise in the mind of a writer in his preface are innumerable; the temptation is to stand at all the points of the argument and try to foresee and anticipate every possible consequence. That, however, is scarcely possible with a subject so wide in scope. Suffice it to say that the case for a new view of strategy is stated as simply as possible and illustrated from the facts of history. Of necessity, this work is only a beginning in inter-Service strategy, and while it is in no wise intended to be dogmatic, it is born of a long study of the problems of strategy at home and abroad. It is, of course, based on my interpretation of history and is admittedly an individual view of more recent events: this is my own view of strategy and must in no way be regarded as the official one.

Throughout this study the Soviet bloc has been posited, for reasons which will be evident, as the power most likely to disrupt world peace. There are only a few major powers who could contemplate becoming involved, in isolation, in a large scale conflict. France and Western Germany have been posited as essential countries in NATO, and it should be noted that if, for example, France or Western Germany were to withdraw from NATO this would disrupt the whole present fabric of the defences of the free nations in Western Europe. The countries of North America, the British Commonwealth and the other free countries would then have to do some radical rethinking and readjust their whole concept of strategy in the preservation of world peace.

The pattern is at present clear, if not altogether clear-cut, of the alignment of Soviet Russia and Communist China and certain states of Eastern Europe against the Western powers in Europe allied with the United States. It is possibly an over-simplification to say that it is the Communist against the non-Communist half of the world when communism itself may be more properly regarded as a facet of the threat. Throughout the world there is such a variety of shades of allegiance as well as many countries uncommitted either to Western or Soviet values. The enemy here considered is not simply embodied in an ideological threat but rather it is the State called Russia: that is, Russia as a power: a Russia expanding and desiring to extend her sphere of influence: a state posing as the symbol of all manner of ideals. It is Russia as a fighting force, an organized community, and a power or state in the most autocratic and absolute sense with which we are concerned.

It would be irrational not to allow Russia's leaders the best of motives even when they clash with our own interests, always remembering that they *are* Russian motives. But we must watch that they do not clash too much or too often and to our disadvantage. It is for these reasons that this book has been written in its present shape and has been related to the political, diplomatic and military assessment of today.

As time passes, political events may so change strategic alignments in the world that Russia is no longer the chief danger to world peace and some other power may rise to an eminence which threatens our security. Nevertheless, the factors identified in this book are still valid and the resilience and adaptability advocated can scarcely be gainsaid.

It should be remembered that the continuous changing of events and human destinies has never been so rapid as in the present era. A hundred years ago the wheel of events turned more slowly so that its chief features could be remarked and noted. Today, however, is not the easiest time to write about global strategy. While the pace of life today is more rapid the prizes it offers to man are often very great. These are offset by the horrific possibilities to mankind of nuclear weapons and of nuclear power. The changing background of the political scene, such as, for instance, the emergence of China as the ultimate balance to Soviet power, might well prove any present day writer hopelessly wrong in his assessment. It is not always easy to see the ultimate outcome of political shiftings and movements though their aim is evident. The outcome of the Bagdad Pact, for example, is itself problematical. Whether it will in fact develop into a useful peacetime organization to counter Soviet penetration in the Middle East, or whether it might become an adjunct to NATO, perhaps in the form of a 'METO', for the defence of the Middle East, remains to be seen.

At first glance an attempt to grasp the stupendous ebb and flow of events may seem as futile as trying to make a rope of sand. One soon finds, however, that there are trends and tendencies which yield their rewards, and that there are foundations on which may be built a structure capable of ensuring that the policy and strategy of Russia will not ultimately dominate the world.

Whatever the political changes which may occur in the next generation there remain the basic strategic necessities. New states may come into being and others vanish but geography will remain fundamentally unaltered. Time and space will continue to dominate basic strategic ideas and the medium and the instruments evolved to encompass them whether land, sea or air. That is why geographical zones are so broadly dealt with in this book, and what is true of geography is also true of history, that though emphasis may change, history is the indispensable link in the strategic pattern.

If victory had gone to the Germans in either of the two great wars of our own time how different might have been the strategical problems in the world today. Had Germany won the First World War, Britain and the Commonwealth would now be submerged. On the other hand, it is likely that Europe would then have become the most powerful military and economic unit in the world with the current integration problems of the Western European countries completely, though brutally, resolved. Europe would then have controlled great overseas resources of raw materials as well as strategic bases. Under these conditions, Western Europe, which at present is no more than a second class and not very co-ordinated power in world influence, could certainly have become a world giant. In whatever way the power and might of the United States may have developed, the present

Soviet Russian threat to world peace would not have matured as it has done.

Had Hitler won the Second World War, the Russian menace would most certainly never have arisen and the struggle for world economic domination would have been between Europe, with Africa and possibly Asia under her domination, against the countries of North America. Thus, we can see clearly how the outcome of war and changes in political alignment and policy can affect the strategic problems of the future.

In either of the above cases the implied freedoms of democracy, with which we are so much concerned, would be non-existent, and the steam-roller of autocracy would have ironed out every national difference in Europe. Not an attractive ideal of unity. Indeed, Europe today prefers to negotiate every step and countries seem determined to retain their national sovereignties and liberties. Here the chief problem of our age is reflected. It is whether the NATO countries and the United States can now decide voluntarily to give up something of that national interest and national sovereignty which they would resist in the face of force.

The strategical implications of the world situation today are outlined in Part One of this work, but the problem of squaring up to the possibilities raises in turn a variety of complications. The task of elucidating these and the solutions thereto is essayed in Part Two.

The action we must take to solve our strategical difficulties, which are of an ever-increasing complexity, is first and foremost an Allied responsibility. Of that there can be little doubt. Hesitation among the Great Powers to deal promptly and adequately with the immediate problems of Allied combined strategy in all spheres may lead to something worse than vacillation on the part of lesser powers who are at present friendly to our aims and purposes. Unfriendly powers on the other hand could not fail to be impressed by resolute action.

Strategy has evolved through the ages from the aims and means of the most primitive of armed forces, through the developed strategies of specifically armed services, to the often hastily improvised combined strategies of allied nations. Improvisation may occasionally yield the pleasant surprise of success but all too often it has led to repeated reverses and a very great waste of men and resources. Thus in an age which has as its chief military feature Allied nations seeking to protect themselves from or to overthrow other combinations of powers, the first essential is to discover a basis on which Allied combined strategy may function not only smoothly but effectively, and, most importantly, may function in any area of the globe. To secure the Allied concept will not mean that our troubles are over but they will be considerably lessened. Service strategies instead of dominating National strategy will be controlled by it and will make for a closer unity of aim and function. This approach to strategy in the free world, that is resolving the most important concepts first instead of endeavouring to fuse a variety of less important and sometimes inimical strategical concepts into one workable whole, will make for an all-important economy, not only of effort, but of resources. This is a consideration which must weigh heavily with nations already impoverished by two world wars.

Having established the principle, it is necessary to go a step further and examine the various strategies and consider how they will be affected in terms of contemporary and foreseeable future weapons and present-day tasks. A change of emphasis will be noticeable in the second part of this work. In Part One the strategies of the past by example and precept point the way to a solution of our strategical problems *in the abstract*. In Part Two a more concrete attempt is made to visualize the principle outlined as a fact.

No military subject could deserve a more genuinely international approach than Global Strategy. Nevertheless, of necessity, this work is limited to the national approach of a British officer who believes that one of the greatest factors which might affect Allied strategy is the future position of Great Britain herself. Some defeatists claim that Great Britain is fast losing her power and possessions. Certainly the vastly disproportionate efforts given in the two World Wars have most grievously impaired the economic prosperity of Great Britain. We have already given up a number of valuable overseas possessions in the Middle and Far East and may have to withdraw still further. Today we are carrying alone too great a financial burden in the defence of the Commonwealth and Allied overseas regions.

It would seem that the British Commonwealth as a whole must take a much more equal share in contributing to global strategy; and it is likely that Great Britain will find her true place, in making her very valuable contribution in Allied strategy, as an Allied member rather than as an individual country.

In war there are already too many features which are entirely fortuitous and anything which can be done to minimize the chance and mischance of war should be undertaken. How much we, as a nation, have left to chance is amply illustrated in the lessons of history, and in the inspired conviction, though an irrational one, that we can always win the last battle. This attitude may not be the only factor which has contributed to our present difficulties but it is certainly one of them: it, too, must undergo a change, since the first battle of a new war may also be the last one.

I would like to acknowledge my indebtedness to those individuals whose comments and criticisms as well as encouragement have helped to make this book possible. In particular, I am grateful to Professor N. H. Gibbs, M.A., D.PHIL., Chichele Professor of the History of War, Oxford. Also to my former colleague, Air Marshal Sir Philip Wigglesworth, K.B.E., C.B., D.S.C., and to Brigadier J. Stephenson, O.B.E., who were both kind enough to read through my draft MS. I also gratefully acknowledge the help of Mr. J. C. Nerney, I.S.O., of the Historical Branch, Air Ministry.

I should like to take this opportunity of acknowledging my indebtedness to Professor Sir Solly Zuckerman, C.B., F.R.S. Throughout an important period of the Second World War we were in constant touch with each other and the many discussions we had on strategy in general served to broaden my view and enabled me to appreciate the relationship and application of air strategy together with those of the land and sea forces. But needless to say he is not committed to any views which I state in this book, which are entirely my own.

I have also to thank Mr. Morley Jamieson for his great help in preparing the MS. and in reading the proofs. Further, I am also much indebted to my secretary, Mrs. V. Kellas, who undertook the typing, some of it trying and arduous.

Fordel Cottage,   E. J. K.-McC.
  Glenfarg.
July 1st, 1956.

PART ONE

CHAPTER I

The Evolution of War

I

N o two wars take the same form. Another war may be something quite different from any which mankind has so far experienced. The form, as well as the reasons and aims involved, may have altered from those which were previously accepted, demanding new concepts of strategy. War is therefore less easy to define than one may at first suppose. The classical definition that war is armed conflict between nations concerned to impose their *will* on each other, a conflict in which energies of all kinds are mobilized and geared to this dominant purpose, is scarcely adequate for modern conditions. The nature of war itself has developed into several new categories and the once precise boundaries between war and peace are now less immediately discernible.

In this work, the term 'total' war denotes a conflict without limit in its nature, geography or the weapons used. This category includes war where the weapons of mass destruction — atomic, hydrogen, biological and chemical — are used against the enemy including the home front. A war in which these weapons were used would necessarily be a global war.

'Limited' war denotes armed conflict of every kind which does not involve the use of the modern weapons of mass destruction against the home front. Here, while the weapons are restricted, the geography is not limited. This category covers armed conflict such as the Second World War. In future, however, it may also include the tactical use of atomic warfare. The tactical use of atomic weapons would, of course, result inevitably in many cases bordering on strategical employment and whether or not hostilities under these conditions would remain limited or develop into total war, would depend on what each of the belligerents thought would benefit them in particular.

'Local' war applies to hostilities limited in both weapons and geographic extent: the Korean campaign is typical. Though there was a distinct danger that this outbreak in Korea might have developed into limited or even total war, it remained local in which the belligerents restricted operations to the so-called conventional weapons and to the area in Korea itself and the surrounding seas. It is conceivable that today, the tactical use of atomic weapons would be used in this category of war.

The fourth category is 'cold' war in which organized armed forces (save in the narrow sense) do not oppose each other, the military role being primarily concerned in supporting police and security forces or opposing subversive action. Rather than military action, cold war seeks to upset the balance of power or the overthrow of authority by infiltration, subversion and economic and technical penetration; indeed, all action short of war. Such conflicts can be general and cover a world-wide range as in the post-war Soviet communist activities, though efforts are often concentrated in particular areas such as for example in Malaya, Indo-China and the troubles in Cyprus.

Such definitions of the current categories of war, while they are most certainly accurate, introduce an air of simplicity into a discussion of war. They suggest the impression that we have reached the end of discussion when we have in fact only made a beginning. The complexity of war in any form belies simplicity.

In war everything is heightened and intensified: the emotions, energies and morale of a people are deeply affected and those physical factors, such as geography, economics, raw materials, armament, food and numerous lesser everyday things, which we take for granted, and which ordinarily have no profound meaning for us, suddenly take on added and important significance when seen in the light of war. They are part of the problems of strategy. Such rapid changes in strategic significance are easily exemplified in the events of 1914 when many people, perhaps even more than in 1939, were reluctant to consider strategically what lay before them.

In varying degrees, nations are in continual diplomatic, financial, economic and ideological competition with each other. These relations vary constantly from harmony and partnership, through differences and competition, strained relations and rivalry, deterrent and retaliatory actions to hostile acts, and then war. Inevitably, these differing relations result in the grouping of nations into allied, neutral and hostile camps. War, in the sense and meaning it has in the general imagination, has also changed in recent times, because now, total war at least threatens to defeat its own purpose. While it was once a national instrument of policy used to achieve national purpose or more power, total war may now well become an instrument of annihilation possibly to all belligerent nations and to civilization itself. Thus it could well be that cold, local and limited war will continue and that nations will make hazardous gambles round the forms of aggression which come under these terms; and that so long as aggressor countries are opposed by adequate deterrent forces at adequate readiness, they will not dare precipitate war involving the ultimate sanction. We cannot, however, assume this and must study and plan for the whole range of the various categories of war.

II

The functions of our armed forces are related to the political aim. Up to the Second World War, the traditional *political* aim was to secure our interests with the minimum of peacetime forces supported by alliances. We depended on those minimum forces being able to sustain the brunt of attack until they could be relieved, first by mobilization, and then by harnessing all our national resources to the war effort as swiftly as possible. Hitherto our overall peacetime *military* role was to provide at minimum cost a maximum deterrent to any aggressor and a maximum bargaining power for negotiations with our Allies. On this basis we maintained forces within each Service which could fulfil the peacetime chores and also provide adequate nucleus forces which could be readily expanded in war to embody our utmost war effort.

Our armed forces fulfilled their aims by roles which were partly inherent in the nature of each Service and partly traditional. For example, originally we had a single Service in the form of an army for all military purposes. Events and developments resulted in this single Service being divided into two: the navy to control the seas and the army to control land operations. Further developments resulted in the formation of the air force as a third service to control air operations.

Functionally the primary roles of the three services are clear, but numerous secondary roles have been added to complicate matters. For example, among numerous others, the navy had a secondary role in shore bombardment, the army in anti-aircraft defence, and the air force in giving support to the navy and the army. Also the roles of the three Services have become increasingly complicated in terms of cold war, local war, limited war and total war, as outlined above.

The structures of our three armed Services were shaped as a result of the respective primary and secondary roles assigned to them, though they were of course also greatly affected by tradition, sentiment and numerous sectional influences and interests. For example, a powerful navy was not only the primary force which controlled the seas and enabled our merchant marine to bring us great profits and prosperity, but it also enabled us to defeat great continental armies without undue commitments. The deterrent value of a battleship in foreign harbours has been proved repeatedly in the past; more than once our fleet has maintained us in security until our national potential could be developed and the free movement and access of our world trade and commerce has been due largely to the vigilance of the navy. The army's role was territorial in the broad sense: to invade, overrun and hold enemy territory: to fight staged battles and maintain the advantage by policing and patrol. The panorama of pitched battles has sustained the role of the army in the public imagination. Thus our two older Services have built up great inheritances and histories. Air power has not yet had time to create corresponding traditions and was first used to support the navy and army in their traditional roles, but subsequently it has gradually acquired a specific role of striking directly at the home front and war potential of the enemy, and conversely to defend our own country. Today these are the primary roles of air forces.

III

In war, the non-aggressor is invariably at a disadvantage inasmuch as his strategy is more difficult to formulate in positive terms. He can only guess at the strategy of the aggressor, whereas the aggressor at least knows the first move. A consideration of the evolution of war will teach us few lessons unless we consider the development of strategy with this proviso in mind: *that while war and strategy have a parallel development such development is not simultaneous*: a fact amply confirmed in recent years.

For over a hundred years the theory of strategy had taught that the aim in war was to break the *will* of the enemy to prosecute hostilities and that the method of achieving this aim was to disorganize his armed forces by battle. It is this theory which I now propose to examine in its application to present and future conditions.

The basis of a state's *will* to prosecute war varies according to the nature of the state. In elementary forms the *will* has often been vested exclusively in the person of the sovereign, so that his elimination, or the frustration of his purpose, was sufficient to destroy it. This is seen in the extreme case where the death or flight of the monarch, present on the battlefield in person and taking part in the fighting, has often decided the contest, because little or no part of the *will* to war of opposing states resided in the armies or nations. This incarnation of the *will* to war in a single person is symbolized by the primitive institution of deciding wars or disputes vicariously through champions, like David and Goliath in the Old Testament.

Where armies are mercenary, and to a lesser degree where they are professional, the *will* to war of belligerent states is still concentrated in a very few persons, while the mass of the populations passively accept decisions reached on the battlefield. However, where citizen or national armies, imbued with a patriotic spirit, are fighting for a national cause rather than for pay and employment, they themselves share in the *will* to war, which in these cases is broadly based upon the sentiment of the nation at large. This is exemplified in the wars of the democratic city-states of ancient Greece, where the citizen body which declared wars and governed their course was identical with the army which prosecuted them. The more nearly the forces necessary to conduct a war are identical with the state itself, the more widely diffused is the *will* to war.

The *will* to war of a state may not only be more or less widely diffused. It may also vary in its strength and intensity according to the value attached to the prizes at stake. The annexation of a province or the capture of a stronghold will only justify the expenditure of a proportionate quantity of effort and resources. As soon as the prospect of achieving the aim with that expenditure has disappeared, the *will* to war disappears also, unless the aim has by then been replaced by a different one, such as the salving of national pride, which may be worth a higher, but still not unlimited, price. Thus, the more essential appears the aim at stake to the existence of the state the stronger becomes the *will* to war. Where the aim of the war is of supreme importance, as when a state is fighting to save itself from virtual elimination by defeat, meaning the loss of national identity and a long future of suffering for all citizens, then the expenditure of effort and resources which appears worth while is limited only by their physical availability.

It may be observed that while the aims which promote the outbreak of war are often positive and clearly defined on one side, if not on both, the aims which maintain hostilities, once declared, are apt on both sides to become nebulous. Thus the conquest or annexation of a specific territory may be the pretext to start a war, but the war may continue long after the original cause has been forgotten, by both sides being anxious, even to fanaticism, to avoid failure or defeat. Nations are even capable of redoubling their efforts when they have forgotten their original purpose.

The political and economic changes of recent centuries in the nations of the West have tended to transfer power from ruling individuals or classes to the whole body of the nations, and with the transference of political power the *will* to war also passed from individuals or groups to the masses. Parallel with this change the aims in making war have changed. Wars are no longer fought merely for dynastic change or territorial acquisition — aims which normally would not evoke the *will* of the masses. Instead of these simple aims, more complex ones which affect every person in the country are accepted as the cause of modern wars.

An important stage in this process of change was the emergence in modern Europe of great citizen or conscript armies, which replaced the smaller professional or mercenary armies of the past, concurrently with the rise of a militant political creed which sought to revolutionize the constitutions and the way of life of Western European nations. The contemplation of the French Revolutionary and Napoleonic wars which followed inspired Clausewitz to write his great philosophic inquiry into the nature of war and the principles of strategy. Yet ironically enough, the gradual disappearance of the conditions of battle which his theory assumed was heralded by these very events themselves.

The classical doctrine of war, that the aim is to break the *will* of the enemy by the disorganization of his armed forces in battle, rested on the following reasoning. The *will* to war existed in the minds of certain individuals and in a certain intensity. By acting, therefore, upon that *will*, hostilities could be brought to an end long before the physical capacity to make war was exhausted. The method of acting on that *will* was to render useless the instrument on which it relied. The aim could consequently be achieved most easily, speedily and economically by disorganizing the armed forces without any further destruction of men or material beyond what was necessary to achieve that end.

By the beginning of the nineteenth century, however, the armed forces were beginning to lose their separateness from the rest of the nation as the exclusive and self-sufficient instrument for waging war. At the same time, with the deepening or broadening of the *will* to war and widening of the scope of war aims, the difficulty of acting upon that *will* had greatly increased. This is not to say that the principles of classical strategy ceased to be valid at any time in the nineteenth century. Neither the economic and scientific advances nor the political changes of the hundred years after the battle of Waterloo rendered the disorganization by battle of the enemy's forces any less the essential process of warfare than it had been before.

It is true that the functioning of armies and the conduct of war had come to depend not merely upon the wealth but also upon the physical resources and industrial capacity of a belligerent. Thus the home front — the mines, the factories, the transport system, the workers and the civil population themselves — equalled the battle front in importance, because without the support of the home front the battle front could no longer be maintained for any appreciable time. The home front, however, continued to be defended by the deployment of the armed forces on land and sea. Apart from naval blockade, an enemy could act upon the home front only, as in the past, by destroying or routing its armed forces.

It is also true that democratic movements and new methods of political organization and propaganda enabled whole populations to be permeated by the *will* to war to a degree previously unknown, so that the *will* might actually outlive the physical ability to wage it. No fresh methods of acting upon that *will* disclosed themselves, and such changes by themselves were unable to bring about any revolution in strategy. The trends which have been described only produced a practical revolution in the principles and conduct of warfare during the last generation, when far-reaching changes in the weapons with which war was fought and the means of mass production to provide them, combined with the public consciousness, brought a parallel development in strategy.

IV

The science and art of war does not have an easy, or for that matter, a predictable continuity. Throughout history there have been numerous radical breaks with traditional concepts of war as exemplified in the invention of gunpowder, iron and steam ships, breech-loading weapons, machine guns, mines and submarines, tanks, aircraft and electronics. These and other inventions have all had a profound effect, strategically and tactically, in war and on armed forces, always to the advantage of the nation which first appreciated and implemented the new invention. Sometimes the invention facilitated the offensive aspect of war and sometimes the defensive. Seldom, however, does a new invention revolutionize overnight the methods of war, because there is an inherent and national reluctance on the part of the military authorities to discard old and proved methods and weapons for new and untried ones, especially in time of peace.

Today, further new weapons are once more changing our accepted ideas of war in a manner more far-reaching than ever. Perhaps it is natural that succeeding generations view their own inventions as the most epoch-making, but it does seem that the advent of nuclear weapons will bring about changes in the nature and conduct of war, and in the structure of our three Services, greater than ever before. It is important therefore that we have the best possible information and advice on these changes because the most portentous feature is that in this era of new weapons of mass destruction there will be no time to learn from experience in battle.

The full measure of the changes which we must envisage may be realized when it is remembered that the estimated existing peacetime stock of nuclear weapons possessed by the United States has a several times greater destructive power than the total of explosive weapons used in war from the time of their discovery. The discharge of such vast power concentrated within the first few days of war would certainly have unthought of results. Of even greater cataclysmic potency, the hydrogen weapon could bring devastation to humanity and in theory at least could provide a single unit capable of fracturing the earth itself. There is a further weapon development resulting from the urge for increased performance of offensive weapons of which the V1s and V2s of the Second World War were a very primitive form. Before long these future pilotless bombers and ballistic rockets will become an important complement to bombers and eventually they may well become the predominant weapon in an air striking force. For example, the United States already have an inter-continental ballistic rocket under development with a nuclear head containing more destructive power than was dropped by all air forces in the Second World War. Incorporated into the armoury of the three fighting services the new nuclear weapons must increase enormously the power of the offensive. In the hands of enemies prepared to use them, these weapons could, if not effectively countered, wreck the whole of our present civilization within the first few weeks of war. The offensive will enjoy an even further advantage in that motive nuclear power promises radical increases in the offensive potential of warships, submarines and eventually even of aircraft.

As might be expected in this era of astounding scientific advancement, which continues to accelerate, these new weapons are not alone in the effects they are likely to have in war. Another field, which promises to have revolutionary results on strategy and tactics, is the development of guided missiles, which have numerous applications. There will be air-to-air guided missiles for use by aircraft to replace the present inadequate guns and cannon: ground-to-air weapons to supplement or to replace anti-aircraft artillery and fighter aircraft, and ballistic rockets to supplement or replace artillery and possibly bombers. Whatever the problems of air defence against the modern bomber those against the ballistic rocket will be greater by several orders of magnitude. Indeed, although weapon experience in the past has taught us to expect a sufficient counter to every fresh offensive weapon, as yet there does not seem to be an adequate defence against the ballistic rocket when it matures. There seems to be no restraint on this form of attack save the fear of retaliation and retribution. There will, however, certainly be a vital struggle between the offensive and the defensive, though probably without any finality because in some eras developments may favour one of these complementary aspects of war and in some the other. Meanwhile, much will depend on the peacetime decisions taken by the authorities in respect of the scientific effort to be given respectively to the offensive and the defensive. Advantage must be taken of the present and increasing ascendancy of the offensive but the defensive should not be neglected.

v

Perhaps the most profound change lies in the motive round which nations now manœuvre and prepare for war. No longer is the motive of war simply to gain new territories, resources and materials. Today, a prime feature of war or threat of war is a world wide struggle over ideologies: a struggle in respective ways of life which is something like a reversion to the wars of the crusaders though the stakes of this fresh ideological struggle are of quite a different order of magnitude. It is ironic that this fresh impulse to war should emerge in the era of the hydrogen bomb.

The Western powers were slow to square up to the totalitarian threat but the foregoing factors have resulted in a profound change in our peacetime attitude to war. Because of the unreasonable and unscrupulous attitude of the Soviet bloc to any peace proposal and the capacity of modern air power to strike swift and mortal blows, the Western powers are taking defensive action, individually and collectively, never before taken by them in peacetime. They are fashioning their armed forces at great cost so that should the deterrent to total war fail, they can be operated decisively at short notice without relying on a lengthy period of mobilization or war-preparedness. The

Western nations in alliance with other non-communist countries have also established NATO, SHAPE and other Allied headquarters and staffs so that Allied, National and Service strategies can be hammered out and agreed, plans made and forces prepared and trained, in readiness for war.

This unprecedented defensive preparation among the Western powers for the eventuality of total war brings us to the immediate problem of global strategy. What we are faced with today is not merely the local and minor vicissitudes of war as in former days. It is not only the possibility of total war, involving the use of nuclear weapons and their catastrophic consequences, but also limited world war, local wars and cold wars as defined at the beginning of this chapter. The future of humanity as a whole is bound up in strategy which perforce must be considered globally.

The nuclear deterrent and strategic air forces do not cover every eventuality. Wars continue though limited geographically and by the use of conventional weapons. There are local conflicts in which great powers contest each other by proxy, the rivals giving limited and varying support, arms and supplies to the opposing minor states in conflict, but stopping short of deliberate acts which might precipitate total war. In Korea, it is true that major powers were engaged in war not quite by proxy. There the United Nations were engaged in a conflict involving nationals belonging to other powers, namely, China and Russia, who were participating as allegedly non-national irregulars.

Cold war is an ancient form of conflict, the method and advantage of which have only become generally apparent since the rise to power of Hitler, and which embraces all hostile measures short of war. In cold war a minor state may be in league with a great Communist power, and recent examples of this are Malaya where communists encouraged by Communist China have challenged British authority, or in the Indo-China conflict where the communists supported by Communist China hamstrung French authority: and more recently in Cyprus where the Cypriots encouraged by Greece seek to undermine British administration. Often in the early stages of cold war, the nature of the challenge takes such an underground and dispersed form that diplomatic, economic and police methods only are adequate and suitable to counter it. Usually, however, these early methods develop into something against which troops, sometimes on a large scale, have to be used in support of the police. The scope for the employment of naval or air forces in cold war is usually limited to the support of land forces and police. Unfortunately, the essentially secret and subversive beginnings of this type of conflict and the guerilla nature of its operation lends itself admirably to communist or unfriendly expansion into unstable and unprosperous countries as well as many countries in the throes of their own rising nationalism. The Western nations have much to learn of this new form of warfare and of the particular strategy they should adopt to counter it.

By far the greatest influence on war and its conduct is weapon development, both offensive and defensive. This is no more clearly seen than in the present age when weapon development not only revolutionizes the act of war but is dictating a variety of new kinds of war. The development of political and national consciousness which has emerged during the last hundred and fifty years also has its influence on war, and on the way, and the reasons why, war is fought. The final factor which affects the conduct of modern war (and, for that matter, the conduct of peace) is strategy which attempts to make the greatest positive use of all features of war. Strategy dominates the act of war and at the same time grows out of the situations of war and peace as, it is hoped, my next chapter will illustrate.

CHAPTER II

Transition from Classical to Modern Strategy

WHILE in peace, strategy seeks to prevent war or to get what is wanted nationally without hostilities, in war it is the function which imposes or tries to impose on the activity of war a purpose, a plan and a method. It can place limitation on action in war or it can withdraw such limitation; and it can speed up or slow down the tempo of events. Strategy is that which makes the activity of war coherent and articulate. It is not only a tangible enemy with which strategy has to contend, it is with the conditions, irrationalities and intrinsic surprises which war, in fact, is always springing on the belligerents. There are few things more dynamic than the evolution of war and its associated strategy. Thus when we define strategy, which like all definitions tends to limit growth, we must be careful to avoid the risk of being outdated by enunciating dogma or rigid doctrine. Our definition must cover the changing concepts and pattern of strategy as it keeps aligned to the development of war: this is as important, if not actually more important, than being technically correct for the current era.

As the nature of war developed even when countries were still largely self-dependent on their raw materials and means of life, war became an affair of more and more complicated strategy. Inevitably war became a contest for the capture and consolidation or control of territory of one kind or another. Strategy was concerned largely with the creation of armies and their deployment in favourable circumstances on battlefields selected as far as possible to give the best chance of defeating and overthrowing the opposing army. In fact, the essence of land strategy was then to bring a superior army to bear against the opposing army at the right time and the right place.

With the growth of sea power, a new strategy appeared directed to the expansion of overseas enterprise and trade. Apart from being quite dissimilar from land strategy, sea strategy is in many ways more complex. In our early history, sea strategy was primarily concerned with the escort of convoys of merchant ships: not until that was provided for did our great admirals seek out the enemy. The protection of merchant shipping has, then, always been an aim of naval strategy. Nevertheless, to complicate this simple strategy, bigger and bigger warships were built to overwhelm the protecting lesser ships, until the great fleets emerged to confront each other in naval battle. The outcome was to confound sea strategy still further because one fleet, however superior, could not always force the enemy to fight, which in turn led to a further facet of sea strategy: blockade and 'fleets in being'. Subsequently submarines, mines and, later, aircraft confused the methods of sea strategy still more.

An important stage in the development of strategy was the combination of land and sea strategies which enabled the British Commonwealth, in particular, to make use of all the advantages of both strategies and thus confound those of other powers whose strength largely rested on land power. But it is important to realize that the development of the natural affinity of land and sea strategies had not a smooth and easy passage. Inevitably the views of the naval and army elements of our High Commands diverged most seriously over many years. Although Marlborough was the first outstanding leader to make far-reaching use of the joint sea-land concept of strategy, controversy still ranges round this subject. The army has been apt to claim that the navy is primarily a carrying service for trade and land forces, and the navy to claim that the primary aim in all strategy is command of the sea. Although the results of joint sea-land strategy were far-reaching, often they were not so immediate as the results of land or sea strategy applied separately. There is much history which records wars concerning the association of both naval and land forces, but it is of the nature of the two strategies co-ordinated to a greater or lesser extent, rather than one whole strategy.

Although virtually restricted to a combination of sea and land strategies, the First World War brought a new and overwhelming factor into strategy in that, for the first time, the belligerent nations believed and accepted that they were fighting a life and death struggle for raw materials, markets, territories and their economic and national existence; and they were not prepared to accept decisions solely resulting from battle by regular and limited forces. By then the various nations had become more thoroughly democratic, in the sense of becoming more politically conscious, and harnessed the whole of their manpower, resources and potential into fashioning great national armies and great navies, and defeat was only accepted when they were wholly overwhelmed and exhausted. This was, in fact, total war. The advent of air power as we have now come to know it during the First World War might well have complicated strategy still further, but, in the event, it did little more than complicate naval and army strategies by the problems and potentialities of air support. Despite great land battles and tremendous casualties, it was the advantages of our strategic heritage of overseas possessions and resources, and our naval strategy over the failing economic resources of continental Germany which brought us victory. The limited classical strategies of a single battlefield or a single continent were expanded into a strategy reaching over a great part of the world: a concept to be renewed and extended still further in the Second World War.

Germany began the First World War largely for economic reasons, however grandiloquent her propaganda may have been at the time. Hitler's motives were broader and more directly evident, and he embarked on the Second World War to acquire 'living space' and to unite Europe under Nazi rule. It so happened that this was a crescendo period in the evolution of strategy: the act of war itself was being revolutionized and profound changes became necessary in strategy. Between the two wars the air staff had formulated an air strategy for the employment of air forces against the enemy war potential and home front, quite separate from land and sea operations. There was a long and bitter inter-Service controversy over this new strategy which was even greater than the controversy in earlier years over the relationship between sea and land strategies. The air authorities claimed priority for the task of attacking the enemy home front over any air support to land or sea operations, whilst the naval and army authorities maintained that such operations were only of secondary importance and a diversion, and even a waste, of the national primary war effort.

The Second World War showed both contentions to be overstatements. Without question, the air strategy of directly attacking the enemy war potential apart from engaging his armies and navies was established. Equally, too, the air strategy of supporting the army and navy, especially at the time of critical operations, was also established. The flexibility of air power lies in the range of tasks it can perform and a certain freedom of choice with regard to these tasks. This idea of flexibility of air power is one which causes complications in air strategy. Fortunately it has enabled the two aspects of air strategy, established in the last war, to be readily applied. We must remember, however, that the full use of the power which nuclear weapons, guided missiles, ballistic rockets and supersonic aircraft will not be so readily applied to the support as to the strategic role of future air power.

On the heels of the establishment of air strategy came a further immense change. The advent of nuclear weapons showed the way to an air strategy which if they were used might well change conventional war of long campaigns stretching over a period of years into a war where the result could be decided in a relatively short time. Thus, the Second World War conflict brought a new magnitude to total war and the consequences of defeat. In addition to the relentless struggle of armies and navies in battle, air forces brought mortal conflict to whole populations on the home front and to the national life itself.

Arising out of air warfare was the revelation that the home front could no longer be protected solely by sea and land forces. It had long been true that naval strategy played a large part in the life and economies of a nation at war, but the process was slow and often not apparent. Air strategy made it all too clear that war is now waged by civilian populations to as great an extent as by the armed forces. This in turn has brought the need of a new strategy for home defence, military forces and civil organizations to implement this development in modern war.

II

The 'Principles of War' are known to every commander, but what happens in practice is very possibly a mixture of the orthodox action and action inspired by the conditions of the moment. They are less principles than guide lines, and many a commander would be delighted that he had followed, not necessarily with knowing intention, the whole code of the Principles of War. The same commander, having achieved a success, would, however, be less concerned to know that he had done so at the cost of violating some sacred tenet.

The strategic factors which are generally accepted as never changing, and are known as the Principles of War, can be stated briefly:

(a) The selection and maintenance of the aim.
(b) Maintenance of morale.
(c) Offensive action.
(d) Security.
(e) Surprise.
(f) Concentration of forces.
(g) Economy of effort.
(h) Flexibility.
(i) Co-operation.
(j) Administration.

It is easy to find examples which do in fact illustrate the Principles with a facility which is almost too good to be true, because, but this is the important point about them, they can only be really met *once they have been established and determined by events*. Besides, there are two further aspects of these so-called Principles which merit our attention. First, they are in no sense absolutes or constants which may be relied on as existing in their own right only waiting to be exploited: they are, or become, desirabilities, but at no time are they necessarily or easily acquired. They are approximations to those conditions in war wherein we are concerned 'to seize the advantage to ourselves and deny it to the enemy'. Such orthodoxy has within it a prime danger inasmuch as the same conditions of war, viewed from the other side, might afford the advantage to the enemy. Secondly, these factors tend to become contradictory and thus cancel each other out. To take only two examples, if we elect for offensive action our security may well suffer at least in the early stages; or again, concentration of forces can militate against economy of effort and might even prove suicidal in certain conditions — for instance, in an air attack with nuclear bombs or chemical and biological weapons. So it is that a commander

C

in a given situation might discern a dozen desirable contingencies but he can only exploit those he is able to encompass.

In fact these are less principles of war than they are military interpretations of the conditions of war: that is, they underlie what happens in war since they represent natural advantages or disadvantages as the commander sees them. He must have the vital and necessary information of the enemy and of his own forces to be able to take advantage of the conditions which do exist. This is clear when they are considered in the light of their positive and negative aspects. Owing their existence to natural and even necessary conditions, they exist in the very nature of war and as such may be exploited to a greater or lesser degree by the commander in war. They become objects of *intention*, and aspects to be watched and considered: but the commander, however astute, cannot create them or mould any one of them to his military needs if other factors are more weighty, or they themselves are recalcitrant or nugatory. They have become the prerequisites of victory only in so far as they have emerged fully in the actual pattern of war. Their elevation to the status of principles is the work of the military writers and colleges who, in their studies of specific battles or wars, see that victory was won by the employment of one or more of these factors. Their significance is therefore of an *a posteriori* rather than an *a priori* importance. This empirical view of military action is almost irresistible, but it describes the past while the future remains uncomfortably blank. It is most easy to fall into this way of thinking after the event while it is much less easy to plan ahead strictly in these terms because of the very great interplay of conditions and factors, either in the midst of battle or in H.Q. at any time before a contemplated course of action.

The factors which affect the principles vary according to the circumstances and numerous changing values, for example, the relative strengths and weapons possessed by the belligerents: the relative geographical situation and material resources: the relative amount and quality of intelligence: the circumstances and way of life of the home front coupled to the morale of the people and the fighting forces: and the relation between the front line forces and reserve strengths as well as the personalities and creeds of the commanders who control them.

This book therefore is not intended as an exposition of the Principles of War so-called. Indeed, some observations may be regarded as contradicting these factors, and as the circumstances, opportunities and situations differ, a new concept may be found necessary to cover the action essential. In this relation the roles and functions of the three Services present problems of peculiar complexity in a new view of strategy.

III

Today, strategy embraces something more than the practical art of the commander and the most outstanding additions are the peacetime aspects. These include the assessment of the potentialities of new weapons: the assessment and nature of the enemy threat: *the assessment and sympathy of world opinion*: the assessment of cold war problems: fashioning the size and shape of the forces to be maintained in peacetime and their state of readiness for sudden war with special reference to deterrent value: the bases and deployment of our peacetime forces: the scale and nature of peacetime reserves and war stocks: the whole range of home defence problems and their co-ordination with the armed forces: and the place of our national forces in Allied strategy and the co-ordination of the problems which arise from it.

It is clear that this extension of the scope of strategy alters the relationship between the political and military leaders in affairs of war. Indeed, political leaders have to concern themselves with many strategical problems, and military leaders more than ever must take account of the political problems in their strategy: inevitably the two spheres overlap.

Identity of ultimate *aim* between the military strategists and the political direction does not always bring about the desired cohesion largely because the *methods* are different. Thus, save only in the overwhelmingly powerful nations, political direction tends to put more and more limitations on military strategy. War aim, or peace aim, must be clearly defined before military strategy can be accurately and correctly set down. If situations develop which catch the political direction by surprise, and this has happened in cold and local war and may happen in total war, then some form of political expediency follows designed merely to 'catch up' with the new situation. It is not surprising if such political expediency is ill-defined and militates against the formulation of a sound military strategy.

It is conceivable that the military leaders of the West could say to their governments: 'We have now reached a stage where, unless you have miscalculated, there is unlikely to be a total war in the next five to ten years, and if there is a limited, or a local war, again through miscalculation, we have the power to stop it, *if you have the courage to tell us to do so.*' What has happened in recent years in the cold war sphere illustrates the limitations, both actual and circumstantial, of the political direction. The cold war must be largely fought on the political front and the results have neither engendered confidence nor a strong overall military strategy. The chief danger in such a situation is that both political and military leaders may tend to lean on each other and hope that the function of the other contains a panacea for all ills.

Desirable as it might seem to have a concise boundary between the military sphere of strategy and the sphere of political direction of war, today this would be a dangerous division of concepts and responsibilities and at a most vital level. Strategy and political direction must be interwoven into a whole at the highest level. The concern of military leaders in former days to limit their responsibility to the efficient use of the forces made available to them by the political leaders is far too parochial in modern times. The political leaders are responsible for policy and direction of war and it is axiomatic that a strong and sound strategy is dependent on strong and sound political policy.

The military leaders are the political leaders' counsellors in giving military advice and they must formulate strategy together. The military leaders must then implement that strategy loyally and in the most efficient manner.

Strategy in modern times must alter radically preconceived Service, National and combined strategies. To an extent greater than before a particular Service faced by a strategical problem has now to deal with it not simply as an army, navy or air force matter, but rather a joint concern of all three. Such a problem must be viewed in relation to the whole. This does not mean polite co-ordination but an active strategical policy on the part of all three Services together and in conjunction, and devoid of inter-Service wrangle. In fact, what must emerge is a joint strategy. Strategic concepts at the moment are very much the separate strategies of the three Services which are balanced and co-ordinated according to the various influences which dominate our High Command and Politcal Direction at the time. Efforts in the past to achieve integration and cohesion have been largely disappointing inasmuch as they have been initiated by specific Service concepts rather than by a joint or national approach.

Today it is becoming increasingly evident, especially under modern conditions with the need of modern weapons, that we cannot afford to retain the present pattern and scale of our armed forces. If we are to produce the most up-to-date fighters, bombers, warships and armoured forces together with nuclear weapons, defensive guided missiles and ballistic rockets, the national bill would become still more impracticable. Moreover, so far as the United Kingdom is concerned research resources available for defence is at best one quarter of those of the United States, or of Soviet Russia. In this respect we must remember that it takes as much research effort to produce one atomic bomb, one bomber, one aircraft carrier or one armoured vehicle as for ten thousand.

The greatest financial danger is that the United Kingdom and United States will try to continue to economize and compromise in defence by the traditional and most unsatisfactory method: that is, cutting a percentage off each Service budget but leaving the general pattern undisturbed. This is certain to lead to degeneration and decadence.

Although the various fundamentals of Service strategy can be stated simply, in fact serious complications in the respective strategies arise because of the very separateness of the Services, and, paradoxically, their ever-increasing dependence of one another, in particular, because of the ubiquity of air power and its adaptability to each of the Service strategies. Much study based on the lessons of history with theoretical analysis has been given to naval and army strategies, and to a lesser extent to that of the air force. In consequence firm and rooted strategical doctrines have been evolved for each of the fighting Services. On the other hand, all too little study and attention has been given to new concepts of joint and combined theatre strategies. The histories of these all important high level strategies are most inadequate, which is probably a major reason why joint and combined strategies are not at present firmly conceived. It is no exaggeration to state that joint strategy has been little more than the highest common denominator of agreement of the three separate Service strategies. To an even greater extent, combined strategy has been the highest common denominator of agreement of the compromise among National strategies of the various Allies which are often much too heavily influenced by the political considerations and personality and prestige of Allied leadership to the detriment of military factors.

To go a step further: it might appear that the strategies of the respective services of each nation in a combination of allies should be similar or even identical to that of the corresponding services of other nations. This, however, is far from true, not only in the matter of strategy, but in customs, usage, requirements and commitments in each of the several services. There can, in these circumstances, be no easy merger or dovetailing of strategical or military resources without some overall strategy into which the various strategies can fit. As in the case of a National strategy we require an Allied strategy, arrived at in peacetime and without prejudice, in which the various National strategies should not only be accommodated but should subserve the whole. The peculiar state of uneasy peace which surrounds the nations at present amply suggests that we cannot wait till the outbreak of war galvanizes the Political Direction and High Command of our nation generally into making decisions. Decisions in relation to strategy must be taken promptly: and an Allied strategy would ensure that such decisions were not only swift, but, so far as is humanly possible, wise and economical as well. In the present era of technical development such an Allied strategy, with adequate forces, could certainly prevent the outbreak of total, limited and local war in the near future.

IV

There are various levels of strategy. Allied, or what is termed combined strategy, is based on Allied leadership and Allied defence policy. National or joint strategy is based on National leadership and National defence policy. The strategies of the three fighting Services and of Home defence which should also be based on National defence policy. The strategies of the Theatre commander and of the commanders of functional forces, such as strategical bombers, should be based on Allied and National defence policy and the Service strategies. And finally, the strategy of the Battle commander is based on those of the Theatre commander and the respective services.

Our strategy is based on Defence policy and embraces the assessment of the various national military tasks in peace and war: the keeping of those tasks in phase with development and aggressive intentions: the extent and tempo of arrangements for mobilization and harnessing the total potential to the war effort: the allocation and balance of the part of the military force required for each of the particular peacetime and war-tasks: the means and methods of bringing to bear the properly balanced forces wherever and whenever required: and the provision of an adequate Home defence.

Defence policy arises out of three sets of considerations, i.e. National, Allied and enemy readiness and potential. It stems from the leadership, political, economic and moral strength of the nation, and its geographic and other circumstances: from the leadership, nature and strength, the circumstances, common interests and mutual confidence of Allied and would-be Allied nations: from the leadership, policies, circumstances and the current and potential strengths of would-be aggressors.

Today, Defence policy with pacific nations is formulated from four prime strategic aspects. It is designed first to provide a deterrent to total war which otherwise might be precipitated by action by any would-be aggressor: here the instrument is the offensive use of nuclear weapons and the strategic bomber and possibly the ballistic rocket. The second aspect is the ability to deal adequately with the cold war where the instrument, according to the situation, is political and military forces. The third aspect is intended to cover the exigencies of local war and limited world war where conventional land, sea and air forces (possibly the tactical employment of atomic weapons) will be required. The final aspect is framed to give a good account, and, if at all possible, to seize any advantage, if and when total war should begin: here, of course, we rely on stockpiles of nuclear weapons and the strategic bomber and ballistic rocket.

The first and last of these facets of Defence policy are closely related since the conclusive deterrent to an aggressor is the likelihood of defeat in an open trial of strength. The third aspect is not so closely related to these two because, essentially, the strategic use of nuclear weapons is improbable, though possibly not the tactical use of atomic weapons.

This being so, the positive deterrent and ultimate sanction against total war, the hydrogen bomb, is unlikely to prevent the outbreak of cold, local and perhaps even, in time, limited world war. Possibly the best deterrent against limited, local and even cold wars would be an Anglo-American airborne division supported by maritime forces suitably based and kept ready for immediate deployment wherever required. The obvious difficulty of such an international deterrent force is political. To cite two present instances: the United States would have to agree to, and the United Kingdom be prepared to commit forces in Formosa, not only in case of a widespread trouble but to nip it in the bud: again, the United Kingdom would have to allow, and the United States be prepared to commit forces say even in Cyprus. These are extreme and awkward cases but there are many other troublesome areas where the international political difficulties would not be so great and could, in all likelihood, be reconciled, and where such a force would be most effective.

Cold, local and even limited war raise two difficult problems for the Western powers. They place modern weapons at a disadvantage and make a greater call for troops which the Western nations find much more difficult to marshal than do the Communist countries. The persistence of the cold, and local, war, so often sponsored if not actually instigated by communistic countries, also presents the Western non-aggressor countries with the conundrum of what proportion of military expenditure and resources should be provided for the cold and local war and what for total war because the requirements are quite different. Thus we have the continual problem of reconciling total war and cold and local war strategies. Yet they are intimately related in so far as the cold or local war affects our position in regard to total war. In this way cold and local war is something we dare not lose since they could be decisive in themselves both militarily and economically and a global war never fought in our time. In the case of the United Kingdom: since she is more likely to be involved alone and without allies in cold, and to some extent perhaps in local war, she should take care that the shape of her armed forces is adequate for any eventuality in which she might be involved alone and at the same time make a fair contribution to the Allied strength as a whole.

v

There are many who believe, and among their number are some of the greatest men of our own day, that the power and influence of religion transcends the purely physical power and influence of science. Though this far reaching but imponderable facet is outside the scope of this work, however, the power and influence of political and military leadership, which can often transcend that of strategy, should not be ignored. This has been repeatedly illustrated throughout history. For example, Wellington's victory on the field of Waterloo, the crowning battle of his career, was due to his leadership helped by the tenacity of his troops, rather than to his strategy, which, in fact proved faulty. A further illustration of this tenacity of the *will* to war was Hitler's leadership after the Allied breakout from the Normandy bridgehead in 1944. The Allied advance so disorganized Germany's vast forces throughout France and far into Germany for several weeks that the German Army High Command virtually believed their strategy was at an end. It was only Hitler's leadership which carried the German army on and enabled them to re-establish some sort of order and plan. This made for a resistance which continued almost up to the time of Hitler's death and prevailed among his forces until the Allied Armies were within half a mile of his Bunker: long after his strategy was at an end.

Perhaps the best illustration of all time of the influence of leadership over the strength or absence of strategy was after Dunkirk in 1940, in the darkest days of the Second World War. Mr. Churchill roused the United Kingdom to face Hitler's threat of invasion. A portentous contribution to this was his speech:[1]

> We shall go on to the end, we shall fight in France, we shall fight on the seas and oceans, we shall fight with growing confidence and growing strength in the air, we shall defend our island,

[1] June 4th, 1940: *Into Battle*, p. 223.

whatever the cost may be, we shall fight on the beaches, we shall fight in the fields and in the streets, we shall fight in the hills; we shall never surrender, and even if, which I do not for a moment believe, this island or a large part of it were subjugated and starving, then our Empire beyond the seas, armed and guarded by the British Fleet, would carry on the struggle, until in God's time, the new world, with all its power and might, steps forth to the rescue and liberation of the old.

If it is not already clear history will certainly show that the strategic position in the United Kingdom at the time gave no justification whatever for any sort of effective stand against a German invasion. Although the enemy made several serious mistakes, it was essentially the sheer leadership of Churchill which inspired Great Britain to rise above strategical adversity.

Against all the facts in each of the above mentioned cases some element vital to the maintenance of strategy was preserved; and the possibility of a fresh strategy growing out of any new situation, however unlikely it may seem, is always present. While the material factors of strategy are wide, the political, psychological and philosophical are all also significant and may be critical. The strategist must take account of everything which affects the life and spirit of nations, our own, our Allies and those of the potential enemy.

Since the needs of the times brought organized armed forces into being, causing them to become larger and more thoroughly organized, so has history dictated the strategies under which they required to be directed. From a military point of view successive empires and civilizations are largely a record of successful strategies: where strategies have failed empires have disappeared; and it is out of the present conditions and historical lessons, as in the past that an Allied strategy will emerge which in its turn will dominate and influence history during the next few generations. The classical axioms of Clausewitz on strategy are chiefly theoretical abstractions confirmed by those incidents in history which best suited the author's theory once he had formulated it. But Mahan, who greatly stressed the influence of sea power on history (thus emphasising the dictates of various naval strategies on human history) also elaborated the lessons of history which he ultimately translated into an idea of strategy. His method resembled a two-way traffic system: sea-power/history, and history/sea strategy: Clausewitz's method was almost wholly a one-way system. It is not clear that he altogether appreciated the distinction between victory which is the ultimate and legitimate aim of battle and winning the peace which should be the strategical aim in war.

The strategical picture is continuously changing not only in the military sense, but in the political and economic spheres. Even now economic aid by other powers to those areas where formerly our influence was paramount may itself upset the strategical balance which is so important for us and our Allies.

Not only have the Western nations given priority to military over commercial and economic considerations but they have deliberately forfeited commercial benefits to gain advantage in defence. This in itself is a positive enough approach and will yield positive advantages but the Communist powers have lately shown us, as in the Middle East, that we perhaps do not wholly appreciate the relation between economics and strategy. With their economic aid to a variety of countries without the customary ties, restraints and alliances they are laying the foundation, both in material and ideal friendship, which may frustrate the initial efforts on the part of the West to conceive a strong strategy and international harmony, especially in those areas where the goodwill of the peoples is so important to the West.

Tradition is the touchstone for the peoples of these areas: the British are suspect in the first place because of their Empire building in past centuries, while the Americans may be suspect in a more direct commercial sense. The Communist powers, treading in areas to which they are not traditionally habituated, do not appear to have motives other than those of well-meaning fellowship. Western economic aid to the land- and material-hungry Asian who views with some resentment the disparity of his own and the Western standard of living, to the Middle East countries and even within NATO, must not be considered in any way as a sop to conscience. Still less may it be considered an assured investment but that it must be applied is without question.

The Western powers are militarily as strong, if not stronger, and as ready as the Communist powers, a factor of striking deterrent significance. It is therefore all the more important that they should not be edged-out imperceptibly and alienated, not only from the resources but the peoples and areas of the globe on which we have relied and do still rely. The political mechanisms which hold together the free world, NATO, the Baghdad Pact and SEATO should be enlivened by this concern. Besides learning the lessons of past war we should learn those of the present peace.

No one of this or the preceding generation would minimize the immensity of the problems which have been briefly outlined but one invaluable pointer may be given here. It is that in looking at modern war we must fix in our minds the principles underlying the *functions* of the armed services; and of course the functions (to an ever-increasing degree of importance) of the civil authorities on the Home front whose bastion is Home defence. Strategically, it is the function which is of importance rather than the service as such.

A modern view of strategy is the direct antithesis of the strategical theories of Clausewitz. It is not a dead schema conceived only in the study but something continually subject to growth and development. Strategy today must have the best of both worlds: of the past in the lessons of history, and of the future, as in the practical and theoretical vision we are able to apply to it.

CHAPTER III

Strategy and Geographical Zones

I

WHILE the strategical situation in the world may change with the passage of time it is not only useful and instructive to consider the issues which face us today, it is imperative that we should do so. Strategy may be considered the science of war in a somewhat similar way that economics is the science of commerce. Just as the nature of war itself and the very nature and concepts of science inevitably change over the centuries, sometimes remarkably as in the present epoch, so must strategy also change. One of the main purposes of this work is to try to deduce and evaluate from history the patterns of strategy in order to have some basis for forecasting and elucidating the course war will take in the future.

The application of strategy has two aspects, both of which have tended to grow and assume a false independence of each other, fostered largely by differences of view, usage and even terminology. First there are the so-called Principles of War accepted by the three fighting services which lead us to a variety of concepts. In this respect there is a subtle difficulty in a strategy evolved from factors, geographical and otherwise, which a leader can influence and other factors over which he has no control. This distinction may be illustrated by the example in the difference between the French and British retreat in 1914 from Belgium to the Marne which was, at least in some respects, a planned strategy which permitted a stand and then counter-attack, and the French and British retreat in Europe in 1940 which had no Allied plan to stand or counter-attack, and led to the British evacuation at Dunkirk and the collapse of France. Secondly, there are the problems of securing frontiers, buffer areas and bases, which have dominated strategy over the centuries of war; frontiers now appear, however, to have much of their former significance reduced with the rise of modern air power. In peacetime, however, nuclear weapons make frontiers most important because the geographical position of the belligerents at the outset of total war could critically affect the outcome.

Throughout the centuries, the geographical location of military bases have had a dominating influence on strategy. Since the end of the Second World War, several of Britain's vital bases have been challenged by the local nationals and some have been lost and others are in the balance. Also since the Second World War the United States has acquired base facilities in numerous places and likewise some of these are already being challenged: for example Iceland, Japan, Morocco and even the Philippines. These challenges to the security and availability of bases is most serious for the Allies because even though aircraft and ballistic rockets can be made of adequate range to deliver hydrogen weapons effectively from home bases and carriers in total war, regional bases would be important for operating military forces in local and even cold wars. It must be hoped that the free countries throughout the world will see their ways to continue to give the necessary base facilities for the Allied forces. Thus territory and frontiers still dominate the strategy of present-day limited war which in fact closely resembles the unlimited war of former times. Indeed should nuclear weapons ever be abandoned by all nations the territorial aspect of strategy would revert to its former importance.

Today, total war is unlikely to break out between Great Powers taking on each other single-handed though wars limited in their extent may occur between a greater and a lesser power or between lesser powers. In cold, local and limited wars, the strategical concepts of the larger powers will be narrowed and limited by considerations of territory and areas of partial resistance and of absolute defence. These same strategical concepts, which a decade ago might have been considered due for modification, are still made valid by that which might have made them obsolete — the deterrent effect of atomic and hydrogen weapons. The present needs of global strategy make the demand for strategic bombing bases a prime factor and Britain, and to a lesser extent the United States, may be fortunate in having such bases, not only in the United Kingdom but throughout the world, without having to annex them.

As non-aggressors the Western powers are at a certain disadvantage in being bent back on the spring of the defensive. Since the Western powers are unlikely to begin a war, the only threat to world peace today comes from the Communist bloc, that is, Russia, China and their satellites. The pattern thus presented of active and powerful states controlling the vast Eurasian land-mass has destroyed the traditional isolationism of the United States and the diplomatic-military reserve of the United Kingdom. The tendency of the Communist powers to expand their influence, if not their territory, in and beyond the Eurasian land-mass and its periphery posits strategy for the Western powers. It is a strategical problem of global dimensions.

It would be a mistake to suppose that all who are not with us in the present political set-up would necessarily be against us in a general conflict. However, Soviet Russia, China and their communist sympathizers not only occupy the greater part of the Eurasian land-mass but are largely self-sufficient and self-supporting in their means of life, and are capable, through privation and other means, of building up a most formidable military strength. On the other hand, the free countries possess or control a great part of the lands and the seas connecting them which surround the Communist land-mass. In general the free countries depend to a great extent for their prosperity, and in some instances for their very existence, on sea-borne trade. Thus we have the initial contrast between the military problems and the basic strategies of the Soviet bloc and the free countries.

A prime aspect then, of our defence problem today is that we should prevent any further territory going behind the iron curtain involving the loss, not only of friends and potential allies, but of vital supplies of food and raw materials, bases and possible war productive power, and an expansion of Soviet influence. This may seem a simple concept of defence but the strategy associated with it under modern conditions of total, limited, local and cold war is most complicated. The nature of the threat is such that we cannot afford to have an erroneous or inadequate strategy because the stakes at issue with the Communist aggressors are ultimately no less than the continuance of the Western way of life and perhaps even of civilization.

Allied strategy rests on the hydrogen and other mass-destruction weapons as the primary deterrent to total war; and although non-aggressors, it is certain that we would use these weapons in retaliation should any opponent initiate war of this nature.

Allied strategy also rests on the tactical use of atomic weapons in the field; particularly in the NATO area. However much we dislike this strategy we have been forced into it because for financial and other reasons our Allied contingents could not at present compete against any major action of the Soviet bloc without it. Thus, the Allies have come to depend on tactical atomic weapons, certainly in Western Europe, knowing that we would probably have to initiate their use and that this decision could well lead to total war and so risk the end of civilized society. Any decision to initiate the use of atomic weapons would be a most agonizing one and in consequence it would seem that we would only take it in extreme emergency, and even then, according to the place and circumstances, there would be varying degrees of sanction among the Allied nations. It is unfortunate that this strategy must inevitably give our opponents scope and opportunity to use diplomacy and to create situations to the Allies' disadvantage.

However desirable it would seem to develop this strategy into graduated deterrences, it would be unwise, even if practicable, to attempt to define precisely in advance the circumstances in which we would use our ultimate sanction. Certainly we could not rely on the enemy idea of graduated deterrence and graduated retaliation being similar to our own.

Doubtless, in some circumstances, local aggression might be dealt with effectively by local retaliation. This might even involve the tactical use of atomic weapons. Such local retaliation would not inevitably or necessarily lead to total war. As in the case of the hydrogen bomb deterrence, the aggressor must be kept guessing how far he can go with his armed forces without bringing down atomic weapons against them.

Although the tactical use of atomic weapons would often involve the home front of one or more countries varying from primitive to highly developed ones, there is an essential difference between this tactical use and the strategic use of these weapons. Whereas, in the former, the weapons of mass destruction are aimed primarily against military targets offered by the enemy armed forces, in the latter, these weapons are aimed primarily against civil targets such as large towns and other important centres in the home front. Moreover, hydrogen bombs would not be used tactically in limited war.

No one must be deluded into thinking that our tactical use of atomic weapons will not cause casualties and damage on the home front of the countries where the military operations are being fought, in particular in Western Europe, the civilian casualties and damage would doubtless be heavy. The point is that, according to the situation and his plans, the enemy would be free to decide whether he would confine the use of his weapons of mass destruction to the tactical role in the local area, or extend their use to the strategic role, that is, to total global war.

Now that the Great Powers of each national alignment possess the means of immediate and unstoppable retaliation, the effect is to neutralize the mutual threat, and give to the strategic and political world picture an apparent stability. This stability can be overestimated since the balance is most evident in areas which are highly integrated and organized politically and militarily, as in Western Europe for example. The same stability does not extend into those areas where aggression will not provoke instant retaliation by strategic bombing on the heart-land of the aggressor, and where an attack by tactical atomic weapons would not necessarily precipitate total war. Thus it should not be assumed that only conventional weapons will be used in conflicts which occur outside the 'stable' area.

In this respect the decision when and where to go to war is today less a specific geographical line where armies march but rather a contour in events. When the Soviet bloc are aware of the strength of the Allied deterrent forces and that total war is imminent, then that is the maximum contour of penetration into our free way of life. On the other hand, when they are sure that a certain act of aggression does not mean the use of the hydrogen bomb then that is likely to result in local or even limited war where geography and territory play a dominant role as they always have in the past. It is in this latter context that we proceed to examine the geographical penetration.

II

The following has been phrased in terms of the territorial concept, but aggression against NATO or any area which for one reason or another is important to its survival will call forth varying degrees of

D

resistance. The concept behind limited warfare is a conventional one involving the use of conventional forces wherein the Soviet bloc are largely superior; and it is a method of aggression likely to be preferred by Russia, probably even when they have overwhelming superiority in the air and in weapons, including nuclear weapons. Resistance to aggression will mean the use of conventional weapons as well as tactical and strategical use of nuclear weapons, though the use of the latter will be related to the magnitude of the situation. What is being visualized here is the possibility of their use in that order in a rising scale of urgency.

A consideration of our own defence and that of our Allies, though in somewhat general terms, is pertinent to the discussion of the geographical zones under review. In the abstract, probably the correct answer is that our defence is the defence of the territories inhabited by the Allied peoples and the preservation of their democratic way of life.

If the enemies which a country will in fact encounter and the nature and dates at which it will encounter them could be foreseen with complete certainty, it would be a matter of simple calculation to ensure that military preparations were neither deficient nor excessive; in other words, to elimate both risk and waste. In practice, of course, the event is never precisely foreseeable, but must always remain a matter of appreciation since it depends upon a vast number of causes, of which not all can be detected or, if detected, assessed at their true importance. Moreover, the constellation of causes is bound to change, through some coming into view or into greater prominence, while others lose importance or disappear altogether. Appreciations have therefore to be reviewed and altered correspondingly. The duty of a government is to ensure that current defence preparations shall so correspond with current appreciation that there is a maximum of deterrent and a minimum both of risk and of waste.

The difficulties of making sound defence preparations within this definition of the term are greatly enhanced by the reaction of those preparations themselves upon the preparations and intentions of other nations. If it were possible to isolate the nation for which an appreciation was being made, and to regard the rest of the world as something entirely separate, with which relations began only at the outbreak of

Auckland

San Francisco

North
Pole

New York

Sydney

Moscow

Buenos
Aires

Cape Town
Map 'A'

An Azimuthal Equidistant Projection centred on London.
In this projection the shortest distance from London to
any other place in the world is shown by a straight line.
Note, for example, the shortest route from London to
Sydney (Australia) passes north of Moscow: from
London to Auckland (New Zealand) passes not far east
of the North Pole.
Printed by the kind permission of British Overseas
Airways Corporation and Messrs. Stanford of Long Acre.

war, then at least the target aimed at would be a stationary one. As it is, both aimer and target are in political, economic, scientific and military motion, and their respective movements are in part related. From this reaction of the military preparations of one nation or alliance of nations upon those of another arises the *deterrent* effect, the effect in preventing or delaying war.

In framing its Defence policy a nation has to solve at the same time several problems. First it must assess what forces it would require at the outbreak and during the course of an assumed total war as well as limited, local and cold wars, and thence deduce the minimum peace-time preparations to assure the availability of the appropriate forces for each category of war. Concurrently, and even more important, it must consider how far these several preparations or even alternatives thereto will actually prevent or deter the outbreak of war.

The successful negotiation of water obstacles, even as narrow as the English Channel or the straits between Sicily and Malta, is no more practicable under conditions of three-dimensional warfare without command of the air than it was under conditions of two-dimensional warfare without command of the sea. As long as this remained true — then, given the necessary command of the air, defence could be secured with great economy of force on, or immediately in rear of, the contour of a water obstacle. In fact, the United Kingdom and the Dominions enjoyed the protection of continuous water obstacles, with the sole exception of Canada, which marches with the United States along a great land frontier. The Union of South Africa also has the protection of the water obstacle which envelops the African continent. Likewise, the United States is protected by oceans. There was, however, an essential further condition of successful resistance, even upon the most favourable water obstacle. The industrial and economic resources to sustain the war on the contour of maximum penetration must be available and must be defended either against the enemy's surface forces or against his strategic bombing, as the case may be. Today, successful defence against enemy bombers is an even more important condition than a sea barrier.

If the resources which a nation requires to maintain the struggle on or forward of its chosen contour of maximum penetration are not within its control, or if the means of transporting these resources to the places where they are required cannot be commanded, that nation is as little capable of pursuing an independent policy as it would be if the contour of maximum penetration itself lay outside its own territory. Similarly, if any Great Power were in a position to dominate the routes by which oil was conveyed to the places of consumption, that other Great Power would hold a virtual veto over action in those places. Today the same applies to the sources of uranium.

It follows that the places where the essentials for defence are produced — whether food, raw materials or manufactured articles — and the routes connecting them with the places where they are required must be included within the area for which defence, as complete as possible, is aimed at. Thus it comes about that territories outside the alliance may be as much the object of our defence as any part of the alliance itself, if they either contain essential resources or dominate the transport routes. The degree of control which it is necessary to exercise over such territories varies from case to case: in some cases the neutrality of the producing country may be left entirely untouched, if the enemy can be denied the power of interference without measures involving breach of neutrality; at the other extreme, occupation during war or even in peacetime may be indispensable.

To include within the contour of maximum penetration the industrial and economic resources essential for successful resistance and the territories which dominate the essential routes is, of course, not sufficient, unless those resources and routes can themselves be adequately secured against strategic bombing by an enemy. The maintenance of adequate defensive air superiority in respect of these potential targets, is no less a condition of successful resistance than that command of the air which enables the contour of maximum penetration to be held if necessary against superior surface forces. The concentration of essential industrial resources in the United Kingdom, and of essential routes, gives to its defence against strategic bombing a peculiar significance which probably could only be diminished by a far-reaching, and therefore probably very gradual, regrouping of population and industry within the Commonwealth.

III

A factor which to some extent has obscured a large view of strategic need throughout the globe is the varying degrees of importance which the cold, local and limited war assumes for each separate country in different parts of the world. For example, the invasion of South Korea cut across United States interest in the Far East and no doubt prompted their decision to resist this aggression with the aid of UNO. As a contrast, the unrest in the Middle East since the Second World War unquestionably affects British strategic interests though it may not so immediately or profoundly affect American interests which were acknowledged at the time.

Assuming then, as we must, that the enemy is the aggressor, we can deduce what may in general terms to be the form of the early phases of a limited or local war. Being an aggressor, the enemy presumably plans the occupation of territory either from military or ideological interest. Ex hypothesis these objectives will lie within the allied zone of partial resistance; otherwise war will not occur. It is less likely that they will be within the alliance itself, and almost certain that they would not be inside the actual contour of maximum penetration. Before a potential enemy reached the point of being able to contemplate the direct conquest and annexation of vital parts of the alliance, some previous act would almost certainly have resulted in war. For example, the invasion of Poland by Germany was made a *causus belli* in 1939, well in advance of any situation arising in which Germany could have directly invaded the United Kingdom.

Accordingly the aim of the aggressor will be to complete his operations as rapidly as possible, with a view to 'localizing' the war and preventing it from becoming a general world struggle. He thereby not only achieves the maximum concentration of force upon his immediate object, but affords himself the best chance of a peace, if only temporary, which will leave him in possession of what he has gained.

In this initial phase the superiority of the enemy in surface forces must be assumed; for it is hardly conceivable that any but a great military power would be in the position to court an offensive war with the Allies. Unless the enemy could achieve a marked superiority, he would scarcely be prepared to take the offensive, especially as choice of time lies with him. To challenge and if possible to gain the mastery of the air in the theatre of operations would therefore be of outstanding importance. The enemy, seeking to expedite the success of his surface forces by every means, may be expected to devote great attention to air support and to depriving the opposing belligerent of his air support; and the principal form of resistance which it is likely to be practicable for the alliance to offer in the threatened area will be that of support and counter support, by which indeed, if the attack fails directly upon a water obstacle, the issue itself may well be decided.

Throughout the second phase, air support and counter air support will at least retain their importance; the fact that the enemy is able to continue and intensify his threat to reach and break through the contour of maximum penetration implies that his surface forces enjoy continued superiority and that his air support forces have not been rendered ineffective. The effort required to render our own air support effective and frustrate the enemy's could not conceivably be withheld. To take two cases from the corresponding phase of the Second World War, if the Battle of Britain, which was a counter air support victory, had been lost, not even the most brilliantly successful strategic bombing directed against Germany's war economy or civilian morale could have prevented the armies in Normandy and Brittany from reaching and occupying the United Kingdom; or again, when Rommel was driving forward to the capture of the Egyptian delta, the sinking, by aircraft and submarine, of half a dozen supply ships bound for Tobruk was worth more to the survival of the Allies than the obliteration of the whole Ploesti oil-field at that time in the war.

The importance of strategic bombing will in this phase be on the increase. The struggle must from now on absorb by stages the whole resources and energy of the belligerents, and strategic bombing will increasingly be called into play to assist in lowering the level of resources below that of requirements. The less the enemy is enabled by circumstances to derive full effect from his superiority in surface forces, the more he is likely to resort to strategic bombing; nor is it probable that a future aggressor will have neglected, as Germany and her allies had done in 1939-40, to try to secure the means of superiority in strategic bombing, as well as in surface and air support operations.

The employment of strategic bombing and of countering the enemy strategic bombing are really complementary; but it is possible to deduce that the latter would in most cases be of relatively greater importance to Allied defence in the period before equilibrium is ultimately reached. Up to that point, the alliance is likely to be working upon the whole on a narrower margin than its enemies; and it would therefore be the application of strategic bombing to the alliance which would offer the quicker return. Accordingly, from the point of view of the alliance, counteracting of the enemy's strategic bombing must in these circumstances take priority over the development of her own strategic bombing against the enemy, though it will be recalled that counter strategic bombardment includes among its weapons the attack of those targets which most directly bear upon the enemy's own strategic bombing offensive.

Whatever the situation, the role of the strategic bomber grows in importance; and the possibility of limited war assuming the proportions of total war underlines our need of adequate bases. This necessity itself re-emphasizes the strategic anomaly at the heart of the world situation. The Soviet technique of ideological expansion is designed to seize every advantage whether in advance or in retreat and deserves a much closer study. Behind the pattern of cold, local and limited war in the various zones looms the strategy of total war. How long total war will be avoided is a question related to the effectiveness of our strategic approach to the cold, local and limited conflict and to the continued validity of the deterrent.

IV

There are two great strategic ramparts in the strategy of the free countries today, and our problems range round these two ramparts. The strategic importance of any area depends on the extent of national sentiment and moral conviction, productive capacity and the suitability of the area for offensive and defensive strategies. Western Europe stands foremost in all these considerations, particularly in regard to productive capacity and strategical advantage. First, the Western rampart, which embraces North America and Western Europe which together are the citadel and the industrial production bases of the

Western way of life and of their defence resources: this capacity of the Western citadel far outweighs anything the Soviet bloc can produce in our time.

It is important that the communists do not acquire any further part of Western European productive or manpower assets for that would not only reduce our own strength but add to the aggressor's. Any danger there might be of this expansion ranges round infiltration of Western Europe in the *cold war*. Unlike the great benefit Germany acquired in the Second World War, however, the capacity of the new war weapons is such that any possession or occupation of part or the whole of Western Europe in a *total war*, would not bring the enemy any worth-while increase of productive capacity. It is thus evident that the Western rampart or Western zone is highly critical in three respects. The non-European Western powers are bound to Western Europe by strong ties of friendship: the Allies in the West need to retain for their own use and to deny the enemy any advantage of allies or territory: and in Western Europe are the most advantageously placed bases from which retaliation could be made quickly against the military and industrial targets of Russia or her satellites.

Then there is the Eastern rampart which includes the non-communist countries of South-East Asia and the Far East. In these regions there are major sources of strategic and commercial raw materials important to the Western rampart and large food supplies for the vast numbers of peoples who populate these parts so that a power controlling these food supplies would control the peoples. Within the Eastern rampart are vast sources of manpower well suited for the creation of large armies for use in the type of war likely in those parts of the world. The same pattern of concentrated industrial strength as in the Western rampart does not exist in the Eastern rampart: indeed, the East is dependent on great industrial help not only in respect of their armed forces but also for their means of life and prosperity.

Although the Western rampart could in some measure make itself self-sufficient, it would be disastrous to the Western way of life should the communists encroach further westwards beyond their present frontier which divides the free world from the unfree. The great resources of raw materials and food supplies would be threatened, and any loss of the Eastern potential productive capacity to the free countries would be of great value to the communists. The moral effect of such a loss on India and the other free countries in the East would be great and the repercussions on the West would be far reaching. The security of the Pacific and the United States chain of bases would also be placed in jeopardy and the position of Australia and New Zealand in the middle of the zone would become dangerous. Moreover, the Eastern flank of the Middle zone would become vulnerable and a serious embarrassment to both the Middle zone and European strategies. Unfortunately, the Eastern rampart contains the countries and territories whose peoples have the lowest standard of living in the world and, since the emergence of Asian nationalism, are the most vulnerable to infiltration, subversion and other methods of cold war.

Notwithstanding these two strategic ramparts, for convenience we shall now examine our defence problems ranging round the periphery of the Eurasian land-mass within three different geographical zones, though we must remember that even these wide sweeps of the canvas must not be kept in isolation. In particular, it is necessary to examine our strategy within the compass of each of these three zones because, even with the vast resources of the Western rampart, we cannot be strong everywhere along the enormous communist frontier and so must concentrate in strength in particular areas, especially with regard to the cold war and the Eastern rampart.

The fact that the Soviet Union and her satellites confined themselves for so long to menace in the West and cold war in the East tended to take the eye off the importance of the Middle zone. The oil reserves of the Middle East and the untapped resources of Africa, including the largest known reserves of uranium ore in the Belgian Congo, are a very tempting prospect to an ambitious power not merely from a consideration of its richness. Such a loss to the Western powers would not only seriously deplete their strategic resources but gravely upset their strategies of East and West. A drive southwards in this area could turn the flanks of both the West and the East. It is not only the oilfields of the Middle East which are threatened here but the airways and also the waterways, the Mediterranean and the Indian Ocean for example, which are most vital to the Western powers. The great variety of nationalisms in the Middle East which find their expression in cold or local wars suggests that it is most vulnerable and an area which requires a far-sighted policy and a determined strategy.

We shall see that the study of the military problems associated with each of the three zones gives great significance and importance to the formulation of our various offensive and defensive strategies within the framework of sound joint strategy and this in turn within a sound Allied combined strategy.

First, there is the Western zone embracing Western Europe together with the United Kingdom, the American Continent and the Atlantic Ocean and secondly the Eastern zone, which covers the Pacific Ocean and the free countries of its western shores and the eastern part of the Indian Ocean: thirdly, the Middle zone comprising the Mediterranean, the Middle East including the Persian Gulf countries, Africa and the western parts of the Indian Ocean. Problems of the northern part of the Eurasian periphery extending into the polar regions are included in the northern aspects of the Western and Eastern zones where they properly belong in global strategy.

Before we proceed to examine in detail the three strategic zones there is one overall problem which should be considered. Since the basis of Western defence with regard both to deterrents against aggressors in peacetime and military action in war, is long range strategic air offensive against the Soviet and her satellite home fronts, a permanent need is a global pattern of air bases round the periphery of their land-mass of land bases supplemented by carrier bases. Fortunately, the Western nations are well provided with regions throughout the world for this purpose. Satisfactory land air bases are available in the United Kingdom, Western Europe, North Africa, the Middle East and to some extent in the Far East but the areas in front of these bases must also be secure. The fact that the greatest number and best air bases in these regions lie in the United Kingdom, makes this country one of the most likely to be heavily attacked by enemy bombers from the earliest hour of hostilities. The Western nations also have the Atlantic, the Mediterranean, the Indian Ocean and the Pacific as suitable seas from which to operate carrier-based aircraft against the enemy home front. The use of both land and sea bases make an excellent combination and give the Western air forces great flexibility and advantage in an all-out air offensive against Soviet Russia and her satellites.

In contrast to the vulnerability of the United Kingdom where limited area suggests the intensification of defence measures, and paradoxically, even suggests a reasonable degree of successful defence, the vast Soviet and Chinese land-mass provides a definite advantage to these nations. They do not have to defend all of it, though we should need a very great extent of defence for an area only a fraction of their size. The thousands of square miles lend themselves first to dispersal and then concealment and it might prove extremely difficult for a bomber force to hit specific military targets. The great concern of Western nations is that the next war, whether total or limited, will be fought in Europe with the distinct possibility of turning it into a radio-active desert.

The organization needed to deal with the local and cold war is very different from that required for total war because the military-diplomatic picture in local or cold war is quite different from that of an unlimited threat. In the West where the menace is of a very specific reality the organization exists for dealing with both the cold and total war. In the Middle East and South-East Asia the Western powers are more prepared for a general widespread conflict than for the exigencies of containment demanded by the strategical pattern in those areas. The splintered and separate organizations to deal with local and cold wars are amply demonstrated by the fact that three local wars have already been fought in isolation: by Great Britain in Malaya, by France in Indo-China and in Korea which last was the only example of a unified command though mainly United States.

This situation brings us to one of the central problems with which this book is concerned, that is, the need for a new national and Allied strategy. It is generally accepted that the chief weakness of the Western powers in South-East Asia and in the Middle East has been their political approach. Cold war in dispersed areas of the globe lends itself to dispersed national attitudes: a fact well appreciated by the Communist powers; and outside a total war the urgency for unification and organization does not present itself so keenly. The first task of the political power is to create those conditions which will make such a unification, if it ever becomes necessary, as swift and as least irksome as possible. Even in Western Europe where the military-diplomatic organization has become highly complex there is still a great deal to be done to secure the most efficient use of resources, of forces in their functional roles and of raw materials.

There are few differences between the United Kingdom and the United States in the basic aspects of strategy such as weapons, forces and the balance of weapons and forces and their respective roles. The differences occur in the national political concepts and approaches to specific military problems and in the views on the probability of proposed action leading from limited to total war or on the national military parochial approaches, dogma and doctrine, with regard to the military application to specific problems.

In NATO there is virtually no difference in the United Kingdom and the United States strategies. Neither country has any colonial interests in the area and the common threat from Soviet Russia and her satellites is sufficient to resolve any national differences which might otherwise arise. In the Middle East or Middle zone differences arise, on the one hand, from a suspicion engendered in the American mind of British colonial and commercial policy, and, on the other hand, a feeling that the Americans do not wholly appreciate the strategic possibilities, both defensive and offensive, of the area. In the Far East and South-East Asia, however, there are many United Kingdom and United States differences which are due largely to their several colonial and commercial interests in these areas. Parochial views are taken on numerous political issues while many senior United States officers are apt to regard this zone as the concern of the United States and are somewhat jealous of British military concepts based on British colonialism. Because each nation has its own interests and influence in these zones it has evolved its own national strategies to secure them. The threat has not become serious enough to bring these strategies together spontaneously and it is unquestionable that a combined United Kingdom-United States strategy would have a profound influence on the effectiveness and economy of our two national strategies in the area.

Obviously there are large fringe zones beyond the critical perimeters in Europe, the Middle zone and the Far East where there can be more room for give and take and where Russia and China should be kept guessing on the reactions of the Western countries, whatever the nature and degree and locality of the attack spread over the whole range of incidents from infiltration to nuclear attack itself. These fringe zones contain numerous strategic contours of penetration according to the importance of the area. For example, the inner strategic contour enclosing Singapore is of higher importance than its outer associated contour enclosing Indo-China. In Allied strategy Chinese direct attack on the former would certainly bring nuclear retaliation against targets in China whereas retaliation against an attack on the latter objective might well be of a lesser nature.

In military problems as in political we must develop a global view, and regrettably, there is apt to be more heartburning than heart-searching in this respect. We shall see, however, throughout this examination, that the operations of surface forces and those which use the third dimension are inseparably interlocked. Neither alone can be relied upon in any likely circumstances to secure the defeat of an enemy since the possibilities of effective action by one part of the armed forces are created by the other and vice versa. This interdependence of the various forms of surface and air forces transcends the mere notion of co-operation on the battlefield with which the Second World War has made professional and non-professional opinion familiar.

An attempt has been made here to present the problem of these vital geographical zones rather than to deal with them in detail since a thorough appreciation of the strategical problems involved requires careful and possibly lengthy consideration. A policy of containment is one of peculiar difficulty. The deterrent power of the Western powers consists of two parts, namely, (1) the combat and (2) organizational components: That is, (1) the armed forces, weapons and their necessary resource of materials with which to prosecute war of any kind in any eventuality; (2) the organizational component is the element of command, the military planners and the framers of diplomatic policy who determine when and where the combat component will be employed. With this latter element this work has a special concern, and, in the detailed survey of these geographical zones which follows, it is hoped to show both the strength and weakness of the current concepts of organizational command in relation to the strategy which has emanated from it, and the additional strength it may gain from a new concept of strategy.

CHAPTER IV

Western Europe

I

THE paradox of Soviet Russia preaching peace while pursuing a policy of aggression in Eastern Europe soon shattered the brief illusion of universal amity engendered by the victory of 'comrades in arms' over Nazi Germany and her allies. So emerged the phenomenon of the cold war in its post-war shape which, combined with a large scale threat to the nations of Western Europe, has revolutionized British and American foreign policies and strategic concepts. Since 1945 containment of communist ambition has involved three things. It has meant a guarantee of military aid and protection for independent Governments against attack, as in Greece and Turkey in 1947; providing immediate aid in arms and supplies to any Government attacked by forces under communist supervision: lastly it involves economic aid to Governments trying to combat agitation and unrest by social reform.

Such a policy and principle of containment diverts attention from the key area of Western Europe including the United Kingdom to important but militarily less vital areas of Asia and the Middle East, and as time passes more and more of our forces are likely to be occupied in tasks which are less military than political. It may be successful for one area and a failure in another while at the same time it imposes on the Western powers the strain of dispersing their vital resources both of man-power and material. It lays on them the inflexible strategy of holding the line everywhere in positions sometimes militarily untenable, and it has absorbed the energies of French forces in Indo-China and then in North Africa urgently needed in Europe.

In view of this there is good reason why we should be clear about the importance of the Western zone even though there can be no doubt about it. The apparently static strategy of defence imposed on us by the present exigencies need not after all be an inert one.

In any strategic consideration of a geographical zone some authorities attempt to define where it begins and where it ends, but for our purpose it is more profitable to trace the changing patterns of the zones in their relation to the development of strategy rather than define the precise contemporary limits. Nevertheless, today the Western zone is a vague area which includes the American continent, the Atlantic Ocean extending northwards over the Arctic region; the countries of Western Europe bounded by the western seaboard, and the Iron Curtain from Norway to the Mediterranean, as well as the western regions of North Africa.

Within this area lies the citadel of Allied military global strategy. In North America are the largest centres of industrial and military production, including atomic and hydrogen weapons, in the world. Western Europe, however, where the strategic area is more or less defined by the non-communist countries on the continent, must be accorded a very special place in Allied strategy because, not only is it second only to America in industrial production, but from it spring the culture and values of the whole of Western civilization. The piecemeal acquisition of Western Europe by Russia would not simply spell disaster for the free European countries but even the might of America would be threatened, so great would be the advantages of man-power, productivity, resources and strategic positions which would accrue to the Soviet. Moreover, it would be unwise to overlook the fact that while there are some of the most satisfactory bases for land and expanses of sea for carrier-based nuclear offensives against the critical target systems of the Soviet bloc in the West and Asia Minor, the Western zone contains numerous vital and vulnerable target centres for attack by the Russians with nuclear weapons.

II

This brings us to our first major consideration in dealing with the Western zone, the vulnerability of the United Kingdom. Though geographically the United Kingdom lies at the outer edge of Europe it represents a power which transcends those nearer neighbours of Soviet Russia on the continent. The conquest of Europe would be far from complete without the defeat of Britain and conversely, if such a defeat could be brought about at the outset of a conflict, the rest of Europe would fall into the lap of communism. The fact that Hitler began by over-running Europe and so leaving Britain a breathing space which ultimately meant his downfall is something which will not be lost on the Russians.

The United Kingdom defence system is said to be the most efficient in the world yet there is no question but that it is most vulnerable to the menace of the strategic bomber and the ballistic rocket. For the use of atomic or hydrogen bombs a much smaller force can be employed with far greater effectiveness than the thousands of aircraft used during the last war. Fighter aircraft are not today capable of taking a large toll of the kind of bomber which would carry these weapons, nor is the guided missile yet sufficiently advanced to guarantee their annihilation, which would be essential. The bomber force sent against the United Kingdom need not be a big one and out of a few hundred it seems certain that a critical number would get through. It also seems certain that something under two dozen hydrogen bombs, dropped on our largest cities and key areas would be enough to break Great Britain's power and the will to resist. Thus, we must take all possible measures to try and ensure that these bombs never fall on Britain. We must make full use of our Allied superior wealth and scientific and productive capacity to fashion forces adequate and in immediate readiness to deter the Soviet from making war, and at the same time capable of exacting the heaviest toll of the enemy bomber forces carrying mass-destruction weapons should the deterrent fail. Notwithstanding the possession of such an Allied force, should total war occur and we cannot prevent the enemy directing the small critical number of hydrogen bombs on Great Britain, we must remember that it would be of little consolation to the United Kingdom to know that the United States Strategic Air Command was then meting out to Russian cities what she had just endured. The awareness of our vulnerability was brought home to us during the Korean conflict when the least irresponsibility on the part of the Americans might have turned a local war into a total one. Our vulnerability with regard to atomic and hydrogen weapons has an anomalous twist in that while we are most anxious to prevent their use, we should

E

ourselves be forced to initiate their use if the Russian divisions tried to overrun Europe.

For something approaching a hundred years British diplomacy has been concerned to find ways and means of keeping Russian power in check without creating a dangerous increase in the power of Germany or France. Then, not long after the end of the last war America joined Great Britain in considering urgently the best strategy to secure Western Europe, lying shattered but still important. Soviet Russian post-war policy determined not only British and American diplomacy but also forced upon us an Allied combined strategy for the Western zone. The very fact that NATO headquarters were established in Paris and not in London made clear that the intention is to render Western Europe defensible and not merely to liberate Europe after it has been overrun. After the last war, the Western countries had demobilized their armed forces down to meagre dimensions compared with the forces retained by the Russian bloc and however they strove they could only redress this unbalance over a period of several years. Fortunately the Western countries had a powerful restraining force at hand. The war spur of Hitler which, temporarily at least, had placed the Western powers ahead of any other country in weapon development, became the shield which saved post-war Europe from the expanding pressure of Russia while NATO was being built up.

Today, the strength of NATO has developed substantially. The direction of NATO strategy is in the hands of two bodies: the Standing Group of the Atlantic Council consisting of representatives of only Britain, the United States and France, and through this committee, the Military Committee of the Atlantic Council consisting of representatives of all the member nations of NATO. Britain attaches great importance to using the Standing Group as much as possible because the direction of strategic affairs, specially in war, can be handled so much better by a body of three than one of eleven members: in fact the latter is impracticable. Also Britain believes she is likely to have more influence in the smaller body when in argument with America than in the larger Military Committee. On the other hand, and probably for the latter reason, America is apt, at least in peacetime, to want to make greater use of the Military Committee than does Britain.

In contrast to the many years of diplomatic attempts to secure

Europe which failed to prevent two World Wars, NATO now promises a way of containing Russia and at the same time harnessing Germany to the orbit of our defences. Not only has the admission of Germany to NATO enabled the Western Powers to adopt a forward strategy in the defence of Western Europe at the Elbe instead of on the Rhine, but the integration of German forces into NATO has secured this control in that they have little potential without the maintenance, supplies and resources of NATO. This is an example of the full significance of combined strategy. Not only is it overcoming parochial service strategies, but it is turning things full circle so that combined strategy is the very power which controls the might of Germany, and keeps her strategy within the harness of NATO.

Britain's acceptance of partnership in the Western European Union is a break with policy of many years standing because her forces are now integrated into the same common organization as the German, French and other continental countries, and to this extent Britain has forfeited some sovereign rights in respect of her strategy in Western Europe. Actually, the sovereign states of NATO even permit an international body to recommend their respective contributions to the common defence effort. Although in recent years Canada has endorsed the idea of a closer unity with the rest of Western Europe the British policy of maintaining the somewhat elusive entity of the Commonwealth has made her hesitate to get too involved on the continent especially as the overseas members of the Commonwealth might not support such action. This latter consideration is held in great esteem since Great Britain knows that she only survived two world wars because of her sea power which enabled her to use her links with the Commonwealth and then later, in each case, with the help of the United States. A primary factor in British change of policy is that the United States is now committed to the defence of Europe as fully as the United Kingdom.

The establishment of NATO and SHAPE has involved a parallel development in the face of a trying demand for recovery and recuperation. It has meant the development of co-ordinated defences and a plan for the integration of forces and war production. Defences have been made and while a great step forward has been taken with regard to new political relationships of Governments, it is here that weakness may assert itself either through the effects of the loosening of tension, general apathy or the barrage of economic strategy and communist propaganda.

III

Although atomic and hydrogen weapons have the cardinal place in the Allied combined and the Western national strategies, the national land forces and air support allocated to SHAPE and the Western European Union are the shield of Western Europe. Without these forces not only would the whole structure of NATO collapse, but the Western European will to resist communist infiltration and piecemeal aggression of every kind would also collapse, even in the cold war and in local war. In limited or total war, the withdrawal of any substantial part of the present Western army divisions would expose the whole of Western Europe to being overrun. Thus, on the one hand, Western Europe would sink so far under the Soviet yoke that little would be left to liberate, and on the other it would dangerously weaken the depth of our air defence at present lying on the Elbe. With Western Europe overrun, not only would Allied strategic bombing against Russian centres become more difficult, but the vital targets and Great Britain itself would be still more gravely exposed to air attack of every kind, both by aircraft and ballistic rockets.

There is general agreement between the British and Americans that neither can stand alone in the defence of the Old World in the same way as America sometimes suggests she can in the Far East. In the areas which flank these two zones, however, the issue over Allied strategic dependence is less clear cut. For example, in the Middle zone which flanks Western Europe and in South-East Asia which flanks the Far East, the British Commonwealth does not hesitate to declare that although these have long been her spheres of influence, today she needs help from America. On the other hand, as made clear elsewhere, the United States has been slow to accept any such responsibility though now the Allied concept of combined strategy in these parts is becoming clearer to both countries. In fact, today the United States accepts that even British-American combined strengths cannot secure the outward pressure along the long perimeter of the Russian and Chinese blocs against cold, local and limited war without an effective combined strategy. It is now acknowledged that in recent years it was the absence of an adequate combined strategy that led the respective countries to political and military differences. This was not so much due to national differences being given to the strategic significance of the various regions of the earth, but to transmitting military thinking and strategy into practical plans. This has come about by the different national opinions and interests at various times, with the consequent different national strategies, resulting in national actions of strengthening one area at the cost of weakening another, becoming out of step within the different zones, but especially between the zones.

It is made clear in a later chapter that there are still some differences in strategy in respect of the flanks of this stronghold area. No differences arise from the northern flank which comprises Denmark and Norway and this is mainly because there are no conflicting Anglo-American interests in this sphere. There have, however, been some serious differences about the South-East flank and it is worth describing these to illustrate the different national approaches to a combined strategic problem. In particular, the United States viewed the inclusion of Greece and Turkey to NATO merely as an extension of the European defence system on the under and South-East flanks. Britain viewed this extension in quite a different strategic concept. In this, Britain seems to have been ahead of America in realizing or at least acknowledging that in total, limited, local and cold war, it is not sufficient for the Allies to confine their strategy to the NATO area. As stated already, Britain looks upon the Middle East as being contained in a second global zone and its security is not only of great importance to the NATO region but also to the interests of the Middle East itself. The British concept of global strategy is that the Middle zone, lying between the Western and Eastern zones, must be considered to be within a separate theatre. Thus, there should be separate supreme commands such as SHAPE for the North Atlantic, the Middle East, South-East Asia and the Far East. Such aspects of the strategies of the different theatres as the allocation of resources between theatres and the issue of directions and the approval of plans, must be adjusted by a central high Allied authority similar to the Combined Chiefs of Staff of the Second World War, or an extension of the present Standing Group of NATO.

Some thought should be paid to the assertion that Britain and America are partners in arms but unrelenting rivals in peace and trade. Defence preparations in the last few years have retarded the smooth economic recovery of the United Kingdom, and there is a body of unmilitary opinion which regards rearmament as a facet of American policy rather than British. This is, of course, nonsense, but a nation already impoverished by two great wars and forced to undertake the gigantic task of 'standing to' in case of another, tends to look forward to a time when the menace or threat of war will be considerably less, and to a return of prosperity. The general fear is that Anglo-American relations are things of the moment, born of the emergency, and whenever amity does return among the nations the British will be furthering preparations for a war possibly never fought; and she will find it increasingly difficult to recover the markets she formerly enjoyed, or indeed find any markets at all. The effect on British economy of the great strain she has already put on it, and will yet have to put on it, will leave her less fitted than in the past for the 'free for all' of competitive trade: and that in the face of the revival of Western Germany and Japan. In view of this attitude the suspicions of lesser nations towards American policy in Europe seem not unnatural. However, except for what seemed to the British to be a hasty and unsympathetic act in cancelling her lease-lend arrangements soon after the last war, the United States merit great esteem for the policy of aid to Europe and the free countries. America's post-war attitude may be regarded as an earnest of her view of the post-emergency period. Meanwhile, whatever may be the economics of peacetime, it is to be hoped that such wise practical vision of America will continue to be extended to the present emergency, not merely in the sense of what she can give Britain, but in the awareness of the unquestionable strength of the United Kingdom. The lessons for Allied strategy here need scarcely be underlined.

IV

Neutrality in Europe is something which the Communist bloc are doing everything they can to encourage *outside* the Iron Curtain: and nothing demonstrates so clearly the communist tenacity of purpose,

as that countries unable to preserve their independence cannot afford
to be neutral. 'Armed neutrality' is therefore an unnecessary emphasis
since neutrality must be armed in order to remain so. Western ideas
of neutrality and respect for it are traditional whereas the communist
attitude to neutrality has been determined by the number of divisions
which the neutral could muster. There is no reason to suppose that
they would respect any 'neutral belt' and would propose such a line
of neutrality only in so far as it would be to their own advantage, as
the situation of isolated and unorganized countries is likely to be.
The more neutrals they can carve out of Europe on the Western side of
the Iron Curtain the better from their point of view: it will only be a
short step to convert such neutrals by adequate menaces into satellites.

There are, however, several genuine neutrals in Europe and foremost
among them are Sweden and Switzerland, who are in spirit and sympathy at least on the side of the Western democracies and spent much
time and trouble in the task of European recovery after the war. They
each possess resolute forces and no one would deny their determination
to maintain their independence.

There is a large question-mark against Spain since she is in no sense
a liberal democracy: but she has a great incentive in preventing the
spread of communism and halting the march of either Russian ideology or Russian troops. Her forces are by no means negligible and
her western and southern coasts could provide ample areas for dis-
embarking Allied forces if more northern ports should be temporarily
closed, and besides being a good general military base she has a number
of valuable naval bases and sites for air bases. The strategic significance
has come to be more widely appreciated by the United States than by
closer neighbours of Spain. The American approach is a much more
realistic one than the British, which, like that of France, is apt to be
coloured by the memory of the Civil War which has been described
as the 'cold war of the 'thirties'. It is also suggested that possibly Spain
is not yet ripe for the role of an ally or a place in NATO, but the truth is
rather that Britain herself and certain sections of opinion on the
continent are not yet ripe enough to accept her.

Leaving aside the new-found neutrality of Austria, a country which
has been neutralized, which emphasizes afresh the different voluntary
neutrality of countries like Sweden or Switzerland, the defence of

her neighbour Yugoslavia to the south-east has a particular significance for the Western powers. Yugoslavia is a most important country in European defence and is a good example of the influence of geography both in relation to NATO defence as a whole, and internally within Yugoslavia itself: because of the layout of the mountains and rivers, most of the communications of Yugoslavia run north and south, which make it easy to invade from the north. It is a communist country which has no common frontier with the Soviet Union and represented in the heart of Europe that most valuable asset, a clash between over-riding ideology of Russian communism and a sound Nationalism. Though throughout the post-war years she has been sitting on the fence gathering what advantage she could both from Soviet Russia and the Western powers she is also a member of the important pro-NATO Balkan alliance. Her vacillations between one camp and the other amply illustrates how political events may change the strategic picture completely. That Tito has been able to deny the Soviet any interference in his internal policy is of the highest importance. The continued improvement in that corner of Europe is strategically correct; and any large-scale attack on Yugoslavia from her communist dominated neighbours would result in an appeal to the United Nations. Her forces are adequate in certain limited circumstances and are capable of dealing with internal or guerilla warfare.

The defence area in Western Europe is shaped roughly like a slice of melon with a specially long flank reaching round to Turkey. Like a melon too, the tenderest part is in the centre and it is here that the defence forces of the West are concentrated. There is a disparity of distance, interest and sympathy between the Scandinavian and Latin countries — a diversity further emphasized by the additional wings of Greece and Turkey. The remoteness of the flanks may tend to lead to demands for aid or forces which cannot well be spared from the defence of the centre where such relaxation would create difficulties for the French and West German Governments. The main strength of the NATO position east of the Rhine is at present in the command of the Mediterranean and the exits from the Baltic and North Sea ports. There are, however, three good reasons why the defence of Western Europe is concentrated in Western Germany. A strategy of withdrawal and liberation is impossible in the mood of post-war Europeans.

There is the vital necessity for the United States and the United Kingdom to show a united front in the area. As already stated a communist occupation would annihilate every worthwhile object, or person capable of leadership, or value, in the countries concerned so that there would be nothing left to liberate.

While France and Italy are particularly sensitive to this last possibility they are hardly more so than Western Germany; and apart from the rearming of Western Germany they feel that the Allies should continue to deploy more and more troops in the vital area. A strategy entirely imposed by political factors is inferior to one which can choose its area of defence within limits set by geographical factors, manpower, economic reasons and national tradition.

v

Germany is now a member of NATO and an integral part of the Western European Union which is dependent on several of the other parts of military strength. But let us not overlook two vital aspects in Germany's growing military power. On the one hand, the great strength, especially in land warfare, she will give to the European Defence Community as her industry and military forces develop. On the other, there is the enormous influence she will have on our strategy. Indeed, Germany will dominate our strategy in West Europe because her central European position together with her war potential makes it easy, and almost natural, for her to play off East and West in order to widen her sphere of interests and influence. Moreover, apart from the central position, sentiment of unity is deep-set and the reunification of Germany is coming increasingly into the foreground as the major issue of politics in Germany and in Europe. So long as Russia is at loggerheads with America and the other Western powers, Germany will play one against the other because it is natural that her policy will be to secure every advantage out of her key position between East and West.

Few Germans today are really resigned to the loss of territory, either in the east or in the west. Germany hardly expects to recover her boundaries of 1941, but she will not be statisfied with less than the boundaries of 1937, and possibly those of 1939. Today, Germany is master of her own fate. NATO strategy must be conceived and directed wisely and generously to ensure that she does not also become the master of Europe's fate. Under the recent Western European Union organization, all Western German forces come directly under SHAPE control. The effective safeguard against any irredentist venture on the part of re-armed Germany is not the Western European Union agency but the logistic power now given to SHAPE: the power to stop the flow of jet fuel through the NATO pipelines, and to cut off ammunition and other supplies. At heart Russia knows that America and Britain are non-aggressors, but she has good cause to fear Germany as she sees her military power developing. Russia must also be anxious that Germany does not drag America and Britain into an alliance to recover her lost territories.

NATO in its beginnings had no capacity to hold any Russian assault and its whole strategy centred round the atomic bomb and the United States Strategic Air Command. Although NATO forces have been greatly extended the shield of NATO strategy remains with nuclear weapons now augmented by hydrogen weapons together with the bombers of the United States Strategic Air Command and the United States fleets as well as the British Bomber Command and British fleets to deliver the weapons. These forces are due to be further strengthened by inter-continental ballistic rockets with nuclear warheads. Inevitably, this shield is now being seriously challenged by similar forces possessed by Russia. It is this mutual challenge which has become the great deterrent to aggression but which, paradoxically, might lead to total war in Europe or elsewhere.

As suggested, the aggressor knows the first move, and that move, in the nature of things, must coincide with what she considers to be her advantage. The temptation and determination, on the part of an aggressor, to seize an advantage despite the deterrent, is the prime danger of the Allied powers in the West.

CHAPTER V

The Middle Zone

I

IN moving on from a consideration of the strategy of Western Europe to an appreciation of other areas the initial impression is not strictly a military one though it is inextricably bound up with strategy. While the Soviet bloc maintains a united political front (synonymous with military unity for them) both in the West and East, the Western powers have so far achieved an appreciable measure of unity only in Western Europe: a unity which is kept alive by the awareness of a common danger. NATO's functions, of course, should not be expected to cover the globe. They are conceived and shaped for the defence of a specific area, but the lessons learnt in NATO could be utilized in the creation of other regional defence pacts, always remembering that there are many differing circumstances and factors. A large part of the United States, and the United Kingdom, strategic policy abroad, and particularly in the Middle East and South-East Asia, is characterized by a lack of positive approach. In contrast to the universal panacea offered by the communists (whatever we may think of it) we offer to nationals in these areas a guarantee of freedom and aid. In these marginal areas we are continually poised on the dilemma of showing our strength and restraining the use of it. In return for guarantees, the demands we make on the various nationals that they make some definite contribution to their own defence are of some political delicacy. Generally speaking, however, confidence in the Allies will increase in relation to the voice with which they speak. A more positive approach to strategy in the Middle zone will come when the United States and the United Kingdom have evolved an adequate Allied combined strategy and so speak with one voice and not two.

The strategic area associated with the Middle East has increased greatly in size with the development of war. In the early days, the

Middle East area of strategic significance was merely the coastal strip, leading from the Balkans to Egypt, of the western seaboard of the Arabian peninsula at the eastern end of the Mediterranean. The vast expanses of desert in all other directions surrounding Egypt except up the Nile itself were not regarded of any value other than as a strategic obstacle. Today the Middle zone comprises that part of Asia Minor known as the Middle East, and can be taken to include those lands and territories between the Eastern Mediterranean and the Indian sub-continent. This means the Arab countries, together with Israel and Iran. The region still provides a landbridge connecting Europe, North Africa and Southern Asia, and the strategic issues are fairly plain, since the northern frontier of this region marches with that of Russian influence for over three thousand miles from Bulgaria to the Pamir Plateau so that any relaxation of vigilance would present opportunities for infiltration or aggression on the part of the communists.

At the beginning of the First World War, our naval and army schools of strategic thought for overseas theatres diverged as substantially as they did at home. Any concept of a National joint strategy in this sphere was even more remote than in the United Kingdom. There is no doubt that the ebb and flow of the prominence of naval and army operations since the downfall of Napoleon had a great influence on the relationship between our Services which resulted in two separate and rather uncoordinated strategies. In particular, both the Crimean and South African wars were primarily army affairs with the naval role being limited virtually to transportation. This, together with the army's problems in India, and, after the Agadir crisis, their great preoccupation with the European threat from Germany resulted in a bias towards army strategy to the detriment of a consolidated joint strategy. Moreover, the size and power of the Indian army played an important part in all our thinking of Middle East strategy.

Thus, at the beginning of the First World War, although our naval High Command had sound views on the place of naval strategy overseas, the army strategic concept was virtually a defensive one of holding our main base in Egypt. So much was this a defensive strategy that the plan was to hold the Suez Canal on the Egyptian side against Turkish attack. It was not until the Turkish army had made several raids across the Canal and Kitchener himself had made a visit from London to the Middle East that the defence concept was widened so that the Canal was protected by holding a line in the desert on the Sinai side. As the war developed, the strategic concept developed also. The first penalty we had to pay for our lack of a well-thought out national strategy, was the army stalemate in Europe. This forced us to joint strategy in the Mediterranean which emerged as the Dardanelles campaign, but this failed ignominiously because the High Command in Whitehall had not yet spontaneously accepted a concept of joint strategy, even in this simple form, but had merely made a hurried and improvised half-hearted plan without the will to see it fulfilled. The disturbing aspect of this particular failure is that the strategic lessons had not been learnt or recorded for the next great war.

Certainly, as the First World War developed, the Balkans, and particularly Turkey, which has so often played an important part in our strategy, re-emerged with fresh significance. Subsequently, the pattern of our strategy extended to Mesopotamia (now Iraq), Palestine, Transjordan and Syria; indeed, to the whole of the Middle East and the waters of the Mediterranean and the Indian Ocean.

II

By the Second World War, the geographic concept of the Middle East had enlarged even wider: that is along the whole length of the Mediterranean on the northern shores from Gibraltar through Spain, France, Italy, Greece, Turkey, the whole of Arabia and thence Iran and into the waters of the Indian Ocean. On the Southern shores of the Mediterranean from Gibraltar, the strategic area stretched through Morocco, Algeria, Tunisia, Libya, Egypt, Sudan, Somaliland, Ethiopia and ultimately South Africa.

By this time we had three Services and this great war found us then with three separate Service strategies in the Middle East. Far from there being a non-partisan overall strategy for this theatre, there was substantial controversy between the respective Service strategies. The navy followed their traditional role and strategy of safeguarding the Mediterranean sea communications and assumed the continued availability of their crucial base at Malta and the continued use of the Suez

Canal for the passage of naval vessels. It was accepted that merchant shipping passing through to the Indian Ocean and beyond would have to use the Cape route, even at the great extra cost in shipping and resources. Whatever wishful thinking there had been about using the Mediterranean for merchant shipping in war was now refuted.

The army view continued to assume that, in most directions, the vast expanse of desert protected their Middle East base from enemy assault. Preoccupied by their strategy in Western Europe, the army had few thoughts for anything more than holding operations in the Middle East. In the event, the crucial importance of the great oil reserves of the Middle East strongly underlined the problems and strategy in safeguarding them. The war also threw into high relief the importance of the Middle East countries and waters as a theatre for most critical operations. Victory in this theatre brought us far-reaching benefits, but our defeat would have brought the enemy benefits perhaps even greater: access to the important supplies of oil, to North Africa and the Mediterranean and the Indian Ocean, the Indian sub-continent and beyond: it would have meant too, the loss of our important base and of the manpower in the Indian Army.

The air force, preoccupied by their strategic concepts of attacking German war potential at its source, and their jealous regard of reducing their effort to provide air support to naval or army operations, led to air strategy in the Middle East being placed as secondary to air strategy in Europe. At this time air strategy was not sufficiently mature to enable air force leaders to grasp the great part waiting for it in the Middle East and other overseas theatres. The war proved all too well the importance of air support to the navy and army, properly balanced with strategic bombing in these parts.

In the Middle East and the Mediterranean Lord Tedder was under great pressure from the navy and army to give air support as they understood it which meant maximum direct air support for every manœuvre or operation the navy and army planned. With very limited air forces he refused to dissipate them in the penny packets the older Services were demanding. Although it may seem a platitude to mention the paramount importance of keeping air forces flexible, at that time the navy and army were each pressing for a fixed and rigid allocation for themselves. At critical times Lord Tedder saw

Map 'B'

This map shows the perspective from which the United Kingdom and Western Europe see their Afro-Asian military and commercial problems. Note the primary importance this view gives to Middle East sea and air communications.

The dotted line along the Iron Curtain shows the contour of maximum strategic penetration of first concern to the United Kingdom —the threat from East of the Iron Curtain.

The arrows pointing Eastwards show the direction of view of the United Kingdom Afro-Asian problems.

the attack against Rommel's lines of communication as the basic role of the air force, with support to the navy and army only when they were fighting decisive battles. As the Middle East campaign developed and the lessons of our catastrophes in Greece, Crete and other operations became apparent he lost no opportunity of bringing the then conditions of modern war to the notice of all concerned in the High Command. He created a new spirit and a new technique of co-operating with the other Services and his contribution to the overall conception, planning and organization of the war in the Middle East and the Mediterranean was considerable.

The outstanding lesson in the Middle East was the ability of air power to render impotent any naval forces operating in a relatively enclosed sea: the extent of the enclosure being determined largely by the range of the aircraft. The situation in the Mediterranean was manageable so long as we had only to deal with the Italians, but once the German air force came into the theatre and acquired air bases on both sides of the Mediterranean our naval force had to retire or be progressively punished. Later, as we became stronger and acquired air bases all along the North African coast, we prevented reinforcements of enemy forces from Europe by sea and ultimately also by air. The battles in North Africa were thus really battles for air bases: a fact which had a direct, positive and vital effect upon our international and inter-Service strategy since it dictated what we could and could not do.

III

Thus we see the changing pattern of strategic problems of the Middle Zone which developed up to the Second World War. But in some ways even more radical changes followed in the post-war period. Although during these years strategy in this zone has been conceived in terms of the military threat of Soviet Russia and her associates, there have been numerous problems affecting this strategy resulting from the rise of nationalism of the contiguous countries. In particular, the serious loss to the remainder of the Commonwealth of the Indian army and of India as a military base, reduced radically British military power not only in South-East Asia, but also in the Middle East, and indeed in the whole world. There has followed the withdrawal of British forces from Palestine, Egypt and the Suez, Sudan, and the controversy with Iran over the oil treaty. On the other hand, the stouthearted and fiercely independent Turkey now lies within NATO and is also allied to Iraq, Iran and Pakistan and, supported by America, she now holds a key position standing guard across the Bosphorus and along the Caucasus mountains to the Iran border: a real bulwark against Russian expansion. The results of these post-war changes have a profound effect on the Middle zone strategy.

It is true that the British were slow in readjusting their strategy in the Middle East to the new forward strategy made possible by the alliance with Turkey and made necessary by modern weapons. Each Service tended to make its own separate rather than joint inter-Service approach to the new situation. The navy hesitated to see further than their old concept of Egypt and its naval bases flanking the Suez Canal and so were reluctant to accept any new strategy. Likewise, the army continued to think along the lines of their many years of occupation of Egypt and the form taken by their strategy during the two world wars. The air force was probably the first of the Services to show the way to a new thinking of a forward strategy.

On the other hand, a strategy to contain any military advance of Russia into the Middle zone is not in itself adequate. The rise of violent nationalism in Egypt and the other Arab countries, and in Israel, calls for some international power to safeguard the free passage of world-wide shipping through the Suez Canal in both peace and war. In consequence, it is unfortunate that before this waterway could be secured, political events forced Great Britain to withdraw from the Suez Canal and adopt a new strategy framed on modern mobility together with a base in Cyprus, as well as base facilities in Libya.

This failure to secure international agreement might well lead to serious trouble before the affairs of the Middle East are brought within bounds. In this context, we would do well to note that the Middle East is an apt illustration of a situation where the Great Powers could become involved in a limited rather than a total war. For example, should Russia decide to use military force to aid the Arab countries against the Western Powers, she might choose to exclude the use of nuclear weapons, or at least to confine their use to a tactical role in the Middle East area.

In this event, the Western Powers might well choose likewise so to limit the use of nuclear weapons. It is of course true that either of the main contestants could at any time decide that, according to the circumstances and progress of the war, it would be to their advantage to initiate the full strategic use of nuclear weapons within or beyond the Middle East. On the other hand, it is quite conceivable that rather than take such measures, the Great Powers would prefer a stalemate or some negotiated peace. Thus, the ultimate sanction of total war might never develop from such a limited war.

The truth is that the Allies had dragged their feet towards a combined strategy in the Middle East far more than the individual Services. It is not surprising that Britain with her years of experience in this zone and virtually carrying alone the interests of the non-communist countries of the world grasped, before the United States, the need of a combined strategy in the Middle East.

To British thinking the Mediterranean has strategic importance as a highway of commerce and the main artery of sea and air communications leading to the Indian Ocean, the Far East, Australia and New Zealand, and then an alternative route to America. The Middle East is also of great strategic significance to the Western nations because from the Mediterranean, Soviet Russia could not only turn the flank of Western Europe from the East, but could strike along the Persian Gulf and thence south into the Indian Ocean, and also south to Africa where there are believed to be large untapped resources of several vital raw materials. In this respect the Belgian Congo contains the world's largest known reserves of uranium ore.

In contrast, the United States pattern of strategic thinking in the Mediterranean has tended to be confined primarily to the southern flank of Western Europe together with the access it gives for their air bases. To the United States, the Pacific is the main artery of communication to the Far East, Australasia and the Indian Ocean. They have been apt to view the Middle East route to the Far East as only a secondary alternative in peace-time and with the Mediterranean, Suez Canal and Indian Ocean links, a vulnerable route in war.

American interest in the Middle East began with missionary and philanthropic activity in the early nineteenth century. In the nineteen-twenties both the United States government and American business began to appreciate the significance of the area since when, in later years, they have moved slowly round to an awareness of its strategic significance. Even so, the United States strategic concept of the area is not wholly formed and they have so far been inclined to conceive the Middle East as a flank or additional feature of NATO, a place for bases from which attacks may be launched in total war and not as an area necessitating rigorous cold- and local-war defence measures. Their attitude with regard to Israel itself appeared almost benign in the face of the conflicting demands which the area made and still makes on the nations concerned with its security. Three problems have stood to the fore for years: the rights of the Jews: the rights of the Arabs: and the security of the zone. The Americans took cognizance of Israel; and while profuse with diplomatic and monetary aid they were reluctant to share the task of military necessity which would attend the establishment of Israel. It is reassuring that recently the United States and the United Kingdom have progressed towards a closer understanding of politics and strategy in the Middle zone.

IV

The post-war Middle zone has been second only to the Far East in troubles from local and cold war. The Israel-Arab conflict, the urge of nationalism, and the intervention of military aid and offers of financial help from the Soviet bloc has disturbed the balance of peace between the contiguous countries and also resulted in repercussions on our own commercial and strategic interests in many ways.

Because of the new rise of Arab and Israel nationalisms and the most bitter hostility against each other; the pressure of the Muslim Brotherhood to return to the strict teaching of the Koran; and the consequential suspicion in the Arab and Israel attitudes to the Western nations, there has only recently emerged a defence organization for some of the Middle East countries which shows the first promise of becoming comparable with the nature and association of the Western European countries voluntarily grouped within NATO. So much is this true that Israel and the Arab countries were prepared to risk communism rather than risk foregoing their newly won independence. It was thought at one time that the Arab Pact against Israel, instigated largely by Egypt and aimed in a lesser degree at the influence of the Western powers, might after all form a basis for the defence of the region. This possibility, however, has not materialized due to the suspicions and dislike engendered among these nationals by the establishment of Israel in their midst, and a general distrust of the aims of the Great Powers concerned in the region. For example, Great Britain is committed by treaty to defend Iraq, Jordan, Egypt, Libya and Saudi Arabia. Great Britain, the United States and France have also guaranteed the present frontiers of Israel, though this guarantee is complicated by the difficulty of determining the actual Egyptian-Israel frontier. Certainly, Israel is the touchstone in the Middle East and it dominates the relations between Egypt and the Western powers. Another country of great strategic influence in the Middle East is Turkey, which stands between Russia and the primary military path to any advance on Egypt. Incidentally, Turkey differs from the Arab countries in that she accepts the new State of Israel as well as membership of NATO. Clearly, we are still far from reaching political and military stability in the Middle East, and major realignments of countries are likely to continue and may be at short notice. The position of Britain's main Middle East base in Cyprus is already associated with any such realignment which has a special significance in our strategy with regard to cold and local war.

Nevertheless, after many disappointments, the free countries have to some extent now in fact bridged the gap in their defence organizations between NATO and SEATO by setting up the Baghdad Council or Pact as an authority to co-ordinate the Northern Tier countries of the Middle East: Turkey, Iraq, Iran and Pakistan together with the full membership support of Great Britain and the liaison, though powerful support of the United States. The three regional defence organizations are different in political, economic and military character, and in their powers and terms of reference because they have been designed to meet the various nationalisms, circumstances, problems and environments with which they are concerned.

The purpose of the Baghdad Pact is to stem the expanding tide of expansionist Russia and her satellites. It is too early to forecast how this pact will develop but clearly the first aim must be to strengthen the Middle East zone in the cold war before proceeding to active preparations against general war. Thus, the first and immense task should be the development and enrichment of the countries which stand in the gap so as to provide the economic strength necessary for any real security against communism. No military Middle East belt is sufficient in itself without this last provision extending throughout the Middle zone. A second aim should be to provide control and regular authority to assess the threat and to knit together a common strategy and tactics for the region to prepare the necessary forces and defences.

Confined at present to the Northern Tier, these efforts should strive to extend their scope to the whole of the Middle zone; in particular, to Egypt and the Suez base. The security of the Middle zone will not, however, be complete until the Baghdad Pact or something equivalent is extended to include the central and southern parts of Africa organized under a Central or Southern Tier of countries.

v

The Second World War in the Middle East probably shows as many lessons in the changing pattern of strategy as any other zone, and illustrates the need of a National joint strategy to weld together in one whole the three separate service strategies. Indeed, this war put the urgent need of this national strategy in relief. But the period since the Second World War has made even more clear a further strategic concept. As already mentioned, the need of an Allied combined strategy has at last been made apparent to our American allies. From this overall combined strategy, the joint strategies of the various nations associated with the combined strategy of the Middle zone can be formulated as soon as the political policies have been formed and approved.

Meanwhile British interests and National joint strategy has taken a peculiar twist in this zone. In contrast to the time previous to the Second World War when Great Britain controlled such countries as Egypt, the Sudan, Palestine and Iraq, today she does not control any of these countries. The burden of our old political, economic and administrative problems of running these countries has gone and our responsibilities are now confined to a chain of military bases: Gibraltar, Malta, part of Libya, Cyprus, Aden and British Somaliland. Today, the three primary British interests in the Middle zone fortunately follow closely the needs of Allied combined strategy. They are first, maintaining geographical facilities for the defence of the zone to contain Russian communist expansion: secondly, securing the oil reserves located in the area: thirdly, maintaining the sea and air arteries from the West to the Indian Ocean and beyond.

The irony of the British national strategy in the Middle East is that while all the free countries are deeply concerned with the maintenance of oil reserves and the air- and sea-ways, Britain is left to sustain, in peacetime, the initial and most important of these interests, the defence of the area, with reduced resources and facilities. Thus, apart from factors which increase our requirement of a through transit passage, especially in peacetime, any consideration of containing the expansion of Russian communism southwards and of preserving the oil reserves in both peacetime and in war, is no longer a partisan British interest, but one of paramount interest for all the Western and free countries. This march of events has brought a radical change in the concept of British strategy in the Middle zone. The full significance and extent of this change of the old idea of leaning on Great Britain will be revealed as the defence of the free countries develops. The Western countries and the free countries in the Middle zone will all have to take their share of the defence burden. In this balance of commitments, it is clear that the Western countries will have to guard against encroaching on the susceptibilities of the newly acquired nationalisms.

It is occasionally necessary to remind ourselves that here we are not simply considering the Middle East. The inflammable centre tends to draw speculation inward when the whole area is highly important, especially the Northern Tier. The concept has widened and the sphere of vigilance extended. If action in this area ever becomes necessary, either in local or in total war, the Western countries' contribution will not simply be the traditional succour as in two great wars, it will be an absolute necessity. They like ourselves will not merely be fighting to preserve a waterway, an air route or an oilfield: they will be fighting for sheer survival. It is therefore fortunate that we have a potential bastion in Pakistan on the eastern flank of the zone. How such a bastion will withstand aggression from a determined enemy will depend greatly on the confidence which the effectiveness of British national and Allied strategy in the Middle zone can inspire.

The key to the present strategy is the speed with which British and the Allied widely scattered forces, in particular the land forces, can be concentrated and deployed in position, not only in the Suez Canal zone, but in Pakistan, Iran, Iraq and Turkey to hold any Russian advance. The difference between the old and new Middle East strategies is that battles of a general war are unlikely to be fought in and around the Suez Canal zone, though there may be some local war and cold war incidents in this area. It is, however, important to remember that the Middle East sea and air routes are unlikely to be safe for commercial use in time of war: the alternative Cape route for merchant ships and the middle African route for civil aircraft must be kept ready and available.

The British withdrawal from the Suez Canal zone, the moving of her headquarters to Cyprus, and the dispersal of her military force in that part of the world, have forced a re-thinking of strategy in the Middle East. The once big concentration of British military force has in the main been dispersed to the United Kingdom to form a strategic reserve, with some infantry residing in Cyprus, the armoured force to Tripoli, and a chain of air bases remains in the Middle East for fighter defence, air support and air transport as well as strategical bombers.

Provision has been made under the treaty for the return of British forces to the Suez Canal zone should the Middle East or Egypt become threatened. The point of this provision is 'threatened by armed forces' and not the threat or actuality of cold war, a distinction not a little disturbing in view of the recent trend of events in the Middle East. The British Middle East Headquarters have been transferred from the Suez Canal to Cyprus though as an operational base Cyprus does not replace the Suez Canal zone. The British Middle East bases have in fact been dispersed between Libya, Iraq and Cyprus as well as the NATO bases in Turkey. In war, Cyprus would be a most important transit base rather than a base from which operations were fought. Such conditions will force us into finding a political solution to the present problem of Cyprus. Notwithstanding, whatever the war problems, under existing conditions, the free countries of the world cannot today assume that Britain can ensure the free passage of world shipping through the Suez Canal even in peacetime. Some international authority is necessary to enforce it.

Whatever the events in Western Europe or the Far East, it seems that the final story of our civilization might well be decided in the Middle East, the area from where our history dawned. It is in this zone that the whole structure of Western strategy can be most easily rent in two.

CHAPTER VI

South-East Asia and the Pacific

I

BEFORE examining strategy in the Pacific it would be useful to go back to the conditions which prevailed before the Second World War. Of the contiguous countries in the Western Pacific Japan was the powerful aggressor. It was appreciated that in a war with Japan, China would remain neutral or be a not very effective ally to us, and also that the South-East Asian countries would remain neutral. Thus, the island nature of Japan and the distances and shipping requirements in the Pacific in respect of the United States and the British Commonwealth dominated our strategy. We required naval and air powers with adequately secure bases before any land operations could be contemplated.

Britain's main base in these regions was at Singapore, with the great army and resources of India nearby. Clearly British advanced bases in China would become untenable under any serious Japanese attack. The United States was if anything even worse placed, for although she had a base in the Philippine Islands, her main base was in the Hawaiian Islands nearly 3500 miles from Japan: her other secondary base in the Aleutian Islands was almost as far distant.

The pivot of British strategy was, therefore, the naval and air base at Singapore and it was believed that this would secure Australia and the neighbouring British and French islands as well as the entrance to the Indian Ocean from the Pacific. With this strategical concept, the British plan in war with Japan was to withdraw to Singapore and to hold this base by its land fortifications and limited naval and air forces. It was contended (which in the event proved wrong) that the nature of the Malayan terrain precluded any Japanese overland threat to Singapore. Also, it was thought that French Indo-China could be held against Japanese attack for some considerable time. In any event, in a European war against Germany, the British and French Governments had little or no scope for increasing the size of the naval, army and air forces they had allocated to the Far East in event of war with Japan. One comfort, however, was the great potential land force reserve of the magnificent Indian army near at hand. Moreover, there is little doubt that the British Commonwealth assumed substantial military assistance from the United States should Japan threaten America's great commercial and strategical interests in the Western Pacific. Unfortunately, however, no Allied strategy had been formulated.

As it happened, the devastating Japanese surprise attack on the American main base at Pearl Harbour brought the United States strategy to nought — her naval and air forces were destroyed and she thus temporarily lost military power in the Pacific. Subsequently, Japan also brought British strategy to nought by using her air forces to sink the United Kingdom main naval forces in the area and then by overwhelming the Singapore base with land forces which advanced through Malaya, thus confounding all concepts for the security of the main base in the Far East. While it is probable that in the circumstances an even greatly superior British strategy would not have saved Singapore, the strategy then was far from being a good strong national one. The pre-war instances of strife amongst the Service strategies mentioned elsewhere are clear indication of this. Even the tactics adopted in the course of defending Singapore fell so far short of an inter-Service concept that it led to disaster: the main naval ships which sailed to their doom went without any support from the air forces which were stationed at Singapore. However, America as well as the British had wrongly assessed the place of air power in strategy in the Pacific with the consequent complete collapse of our Theatre strategy in these regions. With our strategy overthrown the Japanese proceeded to capture the important island bases throughout the Theatre and then to establish their defence at their leisure.

Notwithstanding whatever Japan had done to our Theatre strategy, the British Commonwealth and the United States still had their national strategies such as they were with which to fight back when the necessary forces could be raised and assembled. Greater than all, Japanese political policy and strategy had brought America into war, a country which with her immense resources was to prove the most powerful of all Allies. Thus, British and United States strategies were formulated to recapture the Pacific and overthrow Japan. Thenceforth we had an Allied strategy of sorts, but unfortunately in their early alliance days it was in no way an integrated combined strategy. Indeed, although the United States assembled vast naval, land and air forces in the Pacific, their strategy was not a national one and their Services were in competition rather than in unison. Moreover, not only were the American Services in competition with each other, but they were at variance with those of her British ally as well. For example, it was against the strongest opposition from the American naval high command that President Roosevelt eventually agreed to British naval forces operating in the Pacific in conjunction with the United States naval forces.

'It is an ill wind turns none to good' and so with the United States in the Pacific. Having virtually lost her naval forces she was able to rebuild from a new start without obligations to old or prejudice to modern conditions. Thus it was that the new American naval strategy was conceived round aircraft and aircraft-carriers. Events proved the worth of this strategy and as the campaign progressed, island after island of strategic importance was recaptured in the Pacific and unit after unit of the Japanese fleet and mercantile marine was sunk. Unfortunately, however, throughout the operation the separate Services pursued their own strategies which intensified the marked controversy between the American navy, army and air forces as well as the actual personalities of their Commanders-in-Chief. Indeed, even the high command system to co-ordinate the separate commands and Services deviated more and more from normal organization as the campaign gathered momentum. In essense, Admiral Nimitz's and General Mac-Arthur's commands were based more on a geographical than a functional naval-army division and both were responsible directly and separately to the U.S. Chiefs of Staff for operations in their areas, whether naval, army or air force. Neither Admiral nor General was inclined to agree to any great re-allocation of forces with the swing of requirements as the operations developed. Only the vast war potential and armed forces of America made such a system and such divergent strategies practicable and avoided danger of defeat in detail. None the less, there were occasions when the co-ordination weakness of the strategies and command nearly led to disaster.

II

Since the end of the Second World War there have been far reaching
changes in strategy in the Pacific and South-East Asia. South-East
Asia is a collective name which comprises Burma, Thailand, Indo-
China, Malaya, Indonesia and the Philippines. This re-orientation has
been caused primarily by the change in the power and circumstances
and the alignment of the associated countries. Arising out of this, the
contiguous non-communist countries have become the most vulnerable
testing ground in the present global conflict of ideologies between
the Western and the Communist ways of life. The centre of this
conflict lies round the South-East Asian countries, exalted with rising
nationalisms and often exposed to expansionist communism. This
welter of huge islands and peninsulas twice the size of Europe, enormously rich and densely populated, constitutes a most vulnerable area
since it is in these regions that communism penetrates most easily. It
is for this reason that the Pacific and its South-East Asian appendages
contain a cold war threat even greater than any wide military threat:
indeed, apart from the obvious sapping tactics of diversion it could be
the most deadly challenge to the continued Western resistance. The
free countries could in fact win Europe and yet lose Asia.[1]

Of the foregoing changes, there are two outstanding: the loss of
India and the Indian army to Western democracy and the emergence
of China as a united and expansionist power after many long years of
discord is most outstanding. This is specially so as China is communist
and allied to Russia and there are no countries more adept than they
are in causing trouble with the Western nations by infiltration, subversion and local wars of one kind or another. If China should use
up her strength in expanding South-East in campaigns similar to the
recent one in Korea or become involved in local war with the United
States over Formosa, she will be forced to remain on terms with and
dependent on Russia.

The two most critical zones in the Pacific area are the Japanese
islands and those territories over-run by Japan prior to her entry into

[1] Malayan rubber is the most valuable single industry of the Commonwealth and in
the critical five post-war years, 1947-1951, earned more American dollars than all the
industries and trades of the United Kingdom put together.

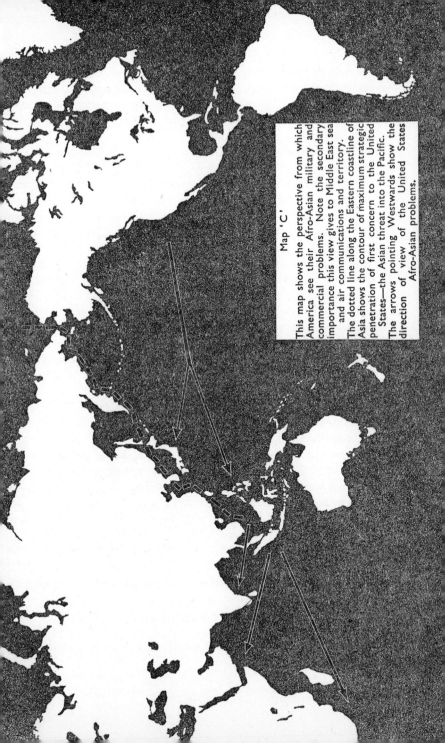

Map 'C'

This map shows the perspective from which America see their Afro-Asian military and commercial problems. Note the secondary importance this view gives to Middle East sea and air communications and territory.

The dotted line along the Eastern coastline of Asia shows the contour of maximum strategic penetration of first concern to the United States—the Asian threat into the Pacific.

The arrows pointing Westwards show the direction of view of the United States Afro-Asian problems.

the Second World War. The Japanese islands have become the sphere and responsibility of the United States: and there is general agreement as to the desirability of preventing Japanese material and military resource falling into unfriendly control. With regard to China, however, there is a wide disagreement. Great Britain feels that China under its communist government should find a place in the United Nations Assembly, and that everything possible should be done to segregate the aims of the U.S.S.R. and China: and that China should have other alternatives to the unrelenting purpose of Moscow.

So far as general war is concerned, it will be a long time before non-industrial China will be able to develop modern military forces which could challenge the Western nations, even with Russia's industrial help. When, however, China does develop her industry and war potential, together with Russia she would present us with a most formidable combination should they remain in alliance. The struggle would be largely in terms of vast land and air forces challenging the military might of the West based largely on air and sea power. Although our sea power would lose much of its old advantage against a vast self-sufficient land-mass, the inherent weaknesses of limited and heavily loaded land communications would give great advantages to our air power.

One post-war example of the Chinese-Russian challenge is the operations in Korea. Here was a clear struggle between the communists and the West for a piece of territory contiguous with both Russia and China as well as Japan. Beginning as a cold war this conflict developed into a local war fought with great ferocity and grievous losses. There were, moreover, numerous incidents that offered an extension to a total war, but neither side dared to make the extended challenge. Indeed, China never committed any Chinese troops as such and limited her intervention to volunteers. The Western nations loaded the dice against themselves by putting a veto on attacking bases on the Chinese mainland and the concentrations of reinforcements beyond the Yalu bridges, and on blockading the Chinese coast as well as on the use of nuclear weapons. Thus, when each side had had enough this local war fizzled out with neither contestant being able to claim victory.

The war in Korea demonstrated how far the communists are

prepared to go and in what circumstances, and it showed a development from the accepted forms of cold war of infiltration and subversion. It seemed that a coup such as was engineered in Czechoslovakia was not enough or not propitious. Guerilla warfare, however admirable for special conditions, may be expected to be superseded by regular armies and organized aggression with headquarters and unified commands. Behind highly organized forces revolutionary governments can be formed whose prime aim is to confuse the peoples' loyalties and to seize power. The Korean conflict considered in isolation might simply have been the result of a miscalculation on the part of the communists of the determination of the United Nations with the United States and Britain at their head. Experience there showed how easily a local war might become a general war and how the outward thrust of communist aims could divert and absorb the strength of the Western powers. It also illustrated that there could be numerous local and even limited wars which need not develop into a total war, and in themselves do not justify the strategic use of nuclear weapons. To use these weapons in such circumstances, however great the temptation might be to cut short the conflict, would certainly precipitate the very thing we have so much interest in avoiding. The Korean war, while showing the dangerous dispersal of our vital forces, also indicated how important it is to have the correctly shaped forces in the right place at the right time. This brings us back to the importance of reviewing the needs of our strategic position in South-East Asia and the Pacific, and trying to determine what is to be defended, to what extent, and in what manner.

In her defence of the Japanese area the United States may gain a considerable advantage in not having the Korean peninsula completely overrun by the communists, but the United Nations went to war there not so much in the wider interests of strategy as with a moral mission. A victory for the United Nations would undoubtedly have consolidated feeling in the Far East for UNO but the stalemate which has resulted there can bring little satisfaction (except that hostilities have ceased for the time being) to either side. Whatever their outcome the Western powers cannot afford many local wars of the Korean type, which is a good example of the impasse into which Communist aggression has forced us. No one will deny that the action of the

United Nations in Korea was morally necessary and that it was essential to show our strength and determination. So it is throughout the whole of South-East Asia and the Pacific. What happens in one area is likely to affect what will happen in another; and it has been acutely observed that how the French fared in Indo-China would affect their position in North Africa, while the success or failure of the British in Malaya will have its repercussions on the events in the Middle East and in Africa. But the question remains how far can the Western powers go? Withdrawal from an area may be strategically sound though it cannot but be interpreted as a sign of weakness while it adds the strain of future recovery. How adequate in fact, is the strategy of the Western powers in these vital areas?

Indo-China is another example of the organized communist challenge. The rise of nationalism in that country made French control especially vulnerable to communist expansion. Great Britain is fortunate in that by wise counsel she avoided similar situations in India, Pakistan, Burma, Palestine and even Iran and Egypt. Like that in Korea, the struggle in Indo-China began with cold war and developed into a bloody though local military war. At the eleventh hour, a face-saving armistice was arranged, but the communists won a partial if not a substantial victory which might develop still further. Indo-China is a good example of how, with the march of events, a country of insignificance can change to one of great importance. Before the advent of cold war, Indo-China counted for little in strategy, but today it has become of great significance for if Viet-Minh, supplied by China, should gain control of the whole of the country, the situation in Thailand and Malaya would be seriously threatened: a threat which could not be offset even by the American stock of nuclear weapons.

Inevitably, Japan, the Western nations' powerful contestant who was eventually vanquished in the Second World War is slowly recovering from her defeat. Although today Japan is dependent on the United States for defence and economic aid, it cannot be long before she begins to re-establish her military forces. Moreover, being the most highly industrialized of the Eastern countries she is making great efforts to conquer markets in China, Russia and anywhere amongst the Western nations. Should it ever happen, clearly a Russo- and re-established Japanese-Chinese alliance could become a crucial threat to the Western nations. Without alliance, however, the old possibility of Japan conquering parts or the whole of China has now receded and seems most unlikely unless China becomes involved in war with the West. Certainly, with the rise of modern China and modern Russia, it does not seem that Japan will resume her previous bid for Asian hegemony or even her foothold in Manchuria or Korea, and without the economic assets of these countries, Japan cannot develop any serious threat to the British Commonwealth in alliance with America. This is a strategic change in the Pacific of first importance.

As with the communist countries, the strategic position of the British Commonwealth has also changed greatly. Hong Kong, her only remaining base in China, is now a mere trading centre which would have little military value in a global war. Nevertheless, in cold war and in local war such as in Korea and Indo-China, Hong Kong is of significant importance.

We have withdrawn from Burma and thus from a strategic position which lies across the back door to both China and India. In the Second World War, Burma became part of a vital supply route to our then Chinese ally. In its new status, Burma remains specially important now that a hostile China stands along the common border with Burma, Assam, Nepal and Tibet. Indeed, strategically, Burma has become a dangerous vacuum in regard to our cold war and local war problems. Even the value of our Singapore bases are threatened by communist infiltration and subversion in Malaya by local nationalisms.

III

The greatest change of weakness in the British position in the East relates to India and Pakistan. Our previous strategic concept of the Indian army as a great land power and of India itself as a great military base for military operations in any part of the periphery of the Indian Ocean, and as a great reserve of manpower for operations wherever required throughout the world, has been confounded for the present. India's and Pakistan's nationalisms together with the struggle over Kashmir has virtually neutralized the Indian sub-continent so far as military strategy is concerned. Nevertheless, the Indian sub-continent together with Ceylon dominates the Indian Ocean and the more important sea and air routes to the East. In the cold war, India still remains a great bastion and is containing the spread of communism. Moreover, India and Pakistan also show promise of being influential intermediaries between the communist countries and the Western nations. These facts of themselves suggest how much a successful strategy in South-East Asia and the Far East generally might owe to the patience, wisdom and friendliness of these two nations.

On the other hand, our strategy in the Pacific in modern times is incomparably stronger than that which existed before the Second World War. In part, this is due to Australia's and New Zealand's new concept and acceptance of peacetime contributions to the defence in the Far East previously carried by Great Britain alone. But much greater than this is the United States' new conception and the vast military power she has deployed in the Pacific together with the further enormous resources she possesses: if conventional weapons are not sufficient to deter China, modern weapons could be brought to bear. As already mentioned, however, it should be remembered that in South-East Asia and the Far East generally the loss of the Indian army is likely to be an immense disadvantage to Britain, especially as her policy there leaves her with many, or even more, military commitments than before.

Basically the difficulty of a sound and strong strategy in the Far East is the weakness of Western political policy in that sphere. This arises from the conflicting interests and doctrines of the several different nations concerned. On the one hand, the United States and Great Britain have many competitive commercial interests as well as divergent strategic concepts resulting from a different approach to the problems. Historic association plays a big part in the way the problems of South-East Asia and the Far East are viewed by the different countries of the Western powers. For example, Britain follows the European influence of the Portuguese and the Dutch in the sixteenth century who approached these parts from the west through the Indian Ocean, whereas the American influence arises from the Spaniards' approach across the Pacific. To Great Britain, the Far East lies eastwards at the end of our sphere of global interests whereas to America, the Far East is the threshold of the military threat of her aggressors. Australian views lie somewhere between these two different views. On the other hand, there are even wider conflicting interests and violently conflicting dogma between the Western nations — the United States, Great Britain and France — and the Asian nations — such as India, Pakistan, Ceylon, Burma and Thailand who are on the rising tide of nationalism and, in varying degrees, are most sensitive to any reappearance of Western imperialistic favour, restrictions, obligations and advice, all of which are suspect. It is clear there is no easy or quick solution to this problem when our different ways of life are remembered: the high degree of political sense and economic prosperity in the West, and the hundreds of millions of primitive, illiterate people of numerous conflicting religions, sects and creeds with an appallingly low standard of existence in the East. Thus, whereas the communist countries have a well-thought-out co-ordinated plan to further their international expansions by infiltration, subversion, local war and all methods short of general war, the Western nations have no overall co-ordinated plan; at most we have only limited co-ordination for a few of our regional problems.

The strength of the Western countries lies in their strategy for total war. So far as the United States is concerned, this is based on overwhelming military strength and the means of applying it, such as the great strategic island barrier which she built up in the Second World War. From these island bases America can use her powerful air and naval forces to dominate any part of the Pacific. America is most sensitive to the security of her chain of bases. For example, Formosa has a political significance so long as National China exists, but probably it is not vital to the United States strategically. Nevertheless, communist possession of Formosa would truncate the American base barrier and would probably have to be recaptured if she ever became involved in a general war with China. Similarly, the loss of the Pescadores would truncate the defence of Formosa. But a more important factor is that the United States could defend Formosa, unlike Korea, effectively and without casualties or strain to herself. Both Communist China and America have stated that Formosa is a vital issue with an essential bearing on their policies, and local war in this area could turn the cold war into a total or possibly a limited one. It would seem, however, that Communist China dare not make a serious challenge to the military power of America on Formosa or elsewhere.

It is therefore not surprising that SEATO, the non-communist organization for the defence of South-East Asia, is radically different from NATO, which exists for the defence of Western Europe and the Atlantic. It is important to appreciate the difference. NATO consists of countries which have to defend themselves against direct attack at the shortest notice in the Atlantic and Europe, while with SEATO only two members, Thailand and the Phillipines, are actually South-East Asian countries. To the other countries in SEATO, the United States, Great Britain, Australia, New Zealand, France and Pakistan, South-East Asia is only an outpost of their own respective defences. Another difference is that NATO has an integrated staff, bases, supplies and stores, and integrated military units *in situ*. These resources are all actively occupied in the defence of Western Europe and are backed by the United States and British powerful strategic air force and fleets with their nuclear weapons and all plans prepared and the forces at immediate readiness. In fact NATO has real and effective military teeth.

SEATO, on the other hand, has no teeth at present and is composed merely of a permanent secretariat to deal among other things with subversion in the area, and there is also an agreement that staff conversations should take place between the interested powers. Progress is being made in stemming the advance of communism in South-East Asia. Not the least successful measure is economic aid in countries where it is badly needed. Also, any further communist advance is certain to make the non-communist countries, who have hitherto tried to remain neutral, see the menace to themselves.

It is, however, important that the Western countries have the confidence and support of the Asian non-communist countries in any measures they take to secure South-East Asia. In this regard, the British feel that America underestimates the importance of India and of retaining India's goodwill. Indeed, Britain attaches great importance to her relations with India and Pakistan and is increasingly focusing her policy and strategy to meet their views. Accordingly, the founding of a military organization for the defence of South-East Asia, if it is to include both Western and Asian countries, will of necessity have to be slow. Anything of the nature of NATO would at present disintegrate SEATO.

More than in any other theatre, the present strategic requirements in

South-East Asia and the Pacific are first and foremost to deal with cold war, though a strategy which can deter and if necessary wage and win a local, limited or total war is also indispensable. It cannot be over-emphasized that while our peacetime problems and troubles centre in the vital and vulnerable areas of the East, should total war ever come our problems, and most vital and vulnerable areas, would be in Europe. Thus strategy in the East is intimately linked and related to that of the West; and what happens in Europe will have its repercussions in the East and vice-versa. The strength of the West as such will be more than an echo in the East if the powers concerned face their mutual problems objectively and with a genuine desire to resolve them.

PART TWO

CHAPTER VII

Allied Combined Strategy

I

ALLIED combined strategy today has two aspects about which it is as well to be clear at the outset. The first of these is the importance of the possession of nuclear weapons by the two major powers in the West, the United States and the United Kingdom. The retention of and determination to exercise this powerful deterrent to total war is the first of these facets of Allied combined strategy and of itself posits a variety of problems allied though distinct from those of the protective organization of NATO. NATO and the military head-quarters of SHAPE are the second feature of Allied combined strategy and are largely concerned with conventional weapons and the accepted forms of mutual political agreement and military protection. SEATO and the Baghdad Pact have yet to develop into effective Allied organizations. As already stressed, the two facets are interlocked and any analysis must reveal the dependence of NATO and SHAPE on the deterrent power held by the two great nations. Thus the United States must figure largely in this essay, not simply because the European continent needs her, but because the British Commonwealth is dependent on her strategic strength.

The foundation of the Allied combined strategy is the strategic stockpile of nuclear weapons, and the means of delivery of them without delay at the vital centres of an aggressor. Until about 1950, the United States' stock of atomic weapons overwhelmed anything possessed by Russia and it was a complete deterrent to aggression. We must now, however, assume that the Russian stock of atomic and hydrogen weapons have now become a deterrent, even to defensive war. Indeed, it now seems possible that we have reached a stage in nuclear weapon stockpiling where the Western Allies and Russia both realize that total war with them is not worth while either to victor or vanquished.

Before strategy at the national and various Service levels can be formulated, the priorities of Allied strategy must be determined for the various types of war. These priorities may change from time to time but the following would seem reasonable at the present time.

First, strategic priority is deterrence against total war; second, cold war; third, local wars; fourth, prosecution of total war should the deterrent fail; and fifthly, limited war. Possibly some authorities would reverse the fourth and fifth priorities even today.

Notwithstanding the foregoing Allied strategic priorities, there are various considerations which result in the individual Allied nations giving a different emphasis, and sometimes even priority, to their own national strategy. For example, under the first priority, the forces required include both stockpiles of nuclear weapons and the means of delivering them, and the NATO land and supporting air and naval forces. The United States accepts that with her vast resources she must provide the bulk of the deterrent strategic air forces. The United States expects the British Commonwealth to provide base facilities for these forces but does not press us to provide any substantial force. Whatever strategic air forces we provide arise out of our own national considerations. On the other hand, in the provision of land forces for NATO, the United States insists that all the Western free countries provide substantial forces. Thus, the British NATO commitment should really be given our national first priority from the Allied overall aspect.

The real threat to the Western free countries is the aim, indeed, the very creed of the Communist bloc to expand their doctrine and control throughout the world. The strategic implications of this is that the greater the effectiveness of the deterrent to total war the greater becomes the communist pressure in cold, local and limited war. Indeed, so great has become the effectiveness of the Allied deterrent measures that the real communist threat has already been transferred to cold war: to expand their ideological influence into the free countries by economic penetration, carefully calculated diplomacy, infiltration and fomentation and exploitation of national movements. This is the greatest problem with which the Western free countries have to contend today to safeguard their way of life. Thus, the strongest national considerations are involved in the cold and local war priorities. In the main, national politics and national interests determine, and even overrule, Allied strategy in these two spheres. In particular, the interests of the respective national government non-military departments each with their own axes to grind overwhelm Allied strategy in peacetime and to some extent even in war.

In consequence, nowhere is Allied policy and strategy more at sixes and sevens than in containing cold and local wars against the Soviet bloc. Indeed, Great Britain must be ready and prepared to *go it alone* with her cold and local war problems and must therefore give high national priority to these fields of strategy. Thus, unfortunately, each Allied nation makes its own piecemeal contribution to its own cold war and local war tasks at great overall cost and disadvantage to the planned and co-ordinated efforts of the Soviet bloc.

In any study of combined strategy today it should be realized that Russia is the only country which can threaten the survival of the Western countries for as long as we can foresee. At the other side of the globe, China may go to war with the West, with or without Russia as an ally, but China herself cannot threaten our survival. Although Russian military thinking in the past has favoured large armies to the detriment of the development of naval and air power, it would be dangerous to assume that she has not revised this attitude in the light of modern experience and developments. Indeed, there is ample evidence that she has assimilated and appreciated the strategic significance of the changes which have taken place in our time. She must consequently be also aware that a third world war with nuclear weapons would possibly be suicide to herself as well as to the Allies. But while she has continued to build up her great forces, to some extent at least, in genuine fear of attack, they have provided her with the ability to exploit all kinds of cold and local war which she has found so profitable. She is also re-arming in readiness for the possibilities of the West becoming disunited, weak or bankrupt.

It is pertinent to consider where the intiative in world affairs now lies. Soviet Russia has no monopoly so far as purely military factors are concerned, and the Western powers have already called her bluff in the military challenge on more than one occasion. In political manœuvre, however, the very nature of the Soviet power gives her a certain possession of the initiative which she is using to her great advantage, when, in view of the potentiality of nuclear weapons, it is an instrument which lends itself all the more readily to the furtherance of her aims.

For example, having decided that the pressure she had been applying in Western Europe could only lead to the outbreak of total war (at a time when possibly she was reluctant to embark on it), Russia shifted the scene and pressure, first to the Far East and South-East Asia, and then to the Middle East through the Indian sub-continent to the Indonesian archipelago. The Western powers, despite their numerous and varied national interests in these zones, seemed powerless to exert any lead in political manœuvre. Their actions lagged behind and were confined to following up the Russian moves with rather tardy and clumsy counter-actions. Somewhat typical of Western policy is their Baghdad Pact, based too much on the military and Maginot Line concept at a time when the primary threat was not military but rather an attempt to win favour with the rising nationalisms of the contiguous countries who require help for their economic development, but at the same time wish to be the arbiters of their own destinies.

When formulating our combined strategy as defenders it is important to bear in mind the initial aggressive war aim of Soviet Russia and the Communist bloc. The nature of the Western nations makes this initial Russian war aim particularly complex for them so long as the Russians have before them the problem of Western Europe with its growing strength of land forces. Besides having all the aggressor's problems of bases and communications in rapidly moving warfare they have the problem of fighting an alliance widely scattered by oceans and strong in sea power to defend them. They have also the problem of confronting an alliance of great strength in air power and with a capacity for carrying the offensive of nuclear weapons, from numerous directions, into the heart of Russia probably superior to anything they themselves could mount.

As a potential aggressor Soviet Russia controls an important aspect of the initiative: that of deciding whether or not nuclear weapons will be used strategically in war. Should Russia agree never to use these weapons and to allow an adequate system of inspection the Allies would be bound to follow suit. Thus Russia is in the position of being able to banish nuclear weapons from the armouries of the world and so confine possible war within the limits and use of so-called conventional weapons. Such a move might present the Allies with the most difficult strategic problem of all, especially when the size of Russian forces are considered. She has an active army of 175 divisions and 25,000 tanks, and an air force of 20,000 aircraft with a programme to keep them modernized, and a navy which is being rapidly expanded and will consist soon of 30 powerful cruisers, 500 submarines and 4000 naval aircraft. Recent cuts in Soviet forces do not materially affect this thesis.

She is therefore not necessarily relying on hydrogen and atomic bombs and rockets though she is building and maintaining a powerful force of these weapons in order to stalemate the Western deterrent force of similar weapons. Rather is she more likely to use her vastly superior conventional forces for limited war, and for local and cold war in selected and troublesome areas where the use of nuclear weapons in a strategic role seems unlikely. In this event, what the Allies must ask themselves is whether the United States would be prepared to withhold the strategic use of her great hydrogen and atomic force and again suffer thousands of casualties? That is the crucial problem, and Russia is feeling her way towards the answer. It is important also for the Western countries to keep clearly in mind their own combined allied initial aim in preparing to bulldoze and retaliate against aggression. We cannot over-emphasize the need to plan, co-ordinate and subordinate the three Services strategies into a national aim within the Allied strategy.

The more effective the deterrent and our defences in Europe the greater the probability of cold and local war developed on the Korean pattern and by infiltration since these are the spheres in which the Soviet bent for world domination achieves most success. In this way the West and its nuclear deterrent could be outflanked and isolated by the gradual transfer of substantial, even enormous, territories, populations and resources from the Western to the Soviet orbit in South-East Asia, the Middle East and elsewhere. Thus, the defence of the territories on the periphery of the Communist land-mass against cold and local war is in itself a major problem in Allied combined strategy.

The co-ordination of Allied combined strategy is specially important in the field of hydrogen and atomic stockpiles so that we may avoid greater provision of joint resources of these weapons than necessary to the detriment of other strategical requirements. For example, if say Russia required a thousand hydrogen bombs to destroy the Allies it would not strengthen our position merely to have ten thousand bombs with which to destroy Russia when possibly only one or two thousand were needed. Such effort would rightly be regarded as wasteful and would be more effectively applied in other fields.

II

At the beginning of the First World War Great Britain was a first class power of great economic and military strength. This country was practically the workshop of the Commonwealth, self-contained in manufactures, and possessed twice the sea power of all other navies combined so that we were at that time able to consider, plan and begin a general war alone. By the beginning of the Second World War, the British financial, economic and military strength had been sapped substantially; she had several rivals in the field of manufacture and productivity, and Germany had greatly superior forces in many respects. Moreover, by this time, the economic strength of the United States had increased tremendously. In fact, although Britain pursued the war alone for many months, she needed American aid to continue and win the war. Relatively, today British industrial and military strength is reduced still further and the potential enemy's strength has increased tremendously. Great Britain is in no sense able to contemplate entering a world war alone, or even to provide forces to deter the enemy without the great assistance of allies. Essentially, she is dependent on allies; she cannot even plan preparations, to say nothing of beginning a general war without American help. Thus, the vital importance of Allied combined strategy to Great Britain today is clear.

In the past Britain was for several centuries very largely independent of allies and in consequence there is little early history on Allied combined strategy. The outstanding exception is the Marlborough wars for it is no exaggeration to say that Marlborough was not only the initiator of allied strategy and allied affairs, as we know them today, but also the first conscious exponent of them. His great asset was his unsurpassed vision in combining naval and army strategies with diplomacy and in making the greatest use of all three. Marlborough had also to face the fetters and pattern of allied interference with his military operations, although their nature and degree were somewhat different from those of the twentieth-century World Wars. He also had to overcome objections to his strategy from his political colleagues, who often had their vision restricted by some local situation. Conviction and the power of persuasion were as important then as today. The similarity of Marlborough's problems to those of the two World Wars of the twentieth century is striking. His activities involved nearly all the civilized people of his time and extended throughout the accessible continents and maritime parts of the world. Just as we have done in the two World Wars, he faced one race and culture who by military power attempted to impose their will and way of life on all others at a time when Europe was impotent without British aid. He faced an England slow but sure in accepting the challenge and fulfilled the role of allied supreme commander as we know it today, because not only was he at the centre of the diplomacy of the Grand Alliance of nearly twenty confederate States of Europe, but he also directed all their armed forces against France for ten campaigns and himself commanded in the great battles. His authority alone secured concerted action.

In earlier times, as with Marlborough, allied strategy depended very largely on personalities rather than on any military organization and co-ordinating or integrating system. Even in the First World War, Allied strategy was much more an affair of good or bad relations between statesmen, commanders and personalities than of any military organization or concept. This is illustrated by the way in which the British and French forces were directed in Western Europe when the two political heads met from time to time with their military advisers and agreed on certain courses and strategy which were then fulfilled with a minimum of co-ordination by the respective national commanders. It was not until the German advance created a most desperate situation in France in 1918 that the Allies agreed to appoint Foch generalissimo to both the French and British forces, though even this amounted to little more than limited co-ordination. When the United States army arrived in France in 1918 allied strategy rose to nothing more than mutual agreement between the French and Americans as to where the latter should be put into the line, and on a very general concept of the co-ordinated strategy to be followed. In the Second

World War Allied combined strategy became a vital problem which forced us to deal with it on its merits. Allied strategy will always be greatly influenced by the political and military personalities of various nationals as well as by specific national war aims, as is instanced by the American attitude to so-called British imperialism in the Middle East; and today, a highly developed Allied organization is necessary to serve these personalities. In combined strategy, Allied problems and difficulties are superimposed on the national problems and difficulties and thus create a most exacting requirement which, like national strategy, depends so much on the personalities of the leaders concerned for its resolution.

III

A fundamental change in the concept of combined strategy emerged when the United States became an Ally of the Commonwealth in the Second World War in December 1941 after the Japanese attack on Pearl Harbour. The formulation of this combined strategy depended of course on agreement between the political heads of the two nations in Allied war policy. Mr. Churchill and Mr. Roosevelt had their first wartime meeting at Argentia in Newfoundland. Subsequently they had nine more momentous conferences in the war years that followed: also about one thousand communications, letters and cables on each side passed between them. They certainly had their arguments, and their mutual exasperations, but they were forever conscious of the stakes at issue. Never in history did Allied policy count for so much in such a shattering crisis and never did it depend on such a close relationship between the two heads of two powerful nations. The great asset of these political leaders is that they understood each other and the fearful strategic problems they faced together.

The first United States-United Kingdom combined operation was mounted for the invasion of North Africa and was named 'Torch'. In Allied operations agreement on the nationality of the Commander-in-Chief often causes great difficulties, but on this occasion, and despite the number of British generals available, Mr. Churchill readily agreed to Mr. Roosevelt's proposal that the Allied Commander-in-Chief should be General Eisenhower. A considerable factor behind Churchill's willingness to accept so readily an American Commander-in-Chief is that the United States had been resisting a strategy of attack in the Mediterranean. Thus, he was delighted at the American appointment. At that time the Allies were in no position to invade Europe and all the evidence of the operation which was mounted for this purpose some two years later and named 'Overlord' proves this. On the other hand, Churchill believed there were numerous opportunities of invade what he called the 'soft under belly' in the Mediterranean and subsequent events also proved this correct.

The strategical background to 'Torch' was that the Western regions of North Africa were occupied by French whose loyalty varied from Nazi, doubtful Nazi to pro-Allied. This somewhat delicate political situation and the existence of the Vichy government was another factor which made the choice of Eisenhower desirable so that 'Torch' should seem predominantly an American affair rather than a British one. It was also believed that a surprise attack on the North African coasts would succeed before Germany could reinforce her strength in that area. As 'Torch' was the first Anglo-American combined operation it was to be expected that in the natural evolution of a combined strategy there were many national facets in military affairs which required adjustment and co-ordination. For example, Britain described the first day of operations as 'D' day, and thence 'D+1' day, 'D+2' day, etc. The United States used the description 'D 1', 'D 2' day, etc. Thus, there was a critical difference of one day in our operational dates. In signal procedure for example, Britain used '12/2' to denote February 12th whereas the United States used '2/12' to denote the same day. Britain used G.M.T. for all overseas operations while the Americans used local time. These and many other operational and procedural points had to be resolved and each nation was reluctant to change its own procedures.

With the actual combined strategy, however, there was little serious difference between the two national strategies. Much of this was due to the give and take between the commanders and staffs which was inspired by General Eisenhower. The organization of his Allied head-quarters and indeed the strategy itself was by no means perfect, but there was a will to get the first Allied operation launched against the enemy. It was perhaps because of General Eisenhower's improvised

H

arrangements for his headquarters that it worked so well. His headquarters was staffed very largely by Allied army officers who served
the General in his dual capacity as Allied commander of all the Allied
three Services as well as those of Commander-in-Chief, Allied armies.
The greater part of naval and air planning and operations was done by
the naval and air commanders liaising with General Eisenhower's
headquarters. This somewhat loose control of the Allied Commander
set the pattern for the Supreme Command headquarters which were
to be formed later, and wherein there are some who would claim
that the control was rather too loose.

IV

Although the actual Allied invasion of Normandy in 1944 ('Overlord') was a masterpiece in combined strategy, there are many useful
lessons to be gathered from a review of the difficulties which confronted
the nations in the preparatory stages: particularly in the Allied political
and strategic backgrounds. Since the retreat from Dunkirk in 1940
our leaders realized that ways and means of re-establishing our armies
on the Continent would have to be found before we could finally
defeat Germany. Some British and American bomber enthusiasts
believed that the enemy's back could be broken before the need to
re-establish our armies arose. Others, including the powerful group
of army leaders in America, believed that invasion against undefeated
German armies would be necessary. Planning which involved much
staff effort to meet this requirement proceeded before and after the
entry of America into the war, though it was not until the spring of
1943 when a Chief of Staff to the Supreme Allied Commander
(designate) was appointed, that such planning could be classed as
realistic.

The main causes for lack of realism of this early planning for the
invasion of Western Europe were failure to agree at the Allied Combined Chiefs of Staff level on what operations should be undertaken,
when and how, and reluctance to make any one individual responsible
for both the preparation and subsequent implementation of operation
plans. Added to this was the lack of resources to meet more than a
fraction of the operations which the numerous Allied plans demanded,

in particular landing craft, which resulted in constantly shifting terms of reference and frequent changes in Anglo-American agreements. A further major problem for the United Kingdom was the danger of prematurely disturbing her defences against enemy invasion so long as any threat remained, and to mount an invasion of France without depleting her own defensive forces.

During this planning period, the British organization for considering and co-ordinating joint operations was involved and complicated. There is no need to reiterate the numerous committees, planning agencies and ramifications which were crying out for direction, authority and decision. Today, Whitehall would not care to explain this chaotic organization. The United States High Command organization had similar problems. Although their inter-Service co-ordination was more difficult than the British, their national military task in respect of the invasion of Europe was easier in that the operation was not on their doorstep, and also with their enormous national potential, they were confident that whatever the hazard of the invasion, Hitler's power was a long distance from the citadel and homeland of America.

Early in August 1942, General Marshall and Mr. Hopkins, representing the United States Government, brought over to England certain proposals for Anglo-American operations regarding invasion of Western Europe in 1942 and 1943 which became known as the 'Marshall Plan'. The plan provided for an Allied force of nearly six thousand combat aircraft and forty-eight divisions as soon as the necessary resources could be accumulated in England — estimated as April 1943. This was not a new idea to the British Chiefs of Staff but the Marshall Plan brought the conception of invasion to the foreground and the General insisted that henceforeward the plan should constitute the main strategic policy of the United Kingdom and the United States.

General Marshall pressed the Prime Minister to lay everything else aside in furtherance of his main objective: the invasion of France. The Prime Minister was, however, adamant on the need for maintaining the defence of India and the Middle East. Indeed, as we have already seen, the Prime Minister succeeded in getting priority for operation 'Torch', the invasion of North Africa, over the invasion of France, and resources were diverted accordingly. Although after this decision M. Molotov urged that the British and Americans should undertake operations for containing forty enemy army divisions in Western Europe the Prime Minister would not go beyond assuring M. Molotov that a 'Second Front' would be opened as early as possible and that we contemplated employing up to one and a half million men.

From the time preparations for 'Overlord' began in earnest towards the end of 1943, the Allied military High Commands had their tasks made the more difficult by the British and American national leaders not giving firm and consistent rulings on the allocation of resources. Much of the indecision at this time was due to high-ranking American generals and admirals clamouring for priority to be given to the Pacific rather than the European theatre.

The biggest inter-Allied and inter-Service conflict ranged round the bombing policy which the Allied political leaders left unsettled. Notwithstanding the invasion of France, the directive from the political leaders to the Combined Chiefs of Staff for the combined strategic bombers, confirmed at Casablanca (January 1943) at the same time as the confirmation of 'Overlord', was the progressive destruction and dislocation of the German military, industrial and economic systems, and the undermining of the morale of the German people to a point where their capacity for armed resistance would be fatally weakened. It is true that at the time of the Casablanca conference, none present had appreciated the strategic bomber effort which would be required in the preparation for 'Overlord', and unfortunately this left much scope for conflict. Much international discord was generated before the Supreme Commander forced the political leaders to square up to the priority problems of the strategic bombing in preparing for 'Overlord'. The postscript is that after the Normandy assault the essential need of the strategic bomber preparations was clear; without it the assault would have failed completely.

v

During America's early and most trying war period Mr. Roosevelt was much impressed by the efficiency, speed, smoothness and ability of the organization of our Political Direction and High Command of war when he first saw it at work during Mr. Churchill's first meeting with him in Washington after Pearl Harbour. He was also particularly impressed by the speed with which information was passed between London and Washington for Mr. Churchill, and by the Prime Minister's Secretariat who produced masterly minutes and then recorded the decisions of the meetings in a surprisingly short time. During that first meeting Mr. Roosevelt decided without hesitation to adopt the British Chiefs of Staff's Committee and Secretariat organization and procedure for himself and also agreed to a combined Anglo-American Chiefs of Staff Committee and Secretariat to be set up in Washington to co-ordinate all Allied strategy, plans and operations for the armed forces. Although on the one hand these decisions were fortunate in that they assured good co-ordination, on the other hand the Combined Chiefs being located in America inevitably weighed heavily in favour of American policy and strategy.

It is clear that the close personal exchange of views by telegram or conversation between the Prime Minister and the President during the Second World War were of the greatest value to the common cause, even though for this very reason the State Department and the Foreign Office at times fell too far into the background. This defect was greatest with the State Department, due primarily to the President's way of conducting business, especially through Mr. Henry Hopkins, his emissary-at-large. Certainly during the latter part of the war there were drawbacks to the method of discussing and often settling so many matters of Anglo-American policy in direct correspondence between Mr. Churchill and Mr. Roosevelt. It must be remembered in this respect that the President shared the common American view, at least to the extent of regarding Russia relatively free and the Chinese as wholly free from the taint of imperialism, whereas he ignored or dismissed as mere self-seeking the whole British contribution to the development of Asia and Africa. He was blind to any sense of responsibility in British colonial policy.

We have seen that in the last war, Anglo-American military affairs were dealt with by the highly efficient Combined Chiefs of Staff Committee. In many of the larger issues involving Anglo-American collaboration, however, the Foreign Office and State Department were at a disadvantage because there was no Anglo-American political liaison corresponding to the Combined Chiefs of Staff Committee.

The need was less clear at the time and in any event it would have been difficult to have created such a political liaison without duplicating the existing diplomatic machinery and thus causing confusion. Notwithstanding, greater co-ordination could have been achieved, in particular at the many important conferences between the Prime Minister and the President. At some of these meetings, although attended by the Chiefs of Staff themselves, the Foreign Office and the State Department were not represented by their political heads and not always by their senior officials. For example, neither the Foreign Secretary nor the American Secretary of State was present at the meeting off Placentia Bay in August 1941 when the declaration known as the Atlantic Charter was proposed somewhat casually: indeed, it is significant that no authentic signed copy of the Charter exists. Again, the Prime Minister and the President signed the document embracing the so-called Morgenthau plan at the second Quebec Conference, in September 1944, without the knowledge of the British Foreign Secretary or the American Secretary of State.

In some respects the United States forces had greater problems even than ourselves, because they had not progressed nearly so far in the technique of co-ordinating their navy and army and planning and working them together. Indeed, there was a real and sometimes bitter divergence of outlook between the United States navy and army, which had been spurred on by the disaster at Pearl Harbour. In consequence, from the outset the American authorities were adamant that their joint operations should have a unified command. This should have been a simpler problem for the United States than ourselves because they had then only two fighting Services, each having its own integrated air forces. As a matter of interest it might be noted that when the Americans entered the war they tried to solve their unity of command problem in amphibious operations by having the admiral in sole command until such time as the general was satisfied that his forces were firmly established ashore, when the sole command was handed over. In fact, this principle was never put into practice in any specifically American national operation.

VI

The United States, now being the greatest power in the world, has in some ways the most difficult strategic problems of all the Allies. She is comparatively new to the role of being the leading world power. Also many free countries, particularly in the East, are suspicious of America's most generous aid and of her every motive. Moreover, with their vast resources of power and almost unlimited mechanical devices of every kind, the Americans are not unnaturally reluctant to sacrifice troops when a bomber, guided missile or naval craft could achieve the task without large loss of life to themselves. Indeed, with their large air force and the high value they place on human life, the United States are not prepared to engage large numbers of troops in conflict with hordes of communist troops whose leaders seem much less concerned about losses. Certainly, the United States intends to use her new weapons of great power to give every support to her land forces. Thus despite her expanding strategy and military commitments, the United States' policy aims to reduce her overseas land forces. They will be replaced partly by indigenous forces raised with American aid among the nationals whose countries are to be safeguarded, such as South Korea, Nationalist China, the Philippines and Indo-China.

In striving towards a closer and closer integration of Allied strategies and smoother working relations between the Allied high political and military authorities, particularly between the United Kingdom and the United States, we must remember that it is natural that different points of view in regard to common problems should result in divergencies, often substantial and sometimes serious. Doubtless the greatest factor in these divergences is the different and conflicting national interests involved. In this, progress can be made only by exploring all possibilities of adjustment and reconciliation, by giving and taking. Nevertheless, on the military level there are other important factors which allow of readier adjustment. Such factors as national traditions, experiences, characters, temperaments and habits all promote international leaders of different types, as well as different methods, procedures and mental approaches to common problems.

In this light arise several international military cross-currents. America's tendency to favour rigid adherence to the written word and to dogma contrasts with the British more flexible practice of adhering to general principles and interpreting the precise meaning of the written word in the light of experience. In actual technique, the American leaders are often forthright and outspoken in their desire for irrevocable directives, while on the other hand, British leaders are in comparison suave in manner. These differences are well exemplified in the American attitude of favouring the system of a Supreme Commander in contrast to the British attitude, whenever possible of favouring the committee system of three separate Commanders with joint responsibility. It is curious in this respect that only recently the British with some reluctance have appointed an independent Chairman to the Chiefs of Staff Committee. What is perhaps the most striking difference in the United States and United Kingdom Service organizations lies in the power placed in the hands of Congressional Committees to investigate, in the broad sense, military establishments and commands. The power of these committees is very considerable and may even place the position of any Commander-in-Chief in jeopardy.

Each of these national systems fails to deal adequately with the parochial views of the respective Services and our combined and joint strategies are handicapped to that extent. The British military high command with its smooth and efficient working committee system seeks to hide inter-Service disagreement and parochial attitudes by finding and accepting the highest common denominator of agreement and the public seldom hear much about military discord. On the other hand, disagreement within the United States Joint Chiefs of Staff is common knowledge in America. Moreover, the dissension of individual members of the Joint Chiefs of Staff from the views of their colleagues results not only from different military premises but from a different approach to policy itself.

Allied combined strategy suffers from the same complexities as British Commonwealth strategy but to a higher degree. Indeed, a basic weakness in Allied strategy is the natural tendency for the Western nations to allow their sovereignty and self-interests to outweigh some of the factors associated with a strong Allied strategy. The fuller the agreement of the respective nations the stronger the strategy is likely to be. For example, a crucial problem on which agreement should be reached between the United Kingdom and the United States is the vulnerability and security of Great Britain in the event of nuclear attack. There could be no strong Allied strategy if the British anxiety of being obliterated in the first few days of a war were not adequately appreciated in the United States; and any suggestion that the United States could survive a nuclear attack and ultimately secure victory for the Allies would be of little satisfaction to a prostrate and devastated United Kingdom. As the United States and her war potential are much less vulnerable than the United Kingdom (though this is not a view widely shared in the United States), it is important for the United Kingdom that enemy bomber bases should be among the first target systems to be attacked and in great concentration. It may be that the United States will be less concerned than the British about the vulnerability of the United Kingdom and may prefer to attack target systems which from their point of view are of greater positive and war-winning value. However, although our two concepts might diverge on this question they are certainly complementary as can be exemplified by the great variety of tasks which can be allotted to the strategic air forces at our joint disposal. British weapons must be of such high quality to earn full respect for Britain's views from both the United States and Russia. Unless Britain makes this contribution she could not be sure that the exact targets of cardinal importance to her would be given the necessary priority in the first few hours of total war.

In considering Allied combined strategy as it may develop in the next decade or two it should not be forgotten that American civilization as such is becoming increasingly American. Lest this should seem a mere platitude it should be pointed out that this is indeed a phenomenon the growth of which began to be appreciated by the beginning of the First World War. The integration of that vast heterogeneous community into one nation is no small compliment to the vision of United States statesmen and the character of the Americans themselves. It has, however, certain consequences and chief among these is the fact that although Britain and America both belong to the West the American way of life is becoming more and more distinct from the traditional European civilization. Less and less do the emigrants look backwards to the older countries either for inspiration or for values. Instead they have found a new value, the United States; and view the rest of the world from the somewhat intoxicating vantage point of optimism. As a result they are more adamant in enforcing their views and to an increasing degree this difference between the new world and the old will affect global strategy and influence the destiny of the whole world.

There does seem one overwhelming obstacle to the build-up and maintenance of a single unified Allied strategy: it is one which has in all likelihood done more than any other factor in the history of Allied combination to vitiate the advantages in such a combination. This is the vast inequality in resources, manpower and weapons among the Allied nations themselves. This scale of disparity, in which the Allied nations are not in fact equals and do not have similar interests and aims, is a most dangerous feature, leading, as it may, not simply to a dissimilarity of interest but to a collision of interest. Today, many are inclined to feel that it is wishful thinking to regard the United Kingdom as having an equal say in the strategy of the Western Alliance in the face of the vast superior financial, economic and numerical strength of the United States. United States national policies, interests and attitudes are greatly different from those of the United Kingdom and of the countries within NATO, or of the Commonwealth and Dominions. It is also felt that, necessarily, the United States as the dominant partner in the Western Alliance will have the greatest say in the political or military strategy, and that strategy will revolve round United States' ideas of what is good for the United States first and the Alliance second.

In no way is this intended as an adverse criticism of the United States, but sooner or later we must face the fact that the United Kingdom is no longer the dominant power in the world, and we must be prepared to accept our position in the Alliance as led by the United States. It would make an hypocrisy of NATO if the British Government were to render allegiance to Allied strategy in times of peace and attempted to pursue a purely national strategy in times of war. Despite the unifying process of NATO and the Western Alliance, governments are still far too reluctant to surrender national sovereignty in favour of Allied unity. This is especially true of the government of a democracy responsible to a people who for centuries have been accustomed to a monarchical system.

The traditional policies of isolationism in the nineteenth century, characteristic of both the United Kingdom and the United States, were designed to avoid military alliances in time of peace and also to keep their peacetime forces to a minimum. By this means they were able to mobilize their strength and conserve their freedom of manœuvre until the moment for necessary and effective intervention presented itself. The United Kingdom turned away from this policy of a free hand early in the present century but only just in time. The experience of the two World Wars has shown how inadequate preparation before hostilities began, both in the organizational and forces sense, nearly meant disaster for us. Had the United States been committed before 1914 to intervene in full strength from the outbreak of European war the First World War would probably never have occurred. Similarly had she been committed in Europe before 1939 it is more than likely that the Second World War would have been avoided. It may be in some degree significant that isolationism in America lasted longer but there can be nothing but admiration for the manner and dispatch with which she has enacted her new policy and her new role.

VII

In some ways the Allied South-East Asia command in the last war had a more difficult problem than the Supreme headquarters for Europe. Certainly, the South-East Asia headquarters had its inter-Allied troubles. Although the British were the predominant partner in this theatre, various arrangements undertaken to meet United States requirements made it the more difficult for the organization to work smoothly. One complication was that the United States army Commander-in-Chief in the theatre was also Deputy Supreme Allied Commander, especially as the American land forces were not under the command of the Supreme Allied Commander. With such a set-up much obviously had to be learned.

In South-East Asia and the Far East the Allied combined post-war strategy is less satisfactory for the reasons already described. Actually, in these regions it is the cold war and the threat of local war rather than the threat of total war that makes combined strategy so difficult. In peacetime many of the free countries of Asia are suspicious of the intentions of the Western powers' political and military activities, believing that they are more for the benefit of the West themselves than for the Asians. Until these suspicions are removed, we cannot expect a sound and comprehensive combined strategy in this area comparable with NATO.

Of the post-war incidents in the Far East, the Korean war in 1950 is of special interest. Here for the first time United Nation forces, though directed by the United States, were operating in a loose Allied combined strategy of many nations. These operations brought out the important lesson of how difficult it is for a Supreme Commander to reconcile changing circumstances with his Allied directive which of necessity must be in broad terms, and vice versa, how difficult it is for the Allied political authority to adjust their broad directive to changing circumstances. One of the main Allied disagreements was the strong desire on the part of many American political and military authorities to adopt strategic bombing, including atomic bombs, north of the Yalu river, which was countered by equally strong desire on the part of most of the other Allies to refrain from this risk of extending the local war into a total one. A second strong difference arose because of the United States military authorities' attempt to advance the land forces to the Yalu river, against British opinion that it was most unwise to advance further than the 'wasp-waist' of the Peninsula.

The Formosa situation of 1955 is another example of national differences in Allied combined strategy, though fortunately patience and perseverance eventually brought the United States decision to defend the China off-shore islands of Matsu and Quemoy round to the British Commonwealth desire to avoid clashing with Communist China on this issue, which was not a critical strategic requirement for the defence of Formosa itself, or for the military power of the Allies in the Far East.

The situation in Indo-China has also caused differences in the British, American and French combined strategy. Then at the critical moment of the campaign when France at last sought for help there was a violent difference between British and American strategies. Fortunately, wisdom prevailed to the extent that France was extricated, at least temporarily, from a hopeless position of complete surrender to the communists. It is well to remember that Indo-China, a region which overshadows China and India, is a key position in Allied combined strategy. The occupation of Indo-China by Japanese forces after the fall of France paved the way for the fall of Singapore and Burma in the last war, and in the same way a similar catastrophe could be repeated.

VIII

The post-war years have shown great advances in Allied military affairs. Never before in peacetime have so many nations agreed to work together in their military affairs as in SHAPE working within NATO. Even more encouraging is the agreement of the Western nations in peacetime to formulate and co-ordinate political policy for the defence of Western Europe. Today the NATO Council has a Permanent Organization in Paris under Lord Ismay as Secretary-General and a Council of fifteen permanent representatives at only one remove from Ministerial level. The Secretary-General is served by an efficient International Secretariat which if given the chance should develop a first-class and powerful organization. It is inevitable that in peacetime NATO cannot have the paramount authority that Mr. Churchill or Mr. Roosevelt had in the last war, but this can be readily defined in a crisis or in war.

An essential in the procedure of the Permanent Organization is that work is not done by votes but by general agreement, using whatever forcing tactics are necessary to get all members to go along with the majority. There is no precedent for the range of international, political, economic and military activities that NATO is covering in peacetime. This has developed from the realization that the defence of Western Europe for total war now covers all aspects of National and international life. It is inevitable that the boundary of the geographical area of NATO and SHAPE presents our nations with difficult problems. In war it is clear that the present artificial limits of NATO's responsibilities would become meaningless. It is equally clear that the free world defence organization and strategy should be extended to cover the whole world.

NATO promises the most likely manner in which Allied Political Direction and High Commands will develop in Europe, and unity in

Allied military affairs is the ideal. We must seek unity with our Allies by streamlined co-operation and find ways of avoiding or minimizing the delays, frustration and cumbersome organizations which are so often associated with this type of unity. International tension and the threat of war make unity by co-operation far more easy because each ally is then much more prepared to forfeit national beliefs and self-interests. When the fear of war recedes, trade and other aspects of national life take first place and military unity by co-operation is much more difficult. Thus there is always the risk, as there has been in the past, that unity by co-operation may be too slow and too late.

NATO has laid well the foundations for planning, co-operation and command for international unity of Political Direction and High Command. It is designed to function in peacetime but would also provide the principal structure of Allied direction and command on the outbreak of war. This organization has gradually assumed political, economic, military and financial functions which clearly distinguish it from previous peacetime alliances. Its role in peacetime is to plan, train and organize in readiness for war, and, in war, it is the nucleus of the organization which would direct the strategy of free Europe.

Recent events, notably the wars in Korea and Indo-China, have emphasized the limitations of the Allied defences. The invasion of South Korea by a communist army from the north, well trained and equipped with Soviet armour and artillery, brought home to the NATO High Command and Political Direction, and to the man in the street, that the free world was not organized to deal with cold or local war, and that communist strategy in more remote parts of the world can seriously weaken the free world's defensive strength in Western Europe. Events in Indo-China and more recently in the Middle East and North Africa, re-emphasized this weakness. We have been forced to realize that the cold war has made the grand strategy of the free world dependent as much on political and economic as on military and geographical factors. It is not now sufficient for a military High Command to co-ordinate military forces: the Political Direction must co-ordinate economic and foreign policy with military matters.

The chief threat of war is always poised at the seat of power and that is amply demonstrated in Europe today but the threat of war finds its more obvious expression in the comparatively defenceless areas of the

Middle and Far East. The emergence of SEATO is an indication of the lessons learnt by the United States, Britain and the Commonwealth and our Far Eastern friends from the growth of NATO. The Baghdad Pact is also an encouraging sign of an effective alliance between the West and some of the countries of the Middle East. It would seem that the free world defence organization is being slowly but surely extended to cover the whole world. The broad outlines of global strategy centre round two main world bastions: those of the Western and Eastern hemispheres. In addition to this, however, three main geographical zones have been visualized, the natural political Western, Eastern and Middle divisions which lend themselves more easily to the study of Allied and national strategies of the various greater and lesser countries concerned. While it is perhaps beyond the scope of this work to argue the shape which our Allied global defences should take it seems that for constitutional and national grouping and interests, and for administrative reasons, it would be best to consider them within three geographical zones. While West and East are easy distinctions they are in fact too simple: strategically they are indeed two bastions but when strategy has to be formed for all areas the Middle zone has a peculiar complexity. It is neither oriental nor occidental and forms on its own account a vulnerable national and geographical area.

IX

Whatever their limitations the existence of NATO and SHAPE means that for the first time since world war became a feature of history we have or can have an Allied war mechanism in being, which can evolve the necessary strategy to combat any all-out attempt to destroy any or all of our Allies.

Besides the deterrent value of nuclear weapons against total war, the Allies must also base their combined strategy on the cold war and the possible outbreak of local war where nuclear weapons are not used by either contestant except possibly in a tactical role. Thus, conventional Allied naval, army and air forces are required. The size and power required of these Allied forces are difficult to assess. In particular, because there is not nearly such a close understanding and agreement between the various Allied nations in this field of political policy and combined strategy as in regard to total war. Indeed, depending on the locality and circumstances, one Allied nation cannot always assume that she will receive help from other Allied nations even in local war and certainly not in cold war. Moreover, it is difficult to assess the locality and the size and nature of military effort our aggressors might establish at the outbreak of this type of warfare, and how quickly they might submit or reinforce for political rather than military reasons.

In assessing the overall size and share of the Allied conventional naval, army and air forces required to deal with local and cold war and the deterrent against these wars breaking out, must also be considered the requirement of conventional military forces in total war and the deterrent against such war. One outstanding peacetime example of this is the Allied forces based in Europe and the Atlantic. These forces would not only be an essential complement to the Allied strategic nuclear weapons and forces in total war, but they are also a great deterrent to Russia in her efforts to nibble away the Western European and Middle East nations piece by piece. It is clear that, in addition to the NATO forces, each of the main Allied nations requires conventional naval, army and air forces deployed in strategically selected spheres together with conveniently placed and adequate reserve forces with a high degree of mobility. The greater the Allied co-operation in providing these forces and in assessing the local and cold war problems, the greater the economy of force. The more the aggressors understand the firmness of the national and international determination to use these forces without delay, the greater will be the deterrent against this form of warfare.

Geography, national resources, general topography, accessibility and communications and changing circumstances in the countries and areas concerned are further factors which can substantially affect Allied combined strategy with regard to strategic bombing. Also geography and national resources determine the need of sea communications. For the Allies, sea communications are vital over a great part of the world whereas for Russia they play a very small part. Thus, combined Allied strategy must be framed to secure the seas in contrast to Russian strategy to deny them to us. Sea communications give us the advantage of being able to establish and use naval, air and guided missile bases on a periphery round the greater part of Russia and within air striking distance of even her most remote vital centres. Moreover, these communications enable us to use aircraft carriers as highly mobile bases for the operation of bomber, reconnaissance and guidance aircraft and guided missiles in remote regions. In local and cold war in distant parts, sea communications are of immense value to us. Again, geography has a most important influence in the depth available for early warning and air defences, and for the land defences to the Allies and to Russia and her satellites respectively. All these considerations are most important factors in the formulation of Allied combined strategy.

Our combined strategy today is based on the following concepts. The hydrogen weapon has raised the power of the offensive over the defensive to such a degree that total war is likely to be suicidal to all concerned and thus will be the end of civilization. Our best and only means of defence is a deterrent strategy which makes this fact crystal clear to the potential aggressor. The acme of this deterrent for the West is achieved by having a nuclear bomber force supplemented by ballistic rockets which is at immediate readiness and capable of mortal retaliation. The Soviet bloc must not only be aware that we are determined to retaliate but that we are in a position to retaliate effectively. This deterrent can be made still more effective by the provision of an adequate air defence of fighter aircraft and guided missiles, together with an efficient Home defence, a symbol of our determination not to flinch even at the prospect of hydrogen war. Such air and home defence would certainly cause the aggressor to pause and to doubt whether he could achieve a sudden victory by a surprise, and supposedly mortal, attack.

Considerations with regard to the prosecution of total war are very similar to those for the deterrent. The bulk of the strategic air offensive would have to be provided by the United States. There would be little opportunity of the United States and the United Kingdom reinforcing the NATO forces. The extent of the remnants of survival of the United Kingdom would depend largely on the efficacy of our air defences and home defence organization.

So far as can be foreseen, under the present global balance of power, there can be no effective defence for any of the Western free countries if considered or dealt with separately and in isolation. Defence of the

Allied countries can be effective only if considered collectively. Certainly there could be no effective air defence of the United Kingdom in isolation against the whole might of the Soviet Russian power even if we increased our air defence and strategic striking force fourfold or more. Nor could there be any effective defence of the frontiers of Germany, France or any other Western European power separately against the whole might of Soviet Russia. Indeed, there could be no satisfactory defence even of the United States of America in isolation because, under such circumstances, she would eventually find herself aligned against Soviet Russia commanding the whole of Europe, Africa and probably Asia as well.

This is not an exaggerated view of the situation and no one would minimize the difficulties of reconciling a variety of national approaches, not only within an alliance, but the individual national solutions of what must seem essentially national problems. If Allied strategy and Allied defence is resolved first and collectively, national problems and difficulties in isolated areas might lend themselves to a readier and more satisfactory solution. But what is important is that national interests do not cut across the Allied defence concept. The French problem in North Africa or the British problem in Cyprus and even the delicacy of defence in Western Germany would present less difficulty and anxiety if the Allied concept was not only accepted in principle but resolved in fact.

In the case of limited global war which excludes the strategic use of nuclear weapons, obviously the Allied nations would not at present be justified in expending any substantial proportion of the resources available for their defence in this sphere. In any event, such a war would not be decided by a knock-out blow and we could expect a period in which to mobilize and harness our resources to the conflict. There is, however, much scope in this form of war for planning nationally and internationally. Should agreement be reached for the exclusion of nuclear weapons and for adequate measures to guarantee such agreement, then obviously a high degree of priority would have to be given to the preparation for limited global war.

This somewhat brief review of the major problems in Allied combined strategy does at least give some idea of their multifarious complexity. One thing on which we can rely is the fact that total war will be the affair of allies opposing other combinations of peoples and that in itself should forge the validity of the concept of Allied combined strategy. But while many, individuals as well as nations, agree that such an Allied strategy should be established and international agreement made in peacetime, such aquiescence is all too apt to become a half-hearted lip-service to what they may regard as a distant ideal. Let us not delude ourselves: it is not something merely which would be good for us — it is essential to our continued existence.

CHAPTER VIII

National Joint Strategy

I

Britain's changed circumstances and her reduced relative economic strength compared with the United States and aggressive Russia are among the primary reasons for many alterations in her national policy and strategy. In the past Britain was able to achieve military victory with a most inadequate peacetime preparation in many spheres, and even after many serious reverses during the early stages of hostility: until such time as the national war effort could be harnessed to the occasion and win the final phase.

In the past era each of the British fighting services was substantially self contained and both in peace and war were also able to formulate their own strategies very largely in isolation of each other. Moreover, the British services did not assume the help in total war from Allies in anything like the same way and to the same degree as they can, today, take for granted help from the greatly more powerful American armed forces. It is important to take the Allied association and the dependence on their mutual help fully into consideration when formulating National political policy and National joint strategy: indeed, the British financial and economic position, if nothing else, allows no alternative.

In Chapter II of this work there are already some illustrations of how the separate strategies of each service have persisted to the detriment of National joint strategy. Yet as the essence of the strategic concept contained in this book ranges round National joint strategy and its relations with the Services and home defence strategies, it would be well, at the risk of some repetition, to begin this chapter with a brief review of the general pattern of the changing features shown by history in the development of strategy.

In no sense, however, may this review be considered comprehensive of inter-Service operations. There have been many such operations when good strategy and co-ordination have achieved excellent results: perhaps the best example of all of a successful inter-Service operation is the actual assault of the Normandy beaches on 'D' day in 1944. There have also been many unfortunate inter-Service operations, varying from failure to partial success which have not been mentioned. The selection of the examples included in this chapter has been made to give something of a cross-sectional picture of the price which has been paid for partisan strategy and concepts in both peace and war.

The Quebec joint expedition of 1759 is an example of a most successful amphibious operation where naval and army strategies were woven together into an effective pattern. Naval and army strategies were also successfully co-ordinated during the remainder of the Seven Years War (1756-63). There followed, however, a series of unsuccessfully co-ordinated joint operations during the later decades of the eighteenth century, particularly in the Mediterranean and Home waters. The Cartagena expedition of 1741 and the Scheldt expedition of 1809 are two outstanding examples where we suffered from the lack of co-ordinated naval and army strategies. More often than not these campaigns or operations of uncoordinated strategy were in the main due to friction between the respective commanders.

In the war with Napoleon, the British navy and army were fighting a common foe, yet their strategies were virtually separate. There was of course some co-ordination between the two strategies but much better effect could have been achieved at smaller cost had there been a better welding. Unfortunately, even in the critical days at the beginning of the First World War, the first experience of unlimited or total war, there was still in effect two separate concepts of strategy, as there had been since the separation of the British navy from the army. Although this strategy was co-ordinated in varying degrees during the phases of this war, it was never amalgamated. Whatever the casualties or deadlock, or however long the conflict, the army strategy was based on the defeat of the German army in the fields of Europe. Essentially, the naval strategy was opposed to the army slogging head-on strategy: it sought to use command of the sea to launch land attack wherever the enemy was most vulnerable. Typical of this is the example of the Dardanelles expedition which unfortunately ended in a disaster which was unquestionably due to a conflict between naval and army strategies at high level. Although air power appeared in the First World War, the naval and army strategic concept of its value never reached beyond its giving support to the naval and land forces.

Since the time of the sixteenth century, when the army, then the British sole fighting Service, was separated into two Services — the army and the navy — National joint strategy has been jeopardized as the result of partisan naval and army strategies developing individually. Army strategy centred round Alexander's and Napoleon's concepts of capture and consolidation of territory, whereas naval strategy centred round the expansion of overseas enterprises and trade by the control of the sea. As the two services became more independent of each other, their respective strategies diverged more and more even into rivalry and inter-Service conflict. This continued right up to the Second World War, and continues even today.

It is interesting to note that at the British political level there is today little, if any, difference in party opinion on the pattern of strategy, but over a long period of history there were two schools of strategic thought amongst the parliamentary parties. On the one hand, there was the continental army school of strategy, and in contrast there was a strong school of opinion which favoured naval enterprise overseas. The British Tory theory was that it would benefit England to subsidize allies to fight her battles on the continent, while strong naval forces, or rather shipping resources, should be used to capture the enemy's ports and trade. In this Britain succeeded in making trade pay for war.

It was because of these inter-Service problems that the British system of joint command developed: the High Command of each Service being solely responsible for its own strategy and affairs, though both were responsible collectively for the operations as a whole. All the great nations have encountered this problem of co-ordinating their Services strategies, but all have not found the system which worked so well in the past for the British, so satisfactory for their own national temperaments. Ironically, it is because the British joint system of command appeared to work so well in the past, with any inter-Service friction only occasionally becoming unrestrained, that there is a reluctance to make the necessary changes which modern conditions require.

In the post-war years of the First World War, when the air force had been created as a third Service, the lack of a National joint strategy, and the continual thrusting forward of partisan Service strategies were much in evidence. This was associated largely with the potentialities of air power round which great controversy ranged: post-war economies and retrenchment, forcing the two older Services to forgo some of their traditional and cherished prerogatives, made the controversy all the more fierce.

II

The first (1914-18) post-war shock to the old traditional British army strategy was Mr. Churchill's advice that the air force should control Iraq at a fraction of the cost asked by the army. In India, the army strategic concept was so deeply entrenched that nothing could dislodge it beyond a reluctant acceptance that some air support was necessary to efficient army operations. Indeed, great heat was caused in the High Command in India and in Whitehall because the air enthusiasts claimed a greater place than was current for air strategy: unfortunately they later increased their claim unreasonably to the task of taking over the primary role of the security of the North-West Frontier against the hostile tribesmen. An interesting postscript to British strategy in India is that notwithstanding a hundred years of army conflict with the Frontier tribesmen, at very great cost and great casualties, this tribal threat virtually disappeared with the withdrawal of British power from India. The reasons for this remarkable change would merit some discussion, though it is beyond the scope of this book to try to assess how much this was due to change in policy and political background, and how much to changes in strategy. It would be a serious charge to weight the latter over the former consideration.

Another strategic question which caused even greater British inter-Service controversy was the defence of Singapore. Whereas the navy and army pressed for a strategy based on very expensive fixed coastal defence guns, the air force claimed that a strategy based on air power would be greatly superior and much more economical. A great deal of money was involved in this partisan strategic controversy. It is now well known that millions of pounds were poured into the making of these coastal batteries and when Singapore was attacked in February 1942, they never fired a shot: indeed, they were all sited to fire in the opposite direction to the Japanese assault.

A further Service controversy in the inter-war years was the issue between the strategic value of the battleship and aircraft. This is an interesting example of two Service approaches to a national strategical problem. The outcome was that the Second World War found Britain with a substantial number of battleships and few aircraft carriers, greater numbers of which would have been a most valuable asset. The value of the battleship in national strategy was not decided until the Japanese attack on the United States battlefleet in Pearl Harbour in December 1941. The whole field of maritime aircraft in the past and today is conceived and dealt with on a partisan naval and air force basis rather than on any truly strategic concept of the problem as a whole. Outwith the responsibility of the air forces, and born in great controversy, British sea-borne aircraft were subsequently transferred to the navy in part and in compromise. The result is that today the British navy possesses and operates all carrier aircraft and the air force have retained all shore-based maritime aircraft as well as flying boats. This is a most artificial division of functional responsibility created for expediency; and functional, financial and material difficulties accrue more and more with the development of national strategy of modern times. Unfortunately, the British Admiralty and to a lesser extent the Air Ministry concern themselves with the retention if not the aggravation of this division of responsibility for partisan reasons.

Again, adequate progress within reasonable expenditure will not be made in the realm of air power until the authorities show greater imagination and courage in replacing familiar weapons in favour of new and untried concepts and weapons. For example, the Air Ministry were reluctant to order guided weapons and encourage their rapid production because they maintained that these new weapons were not adequately developed and still had many teething troubles, and they allocated their resources accordingly. The fact is that the present and certainly the future generations of fighter aircraft are of the most limited value without the provision of guided weapons: no gun or cannon can be very effective with the present modern speeds. Similarly, the value of ballistic rockets is sure to increase in the coming years and yet the Air Ministry strive to retain their bombers in as large numbers as the Treasury will sanction and inevitably to the detriment of the new weapons.

III

After the First World War, a high standard was reached in the British study of the Service strategies at the respective Service staff colleges, in particular, the Army Staff college. Nevertheless, although a lot of lip-service was given to joint strategy, virtually it was based on a combination of the three separate Service strategies. Seldom was Service doctrine departed from at the expense of Service custom and tradition in favour of a genuine overall concept of national strategy. Few army officers of any seniority, and these included the highest intellectual order of all the fighting Services, would in these pre-Second World War years have agreed that the primary role of a bomber force should be anything other than support to the army and the navy. There were indeed many accepted Service principles, practices and dogmas which were highly partisan. For example, a substantial number of the exercises and studies given to students at the British Army Staff College had been framed many years previously, almost on a Boer War concept, and attempts were made annually by the Directing Staff, amongst whom there were many brilliant officers, to bring the work up to date. The truth is that no revision could put right the original setting. There was one instance when the Commandant at Camberley made the most caustic comment in full audience about the solution of one student to a problem with regard to the use of armoured forces. The student had proposed to use the armoured force to raid the enemy on a circuit several miles deep behind the enemy line. The Commandant's scathing criticism was concerned with what he considered the unjustifiable hazard of passing such a valuable asset as the armoured force so far behind the enemy front line. Subsequently, the student became Lord Montgomery's Tank Corps adviser in North Africa and later for the invasion of the continent in 1944. This instance illustrates much of the trouble with our pre-war strategic concepts and the tactics which stemmed from them.

Likewise, many of the studies at the Naval Staff college had been outmoded by air warfare and other new developments with more serious consequences than even those in the army. On the other hand, the Air Force Staff college assumed the possibilities and potentialities of weapons yet to be developed and suffered from an unrealistic assessment of the limitations of contemporary air forces, which resulted in a tendency to get their heads into the clouds and a failure to appreciate the true place of naval and army forces in the current national armoury. Inevitably all three Service staff colleges taught, fashioned and reflected the ideas and thoughts of the senior members of their respective Service High Commands. Such was the indoctrination of Service strategy at that critical time.

It is a most disturbing thought that in those critical years before the Second World War, there was great intellectual capacity, particularly in the army staffs, but they were in blinkers. During that period, the struggle was for Service priority, not for national priority: each Service strove to justify its own strategy regardless of any overall military concept. Despite a variety of co-ordinating authorities the strategy for the Second World War was fashioned from the three separate Service strategies as individual approaches to the one problem and not as one whole.

A contributory cause of inter-Service controversy, particularly after the outbreak of the Second World War, was the intelligence organizations. Each of the Service Ministries had its own intelligence department co-ordinated by the Joint Intelligence Committee of the Chiefs of Staff Committee. Frequently these multiple intelligence services resulted in the great weakness of vital information of a common origin and of a most tenuous character being translated into appreciations and reports by the various teams of keen, able and less able intelligence officers, competing in many instances to make the best case for the partisan and preconceived ideas of their own masters — so much so that the archivists will surely be confounded.

Inevitably with the three separate services strategies there was much controversy and speculation over strategy during the last war in regard to the employment and achievements of the respective services. Subsequent analysis shows that the Allied strategic bombers reduced German oil production by 95 per cent between spring of 1944 and the end of the war, and the German railway system was virtually brought to a standstill by air power during the same period. It was this latter factor which above all else made possible the land advance across Europe. The course of the Japanese War showed that a decisive land battle was not necessary to her defeat. She surrendered with her army intact and before an Allied soldier had set foot in the Japanese home islands. A most apt illustration of the application of modern sea, land and air power.

It came about that the beginning of the Second World War found Great Britain with three separate Service strategies although there were also references to national strategy. In fact, the highest British military authority was the Chiefs of Staff Committee which was composed of the heads of each Service, for the greater part apparently working in harmony.

The naval strategy, based on the years of experience, still ranged round the control of the sea, though it had failed to keep pace with the developments of aircraft, submarines and mines which was to prove most costly. The army was in a difficult position in that many in authority had learnt the dangers of a strategy which committed the bulk of the land forces in Western Europe. Indeed, this was so much so, that the original British plan was to send a minimum land force to the continent. Some few months before the war, however, British political considerations with the French compelled her to change this plan for one committing a large army to the continent. Events showed that this was a correct political decision because France would never have declared war without the commitment of this British land force, and in turn Britain could not have declared war without her French ally.

British air strategy was concerned mostly with strategic bomber forces to attack Germany and a fighter force to defend the United Kingdom. In this strategy, air support to the army and the navy was only of secondary importance and allocated grudgingly. In the event, it became clear that having committed the British Expeditionary Force to the continent, before the days of Dunkirk, air support was more important during the critical operations than any bombing of Germany. The loss of the British army led dangerously near to our losing the war. On the other hand, the premises on which air strategy was based at the beginning of the war were soon proved faulty: the limited destructive power of bombs and bombers at that time could not have been mortal to the German Home front.

After the German breakthrough at Sedan, serious divergencies appeared within the national strategy over British fighter aircraft. The army, pressed by the French High Command, insisted that substantial reinforcements in fighters to the continent to operate with the British Expeditionary Force was essential, whereas the air force maintained that they could be sent only to the grave detriment of the defence of the United Kingdom. The Battle of Britain subsequently showed that the air force was right in this dispute and that, in any event, the whole of the fighter resources could not have saved the army at that time.

To a large degree, the foregoing faults in British strategy were due to each Service pressing its own strategy into the national strategy with emphasis on their advantages and not to their short-comings and weak points. With the older services failing at times to appreciate the strategical issues it is not surprising that the relatively new air force too should on occasion have been confused and even wrong in its approach.

In the Norway campaign of the Second World War, with which it is intended to deal in more detail, the British air force neglect, over the years, of the air support role for both naval and army operations was clearly illuminated. Indeed, since the amalgamation of the Royal Flying Corps and the Royal Naval Air Service into an independent and fully fledged military service, the air support and air transport roles were given scant concern and this continued right up to and during much of the Second World War.

It was with reluctance and as the result of much pressure from the British army that a meagre and very inadequate air component comprising a few army co-operation and a few fighter squadrons was allocated to proceed to France with the Expeditionary Force at the beginning of the Second World War and this force was strengthened but little during the period up to the German overrun of the Low Countries and France in 1940. Slowly under the pressure of events the air force built up more adequate air forces in the Middle East to meet air support commitments, as well to enable it to undertake more effective bombing operations — strategical and tactical — for the army at Alamein and during the drive along North Africa to Sicily and Italy. Still greater pressure and at the highest political level was necessary to provide adequate air support, the strategic bombers for the invasion of Normandy and subsequently up to the end of the war.

Whatever lessons with regard to air support and air transport aspects of strategy were learnt during the Second World War they seem in large measure to have since been forgotten or ignored by the British air force. Today, the air offensive as first line of our national defence is undisputed, though it is realized that the greater part of any such offensive must rest with the United States Strategic Air Force. Notwithstanding their great strategic bomber strength, the United States have a powerful navy which has its own air support force and they also maintain substantial air support forces for their army. Measured in these terms there are still some British air enthusiasts who give far too complete priority to her bomber forces to the detriment of the needs for air support to her navy and army.

IV

What were the reasons for the regrettable and deplorable direction and conduct of the 1940 Norway campaign? Generally, so far as the individual statesmen and officers who controlled the Whitehall direction are concerned, their personal abilities were very similar to those concerned in the most successful invasion of Normandy four years later. Likewise, most of the Service commanders prosecuting operations at sea, on land or in the air were not inferior in military ability to those who were concerned in the later campaigns. If any criticism may be levelled against the individual statesmen or military leaders of that time it is that they were not wholly alive to the situation and the war conditions which then prevailed. Moreover, Mr. Churchill, then virtually acting in the capacity of Minister of Defence, dominated the Service Chiefs who composed the Chiefs of Staff Committee at that time. As too often in assessing history, we are dependent on all too inadequate information about the background environment of the campaign and the reasons why the various people concerned made their decisions. Certainly, no one could understand how and why failure occurred in Norway without knowing the background picture of the circumstances and conditions under which the Whitehall machine was working.

Here was a campaign in which we were caught unprepared in almost every aspect. If ever there was a joint operation, this was one. Yet, in the first place there was no real joint planning or inter-Service concept to the operation. Each Service made its own partisan approach to the problem.

The British navy followed their own concept of war built up over centuries of successful history. They were primarily concerned in using their sea power for blockade, and to seek out the German fleet wherever it might go. They saw in the Norway project an opportunity of establishing bases of great value and also of preventing Germany from gaining control of the Norwegian coast. Confident and traditionally conservative they carried great weight in the deliberations and councils of Whitehall. They had yet to recognize, accept and be confounded by the full significance of air power.

The British army viewed the project as a diversion of doubtful value from their primary concern of concentrating everything in France. In essence they viewed the operation as a problem of getting land forces ashore at selected points with the view to establishing strategic land positions in the defence of Norway against German land attack from the south. As so often happens in history, they tended to view the naval role mainly as one of transportation of their land forces. The army had also yet to realize the full significance of air power.

The air force was concerned primarily with the air defence of the United Kingdom and the strategic bombing of Germany. In particular, this fight of air superiority and the fear of the 'knockout blow' governed policy thinking. In any event, the air force had inadequate forces for each of these tasks and viewed any such project as Norway as a diversion which should not be encouraged. Moreover, at the time, the air force viewed the air support role as a very secondary one to strategic bombing and air defence.

Operationally, the British navy had been in action in their traditional role since the outbreak of the war. The army was deployed on the continent also since the outbreak of war but virtually had not yet fired a shot. Moreover, up to that time the army had no experience of modern land warfare, both in respect of the use of troops and also the effect on the morale of troops of modern weapons. The air force offensive had been confined to leaflet dropping except for some bombing against naval targets. Moreover, the Second World War was the first major war in which the Royal Air Force, the first national air force, fought since its creation in 1918. The Royal Air Force was eager to prove the claims of air power they had made over the years and already they had been disillusioned about the operational potential and effectiveness of their current aircraft and weapons. They saw in Norway a specially difficult pitch for the application of air power with their existing resources.

If the eight months of so-called phoney war had not lulled Whitehall into inaction, it certainly had not shaken the British Service Ministries and the commanders into highly efficient fighting teams. More than one senior officer selected in peacetime for his key appointment had yet to be found wanting under the strain of war. On the other hand, many of the best staff officers were already war weary from the stress of writing papers and making all too many paper plans. Once the Norway campaign had begun and the plan of operations put into effect, there were far too many futile attempts, which Whitehall should have known were administratively impracticable, to improvise the strategy under the stress of urgency.

In contrast to the British war machine, which was not yet geared for the operations which were to be fought in the Second World War, Germany had prepared in earnest for several years, she had modern concepts, the initiative, the forces, a highly efficient machine for the Direction and High Command of operations, and she already had valuable fighting experience in the current war.

Early in the Second World War, without reaching any decision, the British War Cabinet considered the problem of cutting off by mining and other means the supplies of Swedish iron ore which was being delivered to Germany via Narvik. Then, after Russia attacked Finland, there was much political and military discussion which resulted in a plan and preparations for an Anglo-French force to be sent to help the Finns. The intention was to wrest the initiative from Germany by establishing Allied forces at Narvik, Trondheim and Bergen. In the event, the Finns surrendered a few days before the plan was implemented. Subsequently, as a result of Britain's own desire, together with

French pressure for the Allies to take the initiative, plans were made to mine the Leads with the view to stopping the delivery of iron ore to Germany. To guard against German reactions, the plan included landing Allied forces at Narvik and other ports in Southern Norway: these forces were not organized to operate in the face of heavy German opposition, and at worst, only against light Norwegian opposition.

It happened that at the same time Germany had planned to invade Norway for naval strategic reasons. It is interesting to note that this naval sponsored project involved the enemy in much inter-Service friction, particularly because it would entail the postponement of the main German plan for attacking in the West, from November 1939 to the spring of 1940. Probably it was only Quisling's interview, and the possibility of a rapid conquest which decided the issue for Hitler. In consequence, Germany prepared a bold and brilliant plan for the invasion of Norway through much the same ports as Britain had planned. The German plan was based on great secrecy, deception and speed of execution and the use of airborne troops.

It was indeed unfortunate that intelligence in this campaign was so very incomplete, both with regard to the German plan itself and also during the actual campaign. To make matters worse, each Ministry received its own and all too often conflicting reports and it was some time before the overall intelligence for the campaign was put under the War Office for co-ordination. On the other hand, Germany had a good knowledge of the Allied intentions and, seizing the initiative, they made good use of it. This inadequate intelligence, lack of imagination, and lack of experience in modern land fighting since 1918 were among the primary factors in the Allied failure.

Strategically, any campaign in Norway was difficult for any belligerent who failed to secure the initiative because of the geography of the country; especially the relatively great distances between the important ports, the poor communications and the limited number of suitable sites for airfields or even air strips.

So far as resources are concerned, the Allies were very limited compared with Germany who could outnumber the Allies heavily in troops and had a great predominance of fighter, bomber support and transport aircraft. Apart from aircraft, the Allies were especially short in the equipment necessary to operate squadrons away from their bases. Only at sea were the Allies in superior strength and even this could largely be balanced or nullified by the German air power. Germany did not depend on the goodwill of Norway and other neutrals including America in the same way as the Allies: rather they had the support of the Quislings. Moreover, the Allied bombardment policy limited attack from sea or air to purely military objectives in the narrowest sense of the word.

The actual Political Direction and High Command during the Norway campaign was amongst the worst on record in British history. Certainly there was a complete failure to apply any of the lessons which were so prominent in the Dardanelles campaign in the First World War. The Allied Supreme War Councils composed of the United Kingdom and France had delegated direction and command for the Scandinavian operations to the United Kingdom. Thus, the British War Cabinet was the authority for decisions, though it should be noted that the French used all the pressure they could to keep the war away from France. The main link between the making of major policy, and its execution by the separate Services, was at that time the Ministerial Committee on Military Co-ordination. The chairman of this committee was the Minister for the Co-ordination of Defence until his post was abolished just before the Norway campaign when the chairmanship passed to the First Lord of the Admiralty. The members were the Secretary of State for War, the Secretary of State for Air and the Minister of Supply. This committee was dominated by Mr. Churchill, as First Lord of the Admiralty. In fact he was acting as Minister of Defence though Mr. Chamberlain was not prepared to give open approval to subordinating the War Office and the Air Ministry. The committee were given great powers and took decisions, merely reporting to the Cabinet for confirmation.

The Chiefs of Staff were usually in attendance at the Military Co-ordination Committee meetings. During the early phase of the war, the committee was particularly involved in supply subjects but when the Norway campaign began these items were dropped from the agenda and much time given to the strategy and even technical details of the operation. The committee was unbalanced; ill suited to conduct such day-to-day affairs. Its very composition prevented any common feeling or doctrine which could reconcile the conflict, sometimes

K

serious conflict, of the three Services. Moreover, it was out of touch with any knowledge of what was administratively possible. It was indeed not a good committee for the day-to-day task of running operations even when the Prime Minister took the chair. In the rush of these hectic days of the Norway campaign, sometimes two ill-prepared meetings were held each day. No successful operation of a Single service, to say nothing of three Services with frequent conflicting concepts, could result from such unsatisfactory direction.

Notwithstanding the inadequacy of the composition of the policy-making British Ministerial Committee, the small joint staff which served it was hopelessly overburdened because it had been organized and geared only for the long term policy problems of peacetime. Moreover, even the Chiefs of Staff Committee had not then become fully accustomed to the team work necessary for running current day-to-day operations. They could not issue collective inter-Service orders to any Commander-in-Chief. Indeed, they could not even issue signals with a common serial number. In fact, the Whitehall military machine was attempting to do the work of a Theatre headquarters. Events were to show only too clearly the need of a Theatre Commander for such a joint operation and all subsequent campaigns did in fact have Task Force Commanders or Supreme Commanders appointed.

It is not surprising that there was great confusion with regard to plans, and a rapid and bewildering succession of changing plans and orders which in turn confounded all administrative arrangements. The fog of war was thick and when the Admiralty learned from air reconnaissance that the German High Sea Fleet was at sea they ordered the Home Fleet to sail against it. The troops who had been embarked in warships ready to proceed to the Norwegian ports were hurriedly disembarked but their stores and equipments were left aboard and in consequence could not be recovered for some considerable time. The Committee of Military Co-ordination, and even the Prime Minister, did not know of this Admiralty action until some time later.

Soon it was learnt that German forces had landed in Norway but information about their strengths and locations was conflicting and misleading. Certainly it was some days before the real seriousness of the situation became clearer in London and even then the position was far from being entirely clear. For some days it was thought that

Narvik could still be occupied peacefully and so first priority was given to plans for landing at Bergen which was considered most important on political grounds, with second priority to Trondheim which was most important on military grounds. The British War Cabinet decided, however, not to allow any land forces to sail until the naval situation was clear. It should be noted that there was no air component with the land forces at this phase of the operation.

Due to lack of information and of local knowledge, hasty and often unsound decisions, and gross under-estimation of German air power, this plan was to be changed numerous times which resulted in serious delays and confusion.

When it became known that a German force had occupied Narvik, it was given first priority in the plans over all other ports. It was also decided to explore the possibilities of getting a footing at Namsos on the north side and Aandalsnes on the south side so that Trondheim could be captured by a pincer attack. Separate army commanders, each directly under the War Office were appointed for each of these operations, which must have resulted in some loss of cohesion between sector and sector and between British, French and Norwegian forces. Command difficulties were further aggravated by the fact that Admiral Cork, the naval commander at Narvik, was not only senior, but also of a higher rank, than the C.-in-C. Home Fleet. Among other problems, orders between the two had to be passed via the Admiralty.

The plans were soon to be changed because news came of a naval triumph at Narvik and the Cabinet believed the port as good as captured. In actual fact, the first meeting of the naval and army commanders at Narvik disclosed disagreement in principle both as to their instructions and as to the possibility of executing them: there was no mutual understanding between them. The army commander had received written instructions from the War Office, the naval commander had nothing but verbal instructions. Moreover, there was a violent conflict of personalities between the two commanders. Without adequate local knowledge, Whitehall supported the naval commander and accepted responsibility for losses in pressing the army commander to land in deep snow from ships' boats against machine-gun fire. Late in the day the naval commander was given supreme command of the forces of all the Services in the area, but even then his naval control was circumscribed by the Admiralty to within one hundred miles from Narvik.

The War Office was soon to appreciate that troops would have to be released from the Trondheim area to capture Narvik. Then, as a result of the changing situation, particularly the pressure brought to bear from the Norwegian Government to capture Trondheim quickly, the Committee of Military Co-ordination suggested that the pincer operation at that port should be changed to a joint frontal operation by the three Services. The pincer plan was hurriedly and most inadequately adapted to a frontal plan by Whitehall without reconnaissance or photography. The Committee of Military Co-ordination thought naval guns would silence the shore batteries and that the main air contribution would be met by naval carrier-borne aircraft: in addition, they directed that Bomber Command would bomb the airfields in the area at night as well as the hazardous operation of attack by day. Such was fortune that the army commander appointed to command the land forces suffered a stroke the day he had his instructions and this was followed by his successor becoming a casualty in an aircraft accident.

When the C.-in-C. Home Fleet was consulted about this frontal attack he stated that the operation was not feasible without great loss to the transport ships proceeding up narrow water, because of German air power. He also pointed out that none of his ships had on board the high explosive bombardment shells needed for the task. The Committee of Military Co-ordination overruled the Admiral's objections and the frontal attack on Trondheim was ordered. However, if Whitehall did not choose to appreciate the might of German air power in Norway they were soon forced to do so for when the *Suffolk* reached Scapa after bombarding an airfield near the Norwegian coast, her decks were awash after nearly seven hours' attack by German bombers. Ships operating in the Namsos area also had a nasty reminder of German air power. In consequence the frontal attack on Trondheim was called off and the pincer attack proceeded though this too had to be cancelled because the German air attack made it impossible. Enemy air power made it too dangerous for a few carriers to operate near the shore and one fighter squadron of Gladiators which had landed from a carrier on a frozen lake near Aandalsnes was eliminated by

German aircraft within twenty-four hours of its arrival. There is no better illustration of how much Whitehall was out of touch with administration and practicability of operations than the approval for the establishment of this squadron under such crazy circumstances. Agreed that the lake was the only normally flat area available, but it was suicidal to base aircraft on it in face of bombing opposition. Actually the edges of the lake had already begun to melt but in any event the enemy bombs broke up the ice completely. Moreover, the only supplies to the squadron were through Aandalsnes where the Allied force had no transport except a few horses borrowed from the Norwegians. These administrative arrangements were so fantastic that only Whitehall, certainly no commander responsible for the operation, sanctioned them.

When history is written, controversy as to how much the disastrous Norway campaign in the Second World War was due to faulty political direction will be as great, if not greater, than was occasioned by the Dardanelles campaign in the First World War. Mr. Churchill was a very great war leader but he definitely required independent and courageous advice from the Service Chiefs in the formulation of his strategic concepts and the plans which followed. The strategy for Norway suffered possibly inasmuch that the Chiefs of Staff at the time failed to challenge and check him and that they were dominated by him.

It is right and proper that the political authorities should approve strategy, but an outstanding fault in the direction of the Norway campaign was that the political authorities attempted to formulate strategy. Moreover, to make matters worse they tried to do this round the council table during the rush of panic meetings. Fortunately, by the time of Alamein, the North African operation 'Torch' and the invasion of Europe operation 'Overlord', there had been changes in the Chiefs of Staff which resulted in an able and strong team of military chiefs who challenged and checked Mr. Churchill on every military point.

v

The Battle of Britain and the Battle of the Atlantic were the axes on which the whole of British national strategy turned in the Second World War. The first provided security for the home front and the second the security of the life line of supplies of food and essential materials of almost every kind. From the outset there was a critical shortage of aircraft for the two roles, but the real naval-air force controversy centred on the allocation of the bomber and long-range reconnaissance type of aircraft from strategic attack on Germany to their use with the navy for the security of the Atlantic. The difficulties which became over-emphasized and exaggeratedly manifest by inter-Service strife throughout a great part of the war could, at least to some extent, have been mellowed by a more rational and unified approach to the obstacles presented and to the tactical ability which existed at the time. It is a sobering thought to consider that during these particular years the navy might have lost the war while the air force could not, alone, have won it.

The first occasion of strife arose in November 1940 owing to a shortage of suitable aircraft generally and in Coastal Command in particular. This was in some measure due to the British enforced concentration on fighter aircraft during the Battle of Britain. The Admiralty expressed dissatisfaction at this shortage and demanded both immediate and long term increases in the strength of Coastal Command. At this point the Minister of Aircraft Production suggested that Coastal Command be transferred wholly to the Admiralty.

After consideration at top level and discussion between the Admiralty and the Air Ministry the only result was that the operational control of Coastal Command was placed under the Admiralty in April 1941. This proved little different from the previous state of affairs except that the arrangement emphasized the predominace of the naval element in the maritime partnership. No squadron could be transferred from the Command without Admiralty agreement: and they could determine whether Fleet co-operation should on occasion take precedence over trade defence measures.

The next clash of opinion also concerned the air strength of Coastal Command. Early in 1942 the Admiralty drew attention to the deficiency of aircraft in the Command, this time due to the large reinforcements sent to the Middle East. The Admiralty requested large-scale transfers from Bomber Command including a substantial proportion of the newly operational Lancasters. The position both in the Atlantic and elsewhere at that time was most dangerous and it did seem as if the Allies might lose control of some vital sea communications. The situation in the Middle East and the Far East was also very serious. At home the ability to continue convoys to Russia was under constant threat by a powerful German Task force headed by the battleship Tirpitz, backed by U-boats as well as a strong Luftwaffe bomber force in Norway. This being so, if the Admiralty claim was satisfied, it could only be at the expense of the bomber offensive. In the event, the temporary loan of certain bomber squadrons was made to the Admiralty. At the same time the strategic policy in regard to the bomber offensive was reaffirmed although it could not have been decisive at this time.

Late in 1942 and early in 1943 (during the Casablanca Conference), the Admiralty urged the systematic bombing of the Biscay U-boat bases. This was resisted by the Air Staff on the ground that as all U-boat berthings and maintenance were securely housed under impenetrable concrete it would be a waste of effort. Nevertheless this bombing policy was approved and heavy attacks were made on Lorient and on St. Nazaire. A very large tonnage of bombs were dropped and two towns were devastated but the U-boats were untouched and their operations continued uninterrupted.

Later in March 1943 the Admiralty once more requested the transfer of a large number of heavy bombers for the intensification of operations against U-boats on passage in the Bay of Biscay. Such a transfer could only be at the expense of strategic bombing and it was rejected at top level.

The potential threat from the new construction of prefabricated German U-boats in 1944 brought a renewed request for large scale bombing of assembly yards in Germany. It should be noted that the Admiralty were faced at that time with what appeared to be a most dangerous situation. The inshore campaign by Schnorkel U-boats was being increased and, though not then causing serious shipping losses, it needed the utmost efforts of the Navy and Coastal Command to keep these losses within reasonable bounds. It was considered that if the enemy succeeded in sending fifty of the new type XXI U-boats to the high seas this would result in a most dangerous U-boat resurgence which would be difficult to contain by reason of their technical improvements.

On the other hand any diversion of the bombing effort would have disrupted the growing success at this time of the bomber offensive directed against synthetic oil targets and communications, which was then beginning to have a decisive effect. Thus, after discussion, it was decided that only a marginal bomber effort should be so employed. Ultimately the attacks so made had little effect on the output from U-boat assembly yards. On the other hand arrival of sections for assembly was drastically affected by the disruption of road, canal and rail communications so that planned production for March 1945 of the U-boat types XXI and XXII was more than halved. As it turned out of the hundred and twenty XXIs in commission by April 1945 only one ever became fully operational due to difficulties of design.

The tenacity of the Service view here is all the more astonishing since throughout the Second World War we had to suffer adversity before the three Services pulled together. For example, cohesion and unity of aim did not exist when the campaign was launched in Norway, but when the Allies were forced to withdraw from Norway there was real and genuine service co-operation. Again, such unity did not exist during the early days in France in 1939-40 but it came into being when the Allies were forced to evacuate at Dunkirk – here each of the Services rose to the occasion in a supreme joint effort.

The moral is all too obvious. It is not enough for a spontaneous acceptance of national strategy only when the muddle of partisan Service strategy has largely engineered us into yet another jam. The views of the British Admiralty and the Air Ministry throughout the Battle of the Atlantic might seem natural enough but they were the views of separate Services seeing the problem separately though possibly not entirely in isolation. It must be evident too, that we, as a nation, simply cannot afford a national strategy conceived and dominated by specific Service strategies. We cannot afford the possibility of a débâcle from this cause since there will be no time to remedy it.

VI

The invasion of Normandy, code named 'Overlord', was the culmination of all Allied strategy in the West, and it is not surprising that it precipitated some of the most violent partisan concepts of Service strategy. The British Army High Command advised against this operation for as long as they could, but once committed, they pressed for every resource to be thrown into the pot. The British Navy were most apprehensive about the project, but they had little other strategy to offer to the prosecution of war, particularly as they had had a taste of modern war and the fuller aspects of air warfare in the Mediterranean, and so they were prepared to go along with the army in the assault of Normandy on condition that maximum air support was provided. The most violent conflict in this strategy came from the air forces, both British and the United States. Certainly, this is another example of a Supreme Commander building a reasonable joint strategy out of three or rather two violently conflicting Service strategies.

The seat of conflict between the air forces and the Supreme Commander's headquarters, SHAEF, rested in the air concepts of strategical bombing and the air support required for 'Overlord'. It was coincidence that at the time of earnest planning for the invasion at the beginning of 1944, the British and United States strategic bomber forces had, after many delays and teething troubles, succeeded in building up to great strength. Moreover, at this time there was much influential air force opinion on both sides of the Atlantic which believed that the combined strengths of the two national and complementary bomber forces would knock out Germany by direct bombing and so win the war without the need of any army invasion of the continent. Thus, more than ever, the two strategic Air Commanders-in-Chief were reluctant to have any of their bomber effort diverted from their offensive against Germany to what they considered was the subordinate and secondary role of supporting the navy and the army in the invasion of Normandy.

The real controversy waged round the 'Transportation Plan' which was an important part of the Supreme Commander's plan to slow up the enemy rushing reinforcements to the Normandy bridgehead once we assaulted, for it was appreciated that if unhindered, Germany would win the 'build-up' race of reinforcements by three to one. The 'Transportation Plan' required a substantial bomber effort for a considerable period before 'D' day, entailing diversion from targets in Germany to targets in France at a time when each Bomber Commander had staked his reputation on crippling Germany. The Supreme Commander had to use all his influence to get the strategic bomber enthusiasts over-ruled in their objection to supporting 'Overlord'. Events proved that the air support given to the 'Transportation Plan' has not been surpassed in any operation and assured more than anything else our ultimate victory. The enemy's rail system throughout France and Belgium and into Germany itself was paralysed for long after the critical period.

In addition to the 'Transportation Plan', the air forces had numerous other support tasks both before, during and after 'D' day. They had to neutralize the enemy's formidable coast defence batteries; various headquarters, signal centres, radar stations, beach defences, etc. All these operations were also against the strongest objection of the strategic bomber commanders, and again only the status and personality of the Supreme Commander succeeded in having these objections over-ruled.

Conflict between the army and air strategies continued after the Normandy assault. For example, when the army got bogged down at Caen, the bomber commanders were most adamant against giving bomber support, their argument being that once begun, the bomber forces would be supporting the armies all the way to Berlin instead of performing their proper role of bombing target systems in Germany.

There were also grave differences of opinion in the strategies to be used for our air transport forces. On this occasion the differences were not divided between the air force and the army; they existed within the air forces and armies themselves. One school wished to use the air transport to carry supplies to assist Patton's onward rushing armoured force which was in urgent need of fuel supplies after the breakout from Normandy. The other school wished to use the air transport force for airborne operation, dropping troops from the United Kingdom amongst the retreating German forces. All the foregoing differences in the concepts of strategy were in general due to partisan strategies being pressed into the Supreme Commander's joint strategy.

The controversy between the Service strategies and a National joint strategy continues today, very much on the same pattern as the years before and during the Second World War, and for the very same reasons, and there is all too much partisan strategy motivated consciously and unconsciously by tradition and careers. While the difficulty of conceiving a national strategy free from the partisan approaches, inter-Service difficulties and jealousies is very much a special concern of the United Kingdom, we are not alone or isolated in this matter. The United States Brewster Report (1948) found itself unable to obtain a unified (navy-air) plan of action and makes the astonishing statement that: 'we are not unaware of the fact that the Joint Chiefs of Staff, who individually represent the separate services, may find it difficult to prepare truly co-ordinated and integrated plans. The loyalty of each service to its traditions is understandable, but unyielding adherence to service loyalties at the expense of national security is a luxury the Nation no longer can afford'. Surely there can be no more pointed lesson in the search for a sound and unbiased approach to national strategy, hinging as it does on sound Allied strategy, beginning, as it certainly must, between the United States and the United Kingdom.

VII

Gradually during the last war the air force concept of strategy was impressed on the navy and the army and after the lessons of our catastrophes in Greece, Crete, and other operations became apparent, the advantages of attacking strategic target systems began to be acknowledged.

When the Allied policy decision was taken to form a Task Force to drive the enemy from North Africa and a Supreme Commander was appointed, a clearer pattern of joint strategy began to emerge. In this regard, as would be expected, and as was shown later in other theatres, a Supreme Commander has advantages over the triumvirate organization of High Command when welding the three Services strategies into one whole. Probably this was the first time the advantages of a non-partisan and flexible air strategy became recognized by all three Services: even the air force recognized a qualified importance of air support. Thus, out of this Task Force, a great inter-Service controversy began to.be resolved though the final agreement has not even yet been reached. The concept was a flexible air strategy; during critical naval or army operations the maximum air force support being given to the support role, whereas during the ordinary day-to-day operations of the navy and the army when things were not critical, maximum air force effort was given to strategic bombing against such target systems as the enemy focal centres of communication, ships and bases, which were supplying the theatre of operations. On the other hand too, when critical surface operations are not imminent, maximum air force was concentrated on the enemy home front and war potential. This flexible strategy gave great dividends in the Middle East, for example, at Alam Halfa where at a most critical time it reduced Rommel's fuel supplies to enough for three days only.

Examples of the forcing of the three Service strategies into an indifferent joint strategy can also be drawn from the South-East Asian campaign. Here again there is little doubt that the three strategies would have been scarcely tied together without the appointment of the Supreme Commander, for in this theatre, as a result of the hang-over of a century of a supreme army in India, partisan concepts and doctrine were even stronger than in any other British sphere.

In essence, the divergences of British strategy in the South-East Asian theatre ranged round the cardinal partisan concepts of the three respective Services. Naval strategy was focused to the control of the sea, not in any one geographical area, but anywhere an enemy naval force might appear, including the Indian Ocean, and it was controlled from the Admiralty at Whitehall: there was resistance against the delegation of any but minimum forces to the local theatre commander. Army strategy in this theatre had been moulded over the centuries into jungle warfare absorbing every national resource and effort into this field. Had the army been offered a plan to obliterate Japan by atomic bombs or an amphibious plan to capture Singapore in a similar way to the Normandy invasion of 1944, which in fact was something on the lines of the Supreme Commander's strategy, they would have preferred the jungle warfare. As always, air strategy ranged round strategic bombing and any demand for a diversion from this strategy for air support to the army, including the large scale air supply programme required by the army, was a sacrilege. Fortunately we had a Supreme Commander who eventually steered these diverging strategies into a reasonable joint strategy.

Naval authorities no longer dispute the value of strategic bombing, indeed, nuclear weapons leave no inter-Service dispute on this, except the doubt that these new weapons are so devastating and their effect so far reaching, that they may never be used. There is no longer any dispute between the strategic value of the battleship and aircraft, the inter-Service conflict is now whether the aircraft should be carrier-borne or shore-based: virtually between the aircraft which the navy and air force should possess within their present respective Services for the maritime role.

Likewise, the army no longer dispute the value of strategic bombing and for the same reasons as those of the navy. The army are certainly impressed with the problems and possibilities which tactical atomic weapons have brought to them in the field, but inter-Service controversy now centres round the suitability of modern aircraft for the air support role. There are also wide differences of opinion on the amount of strategic effort which should be given to transport aircraft and helicopters, and who should possess them.

Notwithstanding the partisan strategies of the three British Services, the Ministry of Defence is aware of the need of a National overall, or joint, strategy from which the three Services and home defence strategies are formulated. This need is illustrated by the first parts of the 1955 and 1956 Defence White Papers which are conceived in such a national strategic pattern and gives the nuclear weapons the cardinal place and the starting point for the formulation of strategy. Unfortunately, these papers also illustrate the difficulty of planning a non-partisan joint strategy for it will be seen from the latter parts of the White Papers how the separate partisan Service strategies keep penetrating into the overall pattern.

Air force strategy ranges more than ever round strategic bombing and with the new weapons there is a considerable school who question, more than ever, the need for naval and army strategy in general war. There is, however, no inter-Service argument about the major role which army strategy has to take in cold war, and in local or limited war, though there is great dispute and partisan attitudes about the amount of our resources to be allocated to the cold, local and limited war, and how much to the deterrent and to a global war itself. In effect, these partisan strategies range virtually round the resources which should be directed to the army and which to the air force. Partisan strategies are also adopted to a greater or lesser extent so far as guided missiles are concerned, and yet there is no question but that these weapons will revolutionize present strategy in both the defensive and offensive fields. The former of these functions with weapons in the form of air-to-air or surface-to-air missiles is likely to come first and improve defence strategy greatly, whereas with regard to the offensive, the ballistic rocket is likely to promote a most formidable strategy, and we do not at present see how it may be effectively countered. As might be expected, since the new defensive weapons will supplement and even threaten to replace fighter aircraft, and the new offensive weapons will supplement and even replace bomber aircraft, of the three Services, probably the air force is most sceptical and partisan about the full significance of this new family of weapons on our future strategy.

VIII

British national strategy is the most complicated of all national strategies because of the varied global responsibilities. Not only has British strategy to provide for the defence of the United Kingdom, but it must also contribute to the defence of all her overseas interests as a whole, as well as dovetailing it into the separate strategies of the respective Dominions each with her own sovereign power. Clearly, the strength of British strategy varies according to the overall agreement and co-ordination between the separate nations of the Commonwealth and this may vary from spontaneous and whole-hearted agreement to serious differences and even disagreement. Thus, adjustments must be made in British strategy because, whatever the actual priorities of merit, co-operation cannot be expected from parties whose security is in any way seriously neglected by ourselves. Each member nation or unit must be made to feel that its strategical interests are reasonably preserved within the whole Commonwealth pattern of defence. For example, a British strategy which did not give sufficient and acceptable consideration to the Far East problems in respect of the security of Australia would lose much strength and soon find that Dominion seeking military help from elsewhere. This in fact has already happened to some degree.

Although there are three Services, defence is now one problem and this should be the corner-stone of strategy. Differences between the Services lie in the functions they have to perform and not between the different weapons they use.

With the changing pattern of the Services it is important to resolve the roles of each in peacetime, specially of air power, because scientific and technical advances, organization and training can create forces suitable for the role for which they are designed in peacetime, but if war should prove this role or task wrong, it would be too late and we would find ourselves with the wrong forces as we have done in the past: though then we had time to retrieve the situation, in future there will be no time to do so.

Any British atomic and hydrogen stockpile could not be more than a small and insignificant proportion of the United States stockpile. Likewise, any British strategical bomber forces would be very small compared with the United States bomber force. While the size of British air striking forces should be determined in relation to the size of the Allied striking forces, political as well as military considerations are involved. It is possible that British forces demanded by purely military factors might have to be augmented to meet political considerations. In the formulation of British national joint strategy, the air strategy aspect, that is the stockpile of mass destruction weapons and the means of delivering them, should be based on quality and not on quantity, with the idea of contributing the best possible force to the Allied effort; and also to enlist British scientific genius in contributing to the research and development of these weapons and bomber aircraft. Certainly it must not be assumed that the occasion will ever arise when the British Commonwealth would have to prosecute atomic and hydrogen war without the powerful aid of the United States. The air aspects of joint strategy, other than the offensive, should be formulated in close relation to the air defence of the United Kingdom and our other vital spheres, and to air support for our naval and army forces.

Similarly with naval strategy, British naval forces cannot now compare with the United States or U.S.S.R. forces in numbers and power. It is clear, therefore, that in the formulation of British national joint strategy, the naval component should be based on the security of the approaches and close waters of the United Kingdom and the other regions specially related to Commonwealth commitments and security, leaving the more general and wide oceans and the bulk of atomic aircraft-carrier bases and other naval craft to the United States.

Also with army strategy, British land forces cannot now compare with the size and power of the United States and with Russia and her satellite armies. Britain must formulate the army component of her joint strategy from her local and cold war requirements wherever they are liable to occur, together with requirements to fulfil her NATO commitments in Western Europe. In general, her army strategy must provide small, streamlined and hard hitting land forces with adequate mobility.

As with Allied combined strategy, the interplay of geography, resources, topography, accessibility and changing circumstances has a great influence on National joint strategy. This applies particularly to the United Kingdom where modern weapons have reduced most critically the security which the English Channel once gave to the British Isles. Today this citadel of the Commonwealth is the most vulnerable and worth-while target system of all the nations as regards both air attack and the mining of coastal waters. If ever atomic and hydrogen warfare begins in the present era, the United Kingdom would almost certainly be among the first countries to be attacked, and with the present technical balance between offensive and defensive resources, it is likely that mortal damage would result.

The Middle East provides a further good example of the interplay between geography and changing circumstances. Before the construction of the Suez Canal the slow, limited and tedious camel and bullock transport, together with the sea communications at the eastern end of the Mediterranean and from the Gulf of Suez to the Persian Gulf set a series of strategical problems which were revolutionized when the sea communications of the Mediterranean were joined with the Red Sea. Indeed, this junction resulted in British Middle East strategy being centred round the Suez Canal and Egypt. With the present stage of development in air power, land and air transport, armour and weapons, Egypt has lost much of its strategical significance so far as the defence of the Middle East itself is concerned. Today the Allies have the means of adopting a forward strategy and holding the Middle East from the North along the Turkish southern and the Iranian western frontiers. Incidentally it was political considerations which forced the British military High Command to appreciate and accept this change.

The Far East is another example, though in this region the Allied combined strategy is much more loosely determined. In consequence, the National joint strategies do not stem very strongly from a combined strategy. Fuller agreements in Allied political policy in this sphere would greatly help developments in Allied combined strategy. So far as the United Kingdom itself is concerned the loss of the magnificent Indian army, cold wars and communist activities in Indo-China and elsewhere, the loss of Burma and other Far East territories, the greater Australian and New Zealand peacetime contribution to defence, with India's choice to stand apart in defence and her new relations with the United States have all changed substantially the strategical problems in this sphere in recent years. Moreover, the nature of the terrain and the communist and potential aggressor methods of war make forces fashioned for total war less suitable for our Far East problems than other spheres.

The politico-geographical changes of today are in very striking contrast to the apparent stability of the world scene a hundred and fifty years ago. Then, Napoleon, though he had a strong dynastic urge himself, galvanized Europe with a national and continental ideology as distinct from a purely dynastic or ruling class idea. The aggrandizement of her generals was not what drove France's armies throughout Europe: it was the idea of freedom. Then the chief features of war and strategy were reasonably distinct and unmistakable: today the features of strategy are highly complex. Napoleon's progress and conquests, however, changed the political consciousness of modern Europe. All men of all nations in Europe were in the shortest space of time imbued with the initial political lesson – the idea of freedom, whether it was in resisting him or in acceding to him. That the idea may have preceded the march of his armies or become established when they had passed is merely a commentary on the different ways in which men's minds work. Many groups of men had assumed the idea as their birthright throughout history but not so many men had acclaimed it and fought for it altogether and at one and the same time. This was bound to change the trend of affairs in Europe, and today ideas of individual and political liberties are likely to affect the fate of the whole world.

The management of a nation's internal affairs, its diplomacy and relation to other nations and its concommitant strategy have subsequently become highly involved. When a king could give a command to his forces to go to war, the mechanism for its conduct was the absolute minimum; the only direction was the king's voice. Now however, it is a nation or an alliance of nations which may elect to go to war, and the mechanism which directs their course is of the very greatest importance and complexity. The issues which face the civilized world today make it incumbent that the military and political direction of war should be wise as well as heroic.

The political aspect of the direction of war is therefore of prime importance, and the chapter which follows, though written entirely from a British point of view, is an attempt to elucidate the complexity of modern political direction, and, while admiring its more obvious qualities, to suggest how it may be improved.

CHAPTER IX

The Making of a National Strategy

I

A SOUND national strategy is of the first importance to any nation and it must not be assumed that a national strategy, firmly conceived, is inimical to the needs of Allied strategy. The identity of interest implied in Allied strategy demands the formulation of strong national strategies; and a nation's responsibilities and commitments in the affairs of the world determine, or should determine, not only the strength, but the breadth of its national strategy. The responsibilities of the United Kingdom are considerable and the need of a sound national strategy is all the more imperative. The United States, as the greatest world power, has responsibilities which exceed those of the United Kingdom: and yet even she is far from free from the vagaries of a disparate national strategy and splintered loyalties among her Services. It is not, however, within the scope of this work to attempt any examination of American strategy.

It may well be unlikely that a review of United Kingdom defence in the political sphere will wholly illuminate the problems of other Allied nations but there must be some point at which they touch or where such a review may edify if merely by contrast. The relation of the political machinery to the formulation of sound national strategy may at no time be underestimated; and the ways in which a national strategy is finally arrived at explains much that is otherwise inexplicable in military history or military action and may clarify the issues of political and military responsibility.

To describe as machinery those committees and personalities through which national strategy is evolved may not seem either particularly apt or flattering. Yet it is through this loom of intelligence, plans, meetings and personalities that national strategy must grow and be safeguarded: and it is by these or similar means that it may be vitiated or made capable for the tasks ahead. It is in this sphere that beneficial changes should be initiated so that the cumbersome and out-dated can be swept away and the good ratified and made better.

In peacetime the main forum for paramount discussion and decision of British military affairs is the Defence Committee of the Cabinet, under the chairmanship of the Prime Minister. In time of war it is the War Cabinet. Ministerial attendance is at the invitation of the Prime Minister and is largely governed by the agenda of a meeting, but senior ministers such as the Foreign Secretary and the Chancellor of the Exchequer frequently attend and the Chiefs of Staff are also normally in attendance. The existing organization, which was set up in 1947 to administer the needs of the Defence Committee, follows fairly closely that which worked successfully during the Second World War. An important peacetime arrangement, however, is that the Prime Minister appoints a whole-time Minister of Defence who acts as Deputy Chairman of the Defence Committee and through the Ministry of Defence exercises a general supervision over national defence. This minister is responsible to Parliament for the allocation of national resources between the three Services and for their respective strategic roles. He is the sole representative of the Services in the Cabinet, although the Service Ministers are normally invited to attend Cabinet meetings when defence questions are discussed. The Minister of Defence may preside over the Chiefs of Staff Committee meetings whenever he or they so desire but a recent innovation is the appointment of a whole-time senior serving officer as normal chairman. In time of war the whole-time Minister of Defence and his Ministry are abolished and the paramount defence administration is taken over by the Cabinet offices.

The functions of the Defence Committee concern all matters relating to preparations for war. In peacetime they fall into three broad groups: to deal with current defence problems, including plans for the deployment of the armed forces on their peacetime tasks and the relation of those plans to Political Direction in other fields: to supervise the plans for the expansion of the armed forces and their supply in the event of war: and to examine the war planning of the Civil Departments and ensure that their decisions are duly co-ordinated with the planning of the Services and Supply Departments. In these three fields in peacetime, the Minister of Defence has a special co-ordinating responsibility and on these matters the Defence Committee is advised very largely by committees working under his aegis.

The preparation of plans for mobilizing the nation's resources in war involves the collaboration of almost all Government agencies, both civil and military. This task is undertaken by a system of sub-committees working under the general direction and authority of the Defence Committee. These sub-committees are constituted mainly of officials and include representatives of the Fighting Services, Service Departments and Civil Departments, and, where necessary, persons outside Government service altogether.

The Ministry of Defence is a small Department consisting of civil servants and serving officers of the three Services, who advise the minister in the discharge of his responsibility and provide a secretariat, and in many cases chairmen, for the many committees through which this work is largely done. It also embraces the Chiefs of Staff organization and the staff of several inter-Service outstation organizations for which the Minister of Defence is now responsible. The most important of these later organizations are the Combined Operations Headquarters, the Joint Intelligence Bureau, the Directorate of Scientific Intelligence, the Imperial Defence College and the Joint Service Staff College. The Minister of Defence's principal advisers are the Permanent Secretary, who is the official head of the Ministry of Defence and Chairman of the Joint War Production Committee; the Chairman of the Chiefs of Staff Committee; and the Chairman of the Committee on Defence Research Policy.

The Minister is specifically charged with the responsibility for the apportionment, in broad outline, of available resources between the three Services in accordance with the strategic policy laid down by the Defence Committee. This includes the framing of general policy to govern research and development and the correlation of production programmes; the settlement of questions of general administration on which a common policy for the three Services is desirable; the administration of inter-Service organizations, such as Combined Operations Headquarters, the Imperial Defence College, etc. In recent years the Ministry of Defence has also become more and more concerned in the activities of international defence and today it is the focal point for the consideration and expression of the views of the Government on all military aspects of international affairs. It seems certain that this important role will develop still further and inevitably will have to assume more power from the three Service Departments.

The machinery through which the Minister discharges these functions is designed to ensure that the resources available for defence in terms of man-power, weapons and equipment, works services, etc., are used to the best advantage. A procedure has been developed whereby Service estimates are determined in total for each ensuing financial year in the context of a programme normally covering three years ahead, so as to enable provision for defence to be dealt with as a single problem in the light of the economic position and strategic requirements of the country. As the first step, the Chiefs of Staff advise the Defence Committee on strategic requirements of the country. It is then for the Service Departments to translate these requirements into terms of men, money, supplies and equipment and for the Minister of Defence to co-ordinate the results with the help of the Service Ministers and the Chiefs of Staff, and to present to the Defence Committee a coherent scheme of expenditure which will provide forces in properly balanced proportions. On the production side, the Joint War Production Committee, composed of high ranking officials and serving officers, reports as necessary to the Minister of Defence and through him to the Defence Committee, and also considers the apportionment of production resources for the manufacture of equipment for the Services. The Minister of Defence is thus able to frame comprehensive defence proposals in the form of a consolidated estimate for presentation to the Defence Committee and the Cabinet.

For the handling of administrative questions of common interest to all three Services, a standing committee of the three Service Ministers has been established under the chairmanship of the Ministry of Defence. This committee is served by inter-Service consultative committees of Principal Personnel Officers and Principal Supply Officers, which are also linked up in operational matters to the Chiefs of Staff Committee. Certain other Service co-ordinating committees, for example on medical services and educational services, also report to the Service Ministers' Committee.

To advise the Minister of Defence and the Chiefs of Staff on scientific policy in the defence field there is a Committee on Defence Research policy consisting of those responsible, both from the scientific and operational angle, for research and development in the Service Departments and the Ministry of Supply. Their chairman is a scientist of high standing, appointed for a period of years.

At Service level, the three Chiefs of Staff in commission under the chairman of the Chiefs of Staff Committee are the Defence Committee's professional advisers on strategy, the allocations of defence resources and forces, and all other military matters. In addition, each Chief of Staff has the dual role of being the professional head of his Service and the chief military adviser to his own Service Minister. A complication in this sphere, however, is that each Service member of Council in each of the Service Ministries has a collective responsibility for the Service view, but a direct individual responsibility to his own Minister for affairs in his own Department. The actual working of this complex arrangement depends very much indeed on personalities. The Service Ministries in turn are responsible to Parliament for the administration of their own Service in accordance with the general policy approved by the Cabinet and the Defence Committee, and within the resources allotted to them by the Minister of Defence.

The Chiefs of Staff Committee is served by a number of committees and Joint Staffs' Committees, in particular, the Joint Planning Staff, the Joint Intelligence Staff, the Joint Administration Staff, and the Defence Research Policy Staff. The Joint Staffs are composed of serving officers of the three Services, e.g. the Directors of Plans for the Admiralty, War Office and Air Ministry, which together form the Joint Planning Staff. The Directors of Intelligence of the three fighting Services, together with officials of other intelligence bodies, form the Joint Intelligence Committee. The Deputy Chiefs of Staff at the Admiralty, War Office and Air Ministry form the Air Defence Committee. A basic principle of the present British Organization is that, in the Chiefs of Staff Committee and in their Joint Staffs and Committees, it should be the officers responsible in the three Service Departments for executing the approved policy who are brought together in the central machine to formulate it.

II

In the long term the Civil Service as a collective body control affairs to a considerable extent. Although the Service officers' influence may be more in evidence, it is more fleeting and in the long run only secondary. Moreover, it is typically English that the large part played by the Civil Service rests on its very anonymity. No Civil Servant is encouraged to identify himself in the Whitehall organization, and few such Civil Servants ever become public figures.

In intellect, there is a common high standard among the English, Scottish, Welsh and Irish elements. In character, however, the British Civil Service is associated more closely with the English than with the Scottish, Welsh or Irish. In general, it is suave, prone to moderate or under-statement, unruffled, thorough, reliable, of great integrity, content to wait its time and to allow other people to think they may claim the credit while it works very much with the same precision as a machine. This characteristic in the conduct of things is neither written nor recorded anywhere. It results from a genius of the English which in time evolves from breeding over many years a belief of superiority in themselves. It is no coincidence that this is the very quality which is built into character at the English public schools. It is symbolized in the unpretentious home of the Prime Minister at No. 10 Downing Street. One aspect which is important to note is that because of tradition, long experience, custom and the other characteristics of the British Civil Servant, cold logic is at times allowed to over-ride or discount the more passionate approach of foreigners to our international affairs. Certainly there is a tendency sometimes for the Whitehall machine to fall a little behind, or out of step with, America and other nations. Sometimes this is most justified, but there are occasions when we can be most irritating and to no useful purpose.

III

The Admiralty, War Office and Air Ministry each conduct their affairs in different ways and to some extent the differences reflect the respective characters of the three Services. They are each comprised of a mixture of Service officers and Civil Servants, the former, headed by a Chief of Staff, control all military problems, and the latter, headed by a Permanent Secretary, are responsible for the efficient working of the Ministry as a Department of State and in particular the Permanent Secretary is directly responsible to Parliament for accounting for all monies expended by the Ministry and Service in which he is concerned. A primary difference in the conduct of affairs of the three Departments results from the relationship between the Service officers and the Civil Servants: the latter have great powers in that they control all matters of finance and questions of establishments. These relations are in fact the hair-springs of action. In these relations each Service Department is organized differently, as can be seen clearly from diagrammatic charts, but few thoroughly understand how the whole Whitehall military machine operates and just what the differences are within each Department, for they are large organizations performing highly complex functions. Indeed, the actual relations within the Departments which matter most result from factors most subtle and difficult to fathom: relevant factors such as history and the way the Departments were evolved and developed, tradition, custom, prestige, and the types of character of the officers themselves.

The Admiralty is the Service Department most deeply steeped in history and tradition. Basically the administration of the Admiralty has changed little since the days when the separate organizations of the old Admiralty and the Navy Board were compounded into one Department, with the result that even today the Admirals often carry more prestige and influence with their Civil Servants and the Treasury than corresponds with the Generals in the War Office or the Air Marshals in the Air Ministry. One reason for this is that most Civil Servants in responsible positions learned at school the traditions, glories and power of the British Navy and this learning still remains inherent in their minds. Also, Parliament and the people themselves realize that for centuries the navy has been the dominant power behind the development of the Commonwealth and the prosperity of our trade. In fact, of the fighting Services, the navy has been outstanding in paying its keep even in peacetime. These factors are so strong that they still influence the Admiralty Civil Servants, even if unconsciously, when dealing with the Admirals. In fact, the Admirals are very largely the masters in control and the Civil Servants work with them as servants in great mutual trust and confidence. By and large this system works as a result of the Service officer setting the problems and the Civil Servant then being given great freedom to devil the subject and then develop and prepare the relevant papers for presentation. This relationship between the Admirals and their Civil Servants has one adverse result in that numerous matters of relatively minor importance are referred right up to Council level for discussion and decision.

In its present form, the War Office was organized on the recommendations arising out of the report of the Esher Committee set up after the Boer War to try and overcome the great deficiencies of army organization. The War Office is today well provided with a strong team of highly efficient staff officers who do not have Civil Service counterparts at various levels like their colleagues in the other two Service Ministries. Army officers therefore are alone engaged on the whole range of War Office responsibilities to a high level. Thus the emphasis of Civil Service supervision in the War Office is concentrated at Council level.

The Air Ministry already has a magnificent history, but compared with the older two Ministries the Department is new. Little air force history was taught when our Statesmen and Civil Servants were at school and, in contrast with the navy, this has quite significant consequences. It must also be remembered that the Air Ministry was formed against the strongest opposition of the Admiralty and the War Office, and at a time when there was a most inadequate supply of trained air force staff officers. Moreover, when the Air Ministry was created, some of the more far-seeing officials in the Treasury realized that the problems of the new Department were uncharted and might have the greatest repercussions on our military power and the nation itself. Whatever the real motives of the Treasury, the organization adopted when the Air Ministry was created in 1918 enabled the Civil Servant to give the greatest assistance to the Service officers but it also gave them great power in the conduct of air force affairs. The organization provides for joint Service and Civil control at various levels. The Civil Servants are bedded out throughout the framework of the Department and they have a dual responsibility. They are responsible to the Permanent Secretary through Civil Service channels, and they are also directly responsible to the Service officers to whom they are affiliated at the various levels. To some extent this system may be somewhat extravagant in that Service officers are in some respects double-banked by Civil Servants. On the other hand, the bedded-out system has the great advantage that the administration of the Department can be streamlined so that many minor problems can be decided without going to Council level.

The Ministry of Defence was created after the Second World War to co-ordinate the Service Departments together with the Ministry of Supply, the Home Office and other non-military Departments. It was deliberately given terms of reference framed as only a first stage in co-ordination, leaving much of the real power with the three Service Departments. This new co-ordinating, rather than executive Ministry is a highly complex organization and its subtle working is difficult to describe briefly. Certainly under present practice and procedure the title 'The office of the Minister of Defence' would be more descriptive than the Ministry of Defence.

Although the Minister of Defence is deputy chairman of the Defence Committee and can also when he wishes call a Chiefs of Staff Committee meeting and preside over it, his actual place in the direct chain of responsibility in military operational affairs is open to some doubt. The complication arises because, as professional military advisers of the Government, the Chiefs of Staff Committee report direct to the Defence Committee. The actual wording of the charter is 'On all technical questions of strategy and plans it is essential that the Cabinet and Defence Committee should be able to have presented to them directly and personally the advice of the Chiefs of Staff, as the professional military advisers of the Government. Their advice to the Defence Committee or the Cabinet will not, therefore, be presented only through the Minister of Defence.' Indeed, there are some who would probably argue that the Chiefs of Staff Committee is not strictly a Ministry of Defence Committee, though the wording of the charter reads 'At the same time, the organization on which they rely in their collective capacity will be within the new Ministry, and the Chiefs of Staff will meet under the chairmanship of the new Minister whenever he or they may so desire.' In practice, the problem is evaded by the Minister of Defence seldom attending any Chiefs of Staff meetings, and thus the real power in military matters at present resides in the Admiralty, War Office and Air Ministry whose Chiefs under an independent whole-time chairman constitute the Chiefs of Staff Committee.

It is clear from the foregoing that the relations between the Service officers and Civil Servants within the Ministry of Defence are the most subtle and elusive of those in all the Military Departments. Certainly they are the most difficult to explain, for their functions are primarily advisory rather than executive. It is probably for this very reason that the relation of Civil and Service officials is more closely dovetailed than in any other military Department.

Over the years, the Admiralty, War Office and Air Ministry have set up numbers of committees and working parties to examine and report on their own organizations. Inevitably each has claimed its own model to be the best. Today we require an inter-Service and non-partisan committee to examine the organization of the three Service Ministries collectively and to sort the best and the worst aspects of each. Perhaps the first step should be to give the Ministry of Defence a second instalment of power in the steady evolution of our defence organization. Moreover, a more frequent exchange of Civil Servants between the Service Ministries would also bring its advantages.

IV

As already described, the Joint Planning Staff is an essential part of the Chiefs of Staff organization. It is another typically English institution in that the members belong to their own Service Ministries, upon which their careers depend, though they hold a dual and collective allegiance to the Chiefs of Staff: so far as inter-Services affairs are concerned, this brings with it a real weakness. The Joint Planning Staff have cell organizations in all the Overseas Commands, Washington and the old Dominions. The Joint Staff also has close contact with the Foreign Office and all other interested Ministries in the United Kingdom. Smoothness is the key of all Whitehall activity and this is amply illustrated in the working organization for obtaining and co-ordinating the views at a staff level of all the authorities concerned in any particular problem. Whatever the inter-Service problem, and whether initiated within one of the Ministries, from some other authority, or from the Chiefs of Staff themselves, the Joint Planning Staff are superb in producing co-ordinated papers of all the relevant views without delay and often at the shortest notice. If there is a weakness in this organization it is that, by and large, the Joint Planning Staff co-ordinate Service views but seldom make any original inter-Service approach. They have to find the highest common denominator of agreement between the three Services, rather than the best inter-Service answer.

We have already seen that, in addition to the Joint Planning Staff, the Joint Intelligence Committee, Defence Research Policy Committee and numerous other committees and sub-committees serve the Chiefs of Staff organization. The unifying influence which binds all these various bodies together within the Chiefs of Staff Organization is the Ministry of Defence Secretariat. There are two main divisions: the Civil, which serves the less non-military functions of the Ministry such as the allocation and co-ordination of the financial and supply problems of the armed forces; and the Chief Staff Officer's Division. Within and overlapping these two divisions are branches of the Secretariat, which serve the Joint Planning Staff, the Joint Intelligence Committee, the Joint Intelligence Bureau, the Defence Research Policy Committee and numerous other bodies.

The actual organization and method of working the various divisions and branches of the Secretariat are loose and flexible and can be adapted to any situation. An invaluable asset is that it is unhampered in its work by having to follow rigid channels to the various Service and Civil Departments. If the Secretariat requires advice or information, it goes direct to whoever is best qualified to give it. In association with the Joint Planning Staff it can quickly and easily obtain an authoritative staff view and comment on any military problem from any of our authorities in any part of the world.

Service and civilian personnel are specially selected for the Secretariat and they are of the highest standard. A subtle difference from the Joint Staffs is that whereas the Secretariat owe sole allegiance within the Ministry of Defence, all the inter-Service Joint Staff working in the Ministry of Defence owe dual allegiance — first and foremost, individually to their own Service and secondly, collectively to the

Ministry of Defence, and in actual practice this is a most important difference: and the Joint Staffs work under a great Service loyalty strain. The work of the Secretariat also calls for a special and different technique from ordinary Service Staff work. Their primary requirement is the handling of papers for the various inter-Service meetings which they serve in the Ministry. This includes preparing agenda of the business and the manner in which it is to be tabled, and the minutes of the decisions of high level meetings. They also ensure that the work of their particular committee, sub-committee or working party, is co-ordinated with all other bodies in the Ministry or associated with the High Command. Although in theory the status of the Secretariat does not seem to carry power, they wield great influence by their knowledge, efficiency, integrity and close contact with men of real authority. The Secretariat can ease matters through the Ministry of Defence which even senior members in a Service Ministry would find difficult to implement, working as they do through official channels.

We have already mentioned that each Service Ministry decides beforehand their general attitude to the various items on the Agenda of Chiefs of Staff Committee meetings, and these decisions are taken at what are termed 'briefing' meetings. So far as the three Chiefs of Staff are concerned, the briefing organization of their own Ministries plays an important part in the Chiefs of Staff Committee, for upon them depend the attitudes of the individual Chiefs. Each Ministry has its own system, and speed of working is an important factor, for many problems have to be considered at short notice.

A general inherent conservatism in each Service is natural, but in difficult days of heavy financial entrenchment each Service Ministry is all too prepared to take a partisan view and to jettison too many important things to retain its own established and cherished features. It was because of such issues that our Ministries never squared up to any real collective appreciation of the German threat to meet the Second World War. If there is any notable weakness in our military machine today, it is the triple or inter-Service committee approach to our problems of war. It would be tragic indeed if this country, the first to see the need of separating the air force from the two older Services in order to preserve air power and to give it room to follow its natural growth, should now be behind in realizing that war and circumstances today demand the integration of concept, direction and plans in the truest and widest sense.

V

Much economy and increased efficacy to our three armed forces would result from introducing a further stage to the integration of our national strategy within the Ministry of Defence. The briefest résumé of the Second World War makes this clear, for it consisted essentially of a series of joint campaigns in all aspects—intelligence, plans and operations — many of these were part of a combined campaign. In each of these campaigns the navy, army and air force were involved in varying degrees and inevitably each made their own separate and partisan approach to the problems.

The advantages of further inter-Service integration especially lies in peacetime when each Service is competing for limited resources. This is particularly true in finding properly balanced defence forces today, when the navy, army and air force are each competing in their own efforts to incorporate the new nuclear and guided weapons into their respective services. In particular, in finding the best balance between shore-based and carrier-borne bombers; fighters, guided weapons and artillery; and bombers and ballistic weapons.

A most serious problem today is that it seems inevitable that replacement of any part of the armed forces by modern and future equipments will cost more and more as technical developments progress. The urgent question is, as new and expensive equipments are introduced, what things can be given up to keep the national defence expenditure within reasonable limits. What, for example, should be forfeited in place of the most potential and expensive atomic and hydrogen weapons; the very complicated and expensive future bombers and fighters; the most expensive and promising though yet unproved guided weapons and ballistic rockets. Such problems call for the most exacting considerations. All too often in the past, partisan service approaches have resulted in most unsatisfactory compromises. Today it is imperative to find an economic and strategic balance between the separate Services and the Exchequer.

It is most unfortunate that each of our Services believe that they are contributing their best to the national strategy. They seem unable to make an adequate mental readjustment to modern conditions: especially with regard to modern weapons. For example, the belated provision of an adequate air staff employed on guided missiles compared with fighter aircraft. A similar comment applies to the general staff in the War Office and of the naval staff in the Admiralty who are engaged on duties concerned with guns in relation to those working on guided missiles. Again, the three Services still find it difficult to readjust their old traditional concept of placing one vehicle or equipment in reserve for every three or so in the line.

There is no complete or positive answer to these questions, even from a Ministerial inquiry. Nevertheless, a wide-scope non-partisan review would be certain to produce illuminating results. For example, several examinations with regard to saving overhead charges between naval aviation and the air force's coastal command were unconstructive merely because of a rigid inter-Service concept. Given an impartial national approach based on a genuine joint strategy surely a number of aircraft carriers and a number of shore bases could be saved and the same joint potential forces maintained.

Again, several investigations into the present air force overseas deployment have failed to produce any radical changes, and yet the deployment was formulated many years ago when aircraft were primitive and air mobility strictly limited and unreliable. The organization entails the permanent deployment of bomber, fighter and maritime squadrons in some so called balanced pattern, together with all the associated training, administration and supply establishments and married quarters and welfare organizations being based in each of the Overseas Commands. It would seem on the face of it that numerous new factors cannot fail to call for radical changes. These are the greatly increased cost and consequential reduction in the size of air forces; the diversity of the national total, local and cold war tasks; the new requirements for strategic mobility; the enormously increased potential of air transport; the greatly increased skill required for the complicated maintenance problems; and all the increased complexity and expense of married quarters and the whole range of personnel problems. It would take a full Departmental inquiry to assess the problem, but a serious charge is that, whatever the findings of such an inquiry, in more than one quarter there would be prejudice and opposition against any fundamental changes affecting traditions, customs and careers or any radically new concepts.

Likewise, the army deployment overseas calls for a radical and impartial review. The permanent deployment of land forces at our overseas bases and various other regions of interest now seems to be accepted by our military authorities as axiomatic. Surely, under modern conditions there is not only great scope but an urgent need for a more economic use of our forces. It is true that air transport is being used increasingly to meet emergency situations overseas, but generally, routine trooping is still done by troopship, which is not only more costly than air trooping, but is also a most extravagant way of locking up in the pipe-line a substantial proportion of our troops. But there is another aspect to the present policy of our overseas establishments which should be reviewed. There might well be scope, advantages and economy for the reassessment of many of our permanently established overseas organizations. For example, with modern air transport, costs and manning difficulties might it not be better to reduce the permanent garrisons at say Gibraltar, Malta and the West Indies and to hold mobile reserves in the United Kingdom together with the necessary air transport. Under such a scheme there is scope at several places to augment the reduced permanent garrison of regular troops by increasing the enlistment of local personnel either on a regular or territorial basis.

We have stated elsewhere four general priorities for our national strategy and it is difficult enough to apply these to our current problems. For example, what national effort should be given to the deterrent against total war and what to local and the cold war which often calls for troops on the spot. Only a strictly non-partisan authority can assess this. To make things more difficult, national strategy changes with the changing world conditions and national circumstances. To take account of these factors, a requirement of primary importance in formulating and keeping reviewed sound and economical national strategy in face of the Services and other prejudices, is an adequate central defence organization. There can be no question of the importance of this requirement in view of the strong and deep-seated power and influence of the individual military services wherein, incidentally, home defence is not at present properly represented.

M

Whatever the alternative defence organization, in the interim, we must take account of the present separate Services, Ministries, establishments, customs, traditions and methods of co-ordinating and directing them.

VI

The Ministry of Defence prepares annually a White Paper on defence and this is done without a national strategy. It is simply an allocation of resources to each of the three Services and consists of three separate approaches to national strategy. It is the mean of the partisan demands of the Services scaled down to what is available and what the political direction agree they may have.

Each of the Services have their own War Manuals which describe the policy and strategy of their particular Service. Since the advent of nuclear weapons, however, the three Services have found it particularly difficult to re-write their out-moded manuals. This is not surprising because, today, no service War Manual should even be considered in isolation from those of the other Services. A Defence Manual embodying National policy and strategy must be written before any realistic Service Manual can be prepared. Actually such a national war manual would be of the greatest value because it would force the present separate and partisan strategies into a whole national strategy.

Indecision and uncertainty are invariably laid at the door of the politician and too little thought is given to the possibility that they might arise from causes within the political system itself: and to the informed it is quite plain that all is not well in Whitehall, and that, in respect of Defence at least, this part of the machine creaks audibly.

The three Service Ministries have their own very elaborate staffs from which the policies and strategies of the respective Services are formulated. As we have already mentioned, this naturally causes partisan Service approaches to our national strategy. The problem is how should the Minister of Defence and the Chairman of the Chiefs of Staff Committee get a neutral brief on controversial inter-Service problems, because all the Service prejudices and self interests of the three Chiefs of Staff still remain today. Neither of the two foregoing authorities can obtain an adequately neutral brief from any of the Joint

Staffs who owe their primary allegiance to their own Service Ministry and only a secondary allegiance to the Ministry of Defence. For example, neither the Minister of Defence nor the Chairman of the Chiefs of Staff Committee can demand, ask or even expect a paper from any of the Joint Staffs which is anything more than the highest common denominator of views among the three Service Ministries.

Under present conditions, any question of duplicating any elaborate inter-Service staffs within the Ministry of Defence would be unreasonable. The answer lies in the Ministry of Defence Secretariat. Notwithstanding the Joint Planners' compromise briefs and papers, through the Secretariat outposts within the Service Ministries, the Ministry of Defence Secretariat can obtain a neutral brief for the Chairman of the Chiefs of Staff Committee and the Minister of Defence. These two authorites must be prepared to ask for and use such neutral briefs; if need be even in face of conflict from the three Chiefs of Staff.

The one exception and most vital province where the Secretariat cannot at present obtain a quick, neutral and satisfactory brief is from the Ministry of Supply. It is important that the absence of any such outpost in this Ministry should be remedied without delay. This is particularly necessary because of the present most serious gap between the decision and revision of the formulation of high level technical policy by the Ministry of Defence, and the issue and progressing of Service operational requirements which take several years to implement.

There is of course also the need to co-ordinate military problems with Civil Defence. The Minister of Defence has now been charged with this requirement and he must ensure that the means exist for his Secretariat to obtain the best possible neutral brief in this sphere.

There must be some connection, not only of responsibility but of direction, between the Service Chiefs and the political authorities. The problem is: at what level and where should this be: how can the Government get the best advice and how best can they put their defence policies into force: what is the best method of linking the three Service Chiefs, together with the Civil Defence authorities, to the Cabinet Committee? The appointment of a Service Chairman to the Chiefs of Staff Committee was an attempt to bridge the gap and strengthen the Ministry of Defence. This is in imitation of the United States system which might have its advantages but in Whitehall is only likely to perpetuate the already manifest evils of the system. While the arrangement is in keeping with the spirit of compromise in Whitehall it does nothing to alleviate the central position.

Various ameliorations and isolated solutions are in themselves not enough because the whole problem must be considered. While the chief lesson lies in the realization that solutions ought to be found, and without any great delay, the need for several measures is outstanding.

For example, there is no question that, in addition to Service Annual Confidential Reports, the introduction of an inter-Service Annual Confidential Report at Ministry of Defence level on all officers serving in inter-Service and Allied appointments would have a most substantial influence in making the Whitehall machine more efficient. Certainly the present system is very unsatisfactory for many Allied appointments. In practice this inter-Service Report might well be extended to embrace all officers who have graduated at the Imperial Defence College or the Joint Service Staff College. The administration of these inter-Service Annual Reports would require a small cell of non-partisan judicial status in the Ministry of Defence. In all Services officers would realize at once the significance of these reports, which would have great influence on their careers and yet not be in the hands of their own Service Ministry, where so many of the springs of partisan opinion lie at present. It would change the emphasis and balance of allegiance in inter-Service matters.

Another measure, which goes hand in hand with the former, is a provision for prior consultation with and concurrence by the Minister of Defence when inter-Service and Allied appointment nominations by the Service Ministries are under consideration. Indeed, it is difficult to understand why such a provision does not already exist. A third measure, associated with the previous two, is provision for the Minister of Defence to be consulted on all Services promotions nominated by the Service Ministries within the range of Flag, General and Air rank. In general, officers of this rank either hold inter-Service appointments or appointments closely associated with all three Services. Few would claim that the Ministry of Defence provided with inter-Service records was not better qualified than the separate Service Ministries in giving the final approval for such inter-Service nominations.

Meanwhile it is important that the three Services should overcome their partisan approach to new weapons and new methods: an approach which has existed throughout the history of organized command and remains embedded today in the Service attitude. The immediate problem is that measures be taken to ensure a spontaneous acceptance of the new weapons of today even at the cost of the Admiralty, the War Office and the Air Ministry each sacrificing some of their cherished ideas and interests in proportion to the true overall needs, and not simply on any Service pro-rata basis. Unless there is a change in this respect, true unity of command and the best possible use of our resources are likely to be vitiated. We can no longer afford lack of pre-vision and the groping forward of our Service Ministries in the application of new inventions and new ideas or the wastage of financial and material resources.

Although Allied combined strategy is the greater, under present world conditions at least, National joint strategy is the basic strategy upon which Allied strategy is evolved and from which the Service strategies must be formulated. Indeed, National strategy is at present the keystone of all strategy and, given that we can overcome our partisan Service approaches to the problem, there is good reason for believing that Britain has the genius, power and experience to create a National joint strategy which will contribute substantially to the Allied combined strategy.

CHAPTER X

Theatre and Functional Strategy

I

IN the early days of British Service history, theatre strategy for the army was very much the concern of the Commander-in-Chief appointed for the task. War was then limited and the affair of professional troops, and once the Commander-in-Chief had sailed from the United Kingdom with his directive from Whitehall and his allocation of forces and resources for the campaign, generally he had to rely very largely on himself because communications were slow and control from the United Kingdom was of a loose nature, and any question of reinforcement, support or any other help was also a lengthy business which could not be depended on.

Strategy at sea was much the same, except that the Admiralty always had constitutional power which enabled them to maintain a somewhat tighter grip on affairs at sea. Moreover, they were often in a better position to get intelligence of the movements of enemy ships and forces than the admiral at sea; and they were also better placed to make wider use of the mobility of the fleet and ships and so to adjust inter-ocean and inter-command dispositions according to changing circumstances.

Thus, in general, Whitehall did not normally reckon to exert any great influence on the strategy of an army Commander-in-Chief after he had sailed, whereas the Admiralty always tried to keep control on the strategy of their naval forces wherever they might be. For these very reasons, in the past the control of strategy in joint operations was always tricky. A body of Commissioners from the United Kingdom often sailed with the expedition to co-ordinate the naval and army strategies, but more often than not this resulted in decisions to do nothing, or in some half-hearted measure when responsibility for a decision or disagreement was involved. It was natural that in these circumstances our past military leaders required great individual resource, courage and character as well as magnificence in battle.

Since war ceased to be a limited affair of professional forces and became unlimited and the concern of the nation, the government assisted by its military advisers has assumed greater control on strategy in the field and at sea. More and more, the Commanders-in-Chief have had to submit to direction from Whitehall for both Service and inter-Service strategy, and this continues to increase. This was made possible by greatly improved means of communication of every kind, but if there was any resistance against the changing balance of the direction of strategy between the Commanders-in-Chief and Whitehall, the advent of air power and the creation of the third service, which took place during the same period, decided the issue.

The development of this more centralized control of strategy has not been without its teething troubles, though as might be expected, this was more with regard to inter-Service than Service strategy. The illustration of the Dardanelles campaign in the First World War when indecision and lack of strategy and of planning at Whitehall led to disaster has already been mentioned. The Norwegian campaign of 1940 failed for a similar reason as we have seen.

It was not until the United States entered the war that the problems and handling of combined strategy forced us to take cognizance of the national parochial approaches to joint strategy and joint operations. One of the biggest problems in this regard was the planning and al-location of air support for the navy and the army according to the changing phases of the campaign.

Apart from custom and tradition, the very nature of land warfare, and of land forces and their administrative requirements, dictate that territorially they must be organized under one national or Allied army Commander-in-Chief responsible for all land strategy in the area. We have seen that an army Commander-in-Chief may be responsible directly to his home authorities, or to an Allied Supreme Commander appointed to command and co-ordinate the strategies of the three Services for some particular task.

In sea warfare, the main naval forces are normally organized in fleets of composite forces which are allocated to secure the sea com-munications in areas which may be general or specific. In addition to their maritime duties, the naval forces may be given secondary tasks of supporting land or air operations. As with the army, the naval Commander-in-Chief may be responsible to his home authorities, or to an Allied Supreme Commander appointed to command and co-ordinate the strategies of all the Services. A variation from the army problems, however, is that it is frequently found necessary for the naval Commander-in-Chief to remain responsible directly to his central authority for securing the seas, but when any of his force is required for a support role, to make him responsible directly to the Allied Supreme Commander or the Commander-in-Chief of the land or air force as appropriate for that specific function of his force.

In South-East Asia during the Second World War, the Admiralty in the United Kingdom insisted that all British naval forces operating for the security of the maritime communications in the Indian Ocean and surrounding seas remained under a separate naval Commander-in-Chief responsible directly to the Admiralty. Thus, only the limited naval forces allocated for combined operations were under the Supreme Allied Commander for South-East Asia. The arrangement was that in the event of the Supreme Allied Commander requiring naval help on any specific occasion, the naval Commander-in-Chief would direct the support function of his force to meet the need to the best of his ability, bearing in mind his other commitments.

Thus, we see that the support role adds a complication to the navy, but this becomes far more complicated for the air force because they are mainly organized as homogeneous forces for a specific function, such as bombing, fighting, maritime and transport. Moreover, because of their ubiquity, they lend themselves so admirably to the support role in respect of both the navy and the army.

In the Middle East, during operations in the last war leading up to El Alamein and subsequently, the air force used their limited number of bombers with great effect by employing them on strategic bombing whenever possible, and when the navy or the army were in need, making the support function of the bombers available to them as necessary. During 'Overlord' the support function of the British and United States strategic bombers was made available to the army and navy in great strength during the preparatory period, during the assault and subsequently. Again, although the employment of the

Allied air forces in the Burma campaign of the Second World War will long be a matter of some controversy, this is a further example of the functional control of forces.

II

The changes in the concepts of naval strategy resulting from America's Second World War experience in the Pacific theatre are so radical and far reaching that it is well to outline the lessons of the essential battles of this campaign. The early months of 1942 were very rosy indeed for Japan and they were flushed with victories which had brought a great part of the strategic positions of the Pacific under her control, and in a much quicker time and with far fewer casualties than her planners ever believed possible.

Moreover, Japan believed that she could consolidate control of the vast expanses of the Pacific and also get the oil fields in the East Indies operating before America could recover from Pearl Harbour and develop her strength. The Japanese strategic aim, in which they were over confident, was to annihilate the United States Pacific fleet and to set up air patrols between Wake, Midway and the Aleutians so that they could sail at will throughout the western and northern Pacific and land troops anywhere in the area. The crux of the conflict was the United States fleet. Japan had to destroy this fleet or it was certain the United States could and would in the passage of time fight back as she gained strength from her enormous resources.

The tide of the Pacific campaign began to turn at the Coral Sea battle which was fought as a result of Japan's endeavour to capture Port Moresby, the key position which stood guard over any Japanese advance to Australia. The United States were fortunate in having good intelligence in this operation. The outcome of the Coral Sea battle was a tactical victory for Japan in that they inflicted relatively greater losses than they sustained. On the other hand, the battle was a strategic victory for the United States in that the enemy attempt to capture Port Moresby was thwarted.

Not only was the Coral Sea battle a strategic victory for America, but it also heralded new strategic developments for the future in that it was the first naval operation in which all losses were inflicted by carrier-borne aircraft. No ship on either side sighted an opposing surface ship. It is true that many mistakes were made by both belligerents in this new mode of naval warfare, but the lessons of carrier fighting, and their value to sea power, were an indispensable preliminary to the great American victory of Midway which followed soon afterwards.

Midway Island, the furthest outpost of the Hawaii chain, with its air and submarine bases, stood sentinel to Hawaii, and the Midway battle was a prerequisite to any Japanese offensive towards Hawaii and beyond. In their flush of victory, the Japanese High Command were not much disturbed by their setback in the Coral Sea and believed that they could capture Port Moresby at their leisure. They also believed that their Easter raid on Ceylon had put an end to any backdoor interference from British naval forces. Thus, the Japanese navy proceeded with their plans to capture the Midway Island, to be followed by operations against the Western Aleutians. Apart from the capture of these bases, the Japanese believed that the best way to draw the United States and bring about a fleet action was to attack the Midway — certainly Admiral Nimitz could not let the Midway go by default as he had done with Wake Island.

The Japanese naval Commander-in-Chief continued over-confident and, basing his plans largely on surprise, which had paid such good dividends at Pearl Harbour, he dispersed his forces over a wide area of the northern Pacific and so exposed himself to defeat in detail. Again, Admiral Nimitz was fortunate in having good intelligence which enabled him to base his counter plan to good purpose.

The Midway battle began on June 4th, 1942; a great day in United States naval history because the whole course of the war in the Pacific hinged on the outcome of this battle.

Japan won the first phase of the attack on Midway, mainly because the operations of the American shore-based aircraft, both in bombing and in search, were so disappointing. In the next phase, however, the United States carrier aircraft attacked the Japanese carriers with great determination and, as a result, Japan lost her four carriers and thus the crucial power of her naval force. Even though the remainder of the fleet was intact, Japan were forced to retreat westwards without any big fleet engagement and henceforth they remained on the defensive.

Midway was the second great battle in the Pacific in which aircraft were the primary and submarines the secondary weapons. There was no ship gunfire, except of course anti-aircraft. More even than in the Coral Sea battle, the Midway action emphasized the vital role of carrier-borne air power in modern naval warfare. Although the Japanese fleet had vastly superior gun-power, it was compelled to withdraw without a shot being fired.

Likewise, the Aleutian battle and the other great battles in the Pacific were mainly contests of carrier-borne aircraft. The new primary weapon of American maritime power, and of all other nations, had been forged.

With the submarine, it is interesting to note that although not a single sinking was credited to an American submarine in the First World War, they persevered in their development. In the Second World War, American submarines were second only to aircraft in effectiveness. Nearly one-third of all the Japanese warships destroyed were by submarine, and no less than 63 per cent of Japanese merchant tonnage.

The American naval experience in the Pacific in the Second World War set the pattern for modern maritime power. This power depends first and foremost on aircraft and secondly on submarines. Developments of each of these weapons since the second war have increased their power still more in the sphere of maritime power.

III

A practice which was established in the Second World War and seems likely to continue is for an Allied Supreme Commander to be appointed to deal with theatre strategy for the Allied inter-Service forces allocated for some definite military task. In some ways theatre strategy is the most difficult of all strategies to handle because of several complications. Supreme Commanders are responsible only to the Allied paramount military authority so that national political and military authorities have no direct channel to him. Obviously, until Allied *esprit de corps* has developed to an extent similar to Service *esprit de corps*, these channels according to the personalities concerned can lead to delicate situations. Moreover, the political head of the

Supreme Commander's own country must always be in a position of great influence.

Theatre strategy concerns not only combined strategy but joint strategy also, and as the strategy of one Service of one nation may vary considerably from that of the equivalent Service of another nation, differences of doctrine and opinion may vary or even clash between the Supreme Commander's various Commanders-in-Chief and commanders, not only in joint strategy but also in Service strategies. A further complication is, as already suggested, that a Supreme Commander has often to consider the functions of forces not under his command and marry into his strategy and plans their services such as strategical bombers, naval forces, resistance forces, air transport and airborne forces. Again, because of the reluctance of nations to agree to appoint an Allied political leader for the theatre, political duties usually fall on the Supreme Commander and often take up a great deal of time and distract from the strategical problems.

The Allied political authorities can avoid many of these difficulties by ensuring that their combined strategy relating to the theatre is comprehensive and specific and that the associated political problems are not allowed to accrue and deflect the military plans.

As distinct from the theatre or territorial concept of composite forces, some commands are established with homogeneous forces, which have a specific operational function to perform in whatever theatre or territory they may be required. Of the three Services, air forces are specially suited for these homogeneous forces commands: Bomber, Fighter, Coastal and Transport Commands. Composite air forces are usually only established when specially required to give support to naval and army forces. The British composite air force commands established overseas are the exception for administrative reasons and because the size of the force would not justify the functional organization. The outstanding functional command of all today is the United States Strategic Air Command. This great bomber force wields enormous power both in peacetime as a deterrent to aggressors, and in war as a force which could without delay wreck the enemy war potential and much of his home front and even life itself.

IV

There is still a tendency to regard the power of a nation as something to be measured by the purely individual effectiveness of its navy, army and air force. This popular fallacy measures sea power by the number of its warships, land power by the number of its battalions and air power by the number of squadrons it can put into the air.

Those who have thought on these lines have not thought in terms of modern total war, and they can build no sound dynamic and comprehensive policy either for offensive or defensive action on these ideas. Reliance on the individual strength of the three Services is out-moded, and he who thinks of the Services as entirely separate entities and reckons their strength by their respective numbers is guilty of a grave mistake.

The activities of the respective Services constitute a part only of the war effort. It is the total war power to which everyone contributes which is the real measure of a nation's strength. The total war power of the nation may be defined as its belligerent power, which is the sum of its air power, sea power and land power used co-operatively and collectively, plus its civil power, which in turn is the sum of its home front power and overseas trade power. All the elements of war power are inter-related and inter-dependent. The navy, the army, the air force, the merchant navy, home defence, trade, finance, industry, propaganda, raw materials, food, scientists, designers, communications and indeed all war workers are dependent on each other and on leadership. The true war power of the nation is the single result of organizing, training, balancing, co-ordinating and directing all efforts to achieve the maximum results.

Thus, in modern war it is foolish to judge the strength of the nation by the individual strengths of its separate armed and civil forces. Capacity for making war is greater than the joint strengths of the Services viewed separately. Air power has become the spearhead of belligerent power, able to strike swiftly, sometimes even decisively, in pursuit of a common strategy of total war. Sea power is the carrying power necessary for the maintenance of the whole war effort. Land power is the seizing and holding power. Civil power supplies and sustains the means for waging war in every sphere and form. Each of these constitutent powers is inevitably dependent on each of the others: individually, even in their respective spheres, they are incomplete and impotent. The components of total war power fluctuate in their relative effectiveness, and the extent and importance of the roles they fill in policy, strategy and tactics is continually changing with the alternating efficacy of offensive and defensive technique.

Strategy in air defence is another controversial subject. This is largely a question of the balance of research effort resources between the air offensive and defensive; in particular, between the allocation of air defence resources within the home country itself. It is concerned with the balance between the home and overseas commitments; and the amount of air support to be given to NATO; the army and the navy. In modern times further complications have appeared such as the balance between fighters and defensive guided missiles; and the balance between the defence against bombers and ballistic rockets. The United States have a controversial problem, which has a particularly important bearing on Allied combined strategy. This is the balance between the American deterrent and the air defence resources between the defence of the North American continent and defence of Western Europe; and also the amount of air support to be given to the SHAPE land and sea forces. These problems can be resolved only by adequate Allied decisions which permit the formulation of a sound and economic combined strategy, followed by adequate and unprejudiced national decisions which permit the formulation of a sound and economic joint strategy.

Air power is primarily the affair of air forces which use their main instruments, aircraft and ballistic rockets, to strike directly at the enemy or at his armed forces or at his means of life. But in an increasing degree air power must be measured not only by the ability to strike but also by the ability to maintain the service of air transport in the skies. At the same time the whole of this air strength is dependent on the nation's ability to supply the raw materials for production, on the rate of production of aircraft themselves, on the supply and training of personnel on food, on stores and on communications. The workers on the home front, the merchant navy protected by the fleet and the forces guarding airfields and manning air defences are as much a part of air power as the squadrons.

In the same manner, sea power must be measured by the ability to maintain the passage of the merchant navy, and the ability to strike at the enemy's armed sea forces. The actual trials of war have proved that a squadron of torpedo-bomber aircraft can at times have a greater influence on sea power than a dozen or more destroyers and even larger vessels. A score or two of Japanese shore-based aircraft did in fact outmatch a powerful British battleship escorted by cruisers and lesser craft near Singapore in the Second World War. Sea power must also depend on land power and on air power to protect its bases and to defend its seas. The merchant navy as the carrying agent has a no less essential part to play. Again, civil power is the basis of sea power, for without it there can be no new construction or sea operations.

Land power is the affair of armies with armoured forces, guns, and infantry, whose aim is to overthrow the enemy's forces and to occupy territory. It is now axiomatic that land power depends upon air power for its effectiveness. Indeed air power, with its ability to provide reconnaissance, air transportation and a forward striking force, is often the deciding factor in the effective use of land power. Nor is it air power alone which is joined with the army to produce land power. The navy and the merchant navy have their parts in moving essential supplies and reinforcements across the seas; while the backbone of all land power is again the vast civil power necessary to raise, equip and maintain the land, sea and air forces in the field.

Civil power similarly is dependent on the air, sea and land powers for creating and maintaining the conditions under which it lives. Conversely, air, sea and land power are dependent on civil power for the maintenance of their strength. It is indeed the firmness of the civil power which is the true basis of a nation's strength. When a belligerent power can no longer secure the conditions necessary for the continuance of civil power a nation has to sue for peace.

A typical use of functional organization in the army was the British Anti-Aircraft Command which embodied the artillery provided for the air defence of the United Kingdom. This Command made valuable contributions to our defence in the last war, but, with the greatly increased speeds of modern aircraft and the heights at which they can operate, the heavy and medium artillery ceased to be effective and are to be replaced by ground to air guided weapons. The controversy over the disbandment of the Anti-Aircraft Command was typical of so many partisan Service attitudes. In this case the army contested the air force claim that the larger anti-aircraft artillery had become outmoded.

Compared with the army and the navy, air forces are flexible in their functional roles in that they can, if they are properly organized, trained and equipped, be switched within limits from their primary air force role to one of supporting army and naval forces. This flexibility is the cause of complications in the strategical concepts of air force functional commands. Probably more controversy has ranged round this than any other Service problem since the advent of air power. The difficulty lies largely in prejudices of one kind or another. On the air force side there is inadequate acceptance of the support requirement and on the army side there is inadequate appreciation of the effects of strategical bombing beyond the limits of the theatre of land operations.

It is true that we have reached the stage when the more we develop our bombers and ballistic rockets and weapons of mass destruction for their strategical role, the less suited they are for giving direct support to the army or the navy. Thus, we must begin in peacetime to keep in mind the support task and to ensure that the means are available and the training given to be able to provide adequate support when required. Indeed, this consideration must be taken into account when our national joint strategy is being formulated. Probably with the great strength of the United States Strategic Air Command, the United Kingdom should if anything give any benefit of the doubt to the support requirement over the strategic bombing requirement, which in any case can never be even a fraction the size we would desire. In the Second World War probably the air forces, certainly the bomber forces, gave much greater priority to the strategical bombing role over the support requirements to the armies. Doubtless the old air force-army controversy had something to do with this attitude. It is also true that the current bombers and the training of the aircrews did not lend themselves very well for the support role. Moreover, the armies had not the capacity or experience to follow up and make full use of heavy bomber support. Nevertheless, there is no inherent reason why bomber forces should continue to take this strategical view. Given the right joint strategical concept and determination to fulfil it we can expect a properly balanced air strategy.

A special case of theatre command much interwoven with functional command is Home defence. Forty years ago Britain had a hint of what today is an established fact, that the armed services, merely by virtue of their existence, cannot now protect the home front from enemy attack. Indeed the new weapons expose the United Kingdom home front to a threat far graver and more far-reaching than that to which the Services are themselves subject. No national strategy is complete without the inclusion of Home defence needs and special problems since they are likely to affect the movement, action and even the efficacy of the fighting Services. Thus, in considering the components of national strategy, Home defence must be regarded as an integral part of the whole.

Home defence will be composed of a whole cross section of forces and strategies and falls into several military and civil categories. Air defence, comprising fighters, guided missiles, anti-aircraft artillery and the early warning system. Maritime defences which include the defence of our ports and their approaches: the maintenance of the unloading facilities for cargoes, booms and other seaward defences, and the location and clearance of mines. Land defences mean the direction and army support of civil defences, for the maintenance of our daily life, coastal artillery, beach defences, the location and capture of airborne forces, and the whole army and civil effort in countering invasion.

N

CHAPTER XI

Army Strategy

A REVIEW of Allied, National, Theatre and Functional strategies posits unequivocally the demands that are likely to be made on the Services; and it only remains to visualize how the Services' strategies may measure up to these needs and how they will overcome their special problems. It is not intended here to add to the many works already written on the Services' strategies, particularly those of the army and navy. Where necessary, however, brief outlines are given to illustrate the extent to which respective Service strategies have been conceived and formulated upwards from the basic features of each Service rather than downwards from the larger concepts of national strategy. A reiteration of traditional concepts not only serves to underline the contrast presented by present-day needs but it reveals the strength and tenacity which the customary view has in the deliberations of the High Command. This conservatism, like all fondness for custom and tradition, can be a source of strength, but too often it is a source of weakness.

It was inevitable that force of circumstances related the three Service strategies each to the other in varying degrees according to the various stages of history and to the numerous factors of war and peace. This random relationship proved adequate even though sometimes costly in the past, but under the modern conditions outlined in this book, a much more positive relationship is essential, not only to arrive at satisfactory and properly dovetailed strategies for the three Services, but also from the necessity for economy.

Army strategy, the oldest of the three strategies, is also the simplest in the sense that the issues are generally more clear cut. The prime function of land forces has been the neutralization of the opposing land forces by battle. Under the conditions which obtained before the First World War the army of a belligerent nation safeguarded the other essential elements of its power to wage war and to a more certain degree than the navy could usually be forced to battle. Non-military objectives, such as even the capital city, could be relinquished for a time if their continuous possession was not indispensable to the conduct of the war: to gain victory it was still necessary to seek and destroy the enemy's main forces on the battlefield. This was the predicament of Napoleon in 1812, when his occupation of Moscow failed either to bring about the capitulation of the Russian Government or to force the Russian army to give battle. On the other hand, any non-military objective which was vital to a combatant's power to prosecute the war would be covered by his army as long as it remained in existence, and the way to its capture could only be opened by defeating the field forces in battle. Hence the old principle that the function of an army is to defeat the enemy's army. It followed from this that the business of a commander of land forces was to bring them on to the field of battle and there manipulate them in such a way as to achieve the maximum disorganization of the enemy's army.

Battle itself — and this applied to all forces — fell logically into two phases, though in practice they might be intimately interwoven and extremely difficult to separate. In the first phase neither side gained such ascendancy over the other as to enable it to inflict greater disorganization than it suffered itself. In this phase the losses in personnel and material on either side might be equal or might even be greater on the side of the eventual victory. The second phase began when one side or the other had established a definite ascendancy over their opponents, and continued from that time until contact was broken or the action otherwise ended. It was in this phase that the one side disorganized the other by inflicting heavy losses in personnel and material at the smallest cost to itself.

The handling of land forces in actual contact with the enemy was denoted 'tactics' and this applied to all forces. On the other hand 'strategy', as opposed to tactics, related to the handling of forces not actually in contact. Since a commander could freely move only those forces which were not committed, that is, not in actual contact with the enemy, strategy (at least in this strict sense of the term) was concerned with decisions whether and how to move forces. Further, since the reserves of a lower formation were always, from the point of view of a higher formation, already committed, each level of command had different spheres of tactics and of strategy, right from the smallest subunit, when the movement of a reserve section was strategic, up to the high command, where strategy related to the movement of forces between theatres. This last formed part of what was termed grand strategy, which included the deployment and committal of the total resources of a belligerent. The aim in strategy was to ensure that the result of battle when contact did take place was as far as possible a foregone conclusion, while the aim in tactics was to reduce to a minimum the first phase of battle, which consisted of fighting properly so called, and to augment the length and effect of the second phase, which was that of pursuit and disorganization.

Both in tactics and in strategy, the essential difference between the offensive and the defensive was that forces on the offensive sought the enemy, while forces on the defensive awaited or avoided him. The choice of the offensive or defensive in the strategic sphere would generally depend not only on the full circumstances both of the war and of the respective antagonists, but also upon the object with which a given campaign was being fought. Yet the side which was strategically on the defensive might adopt offensive tactics, and vice versa; for in the tactical sphere, the choice depended upon the temporary situation of the two forces in the particular field of battle. Whether the tactical offensive or the tactical defensive was characteristically the stronger form depended upon the exact state of technique, weapons and terrain at a particular time and might vary in the course even of a campaign and certainly of a war. On the other hand, the strategic offensive — in land warfare at any rate — was characteristically the weaker form, since it exposed the attacker to certain inherent disadavantages such as lengthening communications, the occupation of enemy territory, and the confronting of enemy prepared positions. It was therefore a form which in land warfare, and in warfare generally so far as its operations were regulated by those of the land war, could only correctly be adopted by that side which was stronger in the true military sense. This idea may be found fully developed in the Sixth and Seventh books of Clausewitz.

II

The army will be affected radically by the new weapons though perhaps at this early stage the full range of changes is less clear-cut than in the case of the air force or the navy. In its primary role of controlling land operations by battle, the whole strategy of land warfare will have to be reviewed. The essence of current strategical concept, built on past conditions and experience, is an elaborate field organization of bases, depots and lines of communication capable of supplying a number of not very streamlined armies vigorously engaged in battle, either offensive or defensive, with large quantities of munitions and supplies. Inevitably, this has led to a cumbersome organization vulnerable to modern air attack. With the atomic threat there must be a new strategical concept which will reduce the vulnerability and worthwhileness of target systems and targets on which the army depend in the field. This is certain to include much streamlining of fighting and support formations, less dependence on set battles extending over weeks and requiring vast quantities of munitions and supplies, a great reduction of heavy artillery replaced by atomic guns and guided weapons of longer range which avoid supply problems in forward areas; and also a revised lines of communication organization which relies much more on air transport, including helicopter and vertical take-off aircraft besides much less dependence on large vulnerable field bases and depots.

Fortunately the foregoing changes in the structure of the army necessary to meet its primary role bring benefits to at least some of the more important of the secondary roles. In particular, the cold war task and the peacetime chores lend themselves to the streamlined formations and units: to the increased mobility and flexibility: and they do not demand anything like the same vast cumbersome lines of communication together with the extensive supplies and supporting artillery ammunition required for staged battles. Moreover, air transport, especially short-run take off types required for the army's primary role suits the above two secondary roles admirably under satisfactory air conditions. Again as a result of a recent decision on British inter-Service responsibility for air defence guided missiles, a major part of a further secondary role, anti-aircraft defence of the United Kingdom has already been transferred to the air force, thus releasing many skilled army regulars and large numbers of Territorials for other urgent duties. On the other hand, a secondary role which has become greatly more important by the advent of nuclear weapons is support to the Home front: that is support to civil defence, and the maintenance of essential services and salvage. This will necessitate a much closer and more positive relationship between the army and civil defence in policy, organization and training in peacetime, and in direction and command in war.

Conventional land tactics evolved through a changing strategical and weapon background. For example, the greatly increased fire power of automatic weapons and machine guns in the First World War revolutionized the British Boer War tactics, and to a great extent gave the advantage to the defence for some time. This, together with the vast increase in artillery, resulted in the already mentioned elaborate bases, depots and lines of communication and large reserves necessary to support the staged battles which resulted. Subsequently, in the Second World War, armoured forces restored the balance to the offensive and brought a completely new concept of tactics. Then as the efficacy of air support developed, still further changes resulted in tactics.

It is interesting to consider that in the Second World War the Allies and not the Germans fought the set battles, for example, in Norway, France, Russia, with Rommel to a certain extent in Africa and with Runstedt in Normandy during December 1944. The concept of mobility behind the technique of the blitzkrieg was perhaps the most revolutionary idea in Army strategy to emerge during the Second World War. It was a complete reversal of the technique in the First World War where there was practically no manœuvrability and consequently little generalship in the broadest sense. Then, the form of war amply illustrated the superiority of the defensive over the offensive through fire power: a fact which explains why it became largely a slogging match with the creation of a continuous line with virtually no flanks on the Western Front. Had the Maginot Line been extended to cover the whole of the French frontier it is possible that army strategy if left to itself in the Second World War may have developed in the same way. Indeed the British and French initial approach was to establish and consolidate in the former manner and fight a war of attrition.

How far the thrust of the blitzkrieg technique may be employed in the future is an open question but the initial lesson of surprise, speed and manœuvrability cannot be ignored. Here was an instance of the offensive being superior through mobility and armour. The main lesson, however, is not simply that armour gave the advantage to the offensive but that strategy and tactics should be considered in the light of our own offensive potentialities as well as those of the enemy. The defensive can be again strengthened through the acquisition of nuclear weapons (fire power) but any war of the future is unlikely to be static or confined for that reason. The Germans in the late war foresaw the blitzkrieg: what we must ask ourselves is, what is it that is foreseen by the potential aggressor of today.

The new weapons of this era radically affect land strategy, but they are certain to have an even greater and vital effect on land tactics. The results of the new strategical concept and structure of the army, the application of atomic fission in bombs, artillery, guided missiles and minefields, and the application of the several types of guided and ballistic weapons, will have far-reaching effects in tactics both in the offensive and the defensive. Indeed, of the three Services it is probable that the army will have the most difficult task in assessing and meeting the new tactical requirements. Even the conventional land battle concept must be reassessed for it is possible that nuclear weapons will often be able to overwhelm an army in its preparation stages, before ever land battle can be joined. Modern tactics must certainly enable armies to avoid presenting worth-while targets for as long as possible, and yet be able to gather and strike when and where the Commander so desires: they must also force the enemy to concentrate and expose himself.

Armoured forces require special tactical consideration under the new conditions, not only because of the threat of the anti-tank guided missile, but also because they are the army's powerful offensive arm and yet they can become most vulnerable and worth-while targets for atomic attack.

Notwithstanding all the changes in army problems, tactical air superiority will probably be a more dominating factor than ever before in field operations and the air support they demand. Modern weapons will play an outstanding part in this. Certainly tactics for local air defence in the field call for the closest examination because the greater part of the new and vastly increased threat to land forces arises from air attack in one form or another: whether it be by bomb or guided bomb, or by long, medium or short range ballistic rocket. We have already mentioned that the most careful consideration must be given to the provision of air defence weapons for use in the field: in this respect, the division of responsibility between the army and the air forces is a most important matter.

III

In accordance with our new national strategy, the army strategy necessary to comply with the priorities of maximum deterrent and maximum efficacy should the deterrent fail dictates the shape of our land forces as something vastly different from the shape which evolved from army history and accepted doctrine. The whole concept of army strategy based on mobilization and a period in which to expand a peacetime nucleus has to be discarded. On the other hand, it should not be forgotten that the size of an army which can be maintained in peacetime is limited.

How can the army contribute to the deterrent to total war? Certainly it must give the prime place in this field to air forces with their stock of nuclear weapons. But to rely wholly on the potential of the air effort would be an over-simplification of the problem.

The biggest contribution our army can make to deterrent to total war is without question its place, supported by the tactical air forces, in NATO. In this role it plays an important part in securing some measure of depth for manœuvre, and in the air defence of the United Kingdom, and in forming a land force which challenges the advance of Russian land forces into Western Europe. Concurrently with this, the army contributes to the NATO peacetime forces which not only restrain Russia from cold war encroachment into Western Europe but also inspire the free countries of Europe to resist.

A highly efficient Home defence would make it clear to Russia that we mean to resist to our utmost any aggression; and in total war our land forces would have to play a leading part in this role. Indeed, this is an ideal role the Territorial army, once the field reserve to the peacetime standing army, could undertake most readily and effectively.

Should the deterrent fail and total war occur, an army based on the foregoing pattern, with its tactical atomic weapons and deadly atomic by-products, and supported by tactical air forces, would be well suited to make an effective contribution to our national and allied strategies in waging total war: in particular, in helping NATO to stem the advance of the Russian land forces in Western Europe and also in taking a key role in maintaining the home fronts. The strategic air forces could, in addition, give the land forces tremendous support when required during critical periods.

The one traditional commitment which should certainly be reduced under the new national strategy is the vast and multiple peacetime organizations, stocks of equipments and stores, and plans prepared for raising large non-regular land forces in the months following the outbreak of total war. If for no other reason, they could not in nuclear war arrive in time to be effective, in fact it is doubtful if they would ever arrive, and in any case as mentioned above they would be more effective in helping to support the national life at home.

The new weapons bring a new concept for war readiness for the army in the same way as for the other two Services. Not only in its primary role of meeting its NATO commitments in the defence of Europe, but also in its secondary roles of supporting the Home front as well as meeting cold war problems wherever they might arise. Thus many organizational, training and personnel questions will have to be reviewed in the light of the army strategy, tactics and weapons required by our new national strategy. Moreover, the relations between regular and non-regular personnel and units in terms of the new war readiness requirements will have to be carefully examined. In the role of supporting the Home front for which the non-regulars are well suited, many new training problems will have to be resolved. Another matter resulting from the new war readiness concept is a radical adjustment between the balance and state of first line units and equipments, and those in reserve: this in turn will have numerous repercussions on training and personnel.

It is clear that whatever guided missiles are provided for the army will go to the artillery except those carried and operated by tanks. This should not cause any great changes except some adjustments in the trade structure of the artillery. It is in the maintenance aspect of guided missiles that the biggest difficulties will arise, specially with the peacetime stockpiles. It is too early to say what all the problems will be, but with the limited number of skilled regulars available in peacetime, it would seem that civil contracts or skilled civilians will have to be used wherever possible.

The inter-relation and inter-dependence of the Services are the most obvious when they are considered in their primary roles; and it is here that there is greatest danger to our national strategy when each claims the importance of their particular primary role and demand increasingly the support of the others in roles not only less spectacular but often less vital. But the primary roles are no less linked with the secondary roles: without the support of tactical air forces or the transport role of the maritime forces our armies could be completely immobilized. Conversely, the immense striking power of our air forces could be largely negated without the battalions to consolidate the gains thus grasped. These are simple examples but they bring us back to the ever-recurring problem, particularly in regard to the secondary roles — who is to do what? The importance of the Home front is growing and without the equanimity and balance which the army can maintain in this sphere the most strenuous efforts of the other Services, in their primary or secondary roles, may be cheated of the results they deserve.

We have mentioned elsewhere that the greater the deterrent of nuclear weapons to total war, the greater becomes the risk of local and cold wars in Europe and elsewhere. In such conflicts the army plays the primary role, the air and naval forces being confined to a subordinate supporting role. The British Commonwealth, spread as it is throughout the world, is particularly liable to become involved in these local and cold wars, and to have to prosecute them alone. Thus, she must ensure that her national strategy provides for land forces adequately shaped, equipped and trained, and with the means of being deployed and supported swiftly and wherever required.

If anything, on balance, the new weapons enhance the capacity of the land forces to meet this role. The navy in its supporting role will probably not be greatly changed. On the other hand, while the supporting role of air forces shaped for total war will become more and more difficult in many respects, if tactical atomic weapons are used, the power of air forces in supporting armies would be increased immensely.

A certain complexity characterizes the search for strategic principles due to the fact that we do not know what kind of war we shall be called upon to fight. Cold wars and wars where the fighting can be limited to a specific area we can expect and for which we can prepare. But the nuclear bombs are large question-marks inasmuch as the great powers have agreed at Geneva that there is no future in them. It is likely therefore that aggression in the form of cold and local wars will continue to increase, and, according to the policies of the aggressor and those attacked, may assume dimensions which cannot be strictly termed limited, yet, for one reason or another, without involving the mighty sanction of the hydrogen weapon. This is a distinct possibility even though the hydrogen weapon is poised as a deterrent to all-out aggression. It is conceivable therefore that we may have 'half and half' wars in which nuclear weapons are confined to tactical rather than strategic use and military forces are employed in what is termed the 'conventional' sense.

In this light consider two aspects of the inherent and continual inter-relation between the strategies of the Services with reference to our land forces. First, there is the important contribution which land strategy made to air strategy by increasing the depth of air defence and reducing the distance to be flown for air offensive. This was well illustrated in the Second World War where Eastern Germany was out of effective bomber range until the Allied armies occupied Italy and large parts of Western Europe; and also when the air defences of the United Kingdom were hard put to it when the greater part of the European continent was available to the German forces. The second aspect is the part played by land strategy in assisting air strategy substantially by placing the enemy home front and war potential under great strain. Clearly the more our armies could force the enemy armies to make demands on man-power, equipments and stores of every kind, the more effective would be strategic bombing. In the Second World War, it is worth noting, the German armies demanded over three-quarters of the whole vast German war resources to raise and keep them in the field.

Although the advent of nuclear weapons may have changed the

foregoing factors very greatly they remain valid to some extent at least. Even if the overwhelming destructive power of the new weapons makes it unnecessary for the enemy home front and war potential to be loaded and put under strain by army strategy, our national strategy must be prepared for circumstances such as 'local' war where these weapons could not be used. In any event, there is the factor that depth in air defence is more important than ever; and our defence guided weapons and fighters of the future will be able to use most profitably any extra depth made possible by army strategy.

The comparative directness of army strategy, as outlined in the above terms, is not a little misleading. It is not, as the unititiated might suppose, as simple as all that; though these are its main features. It also lends itself to the suggestion that maritime and air force strategies are equally as straightforward. In comparison, however, the strategies of the air forces and maritime forces are more revolutionary in their complexity.

CHAPTER XII

Maritime Strategy

I

THE confusion which has reigned with regard to the formulation of a sound national strategy is exemplified in the present artificial division of responsibility in the aims and functions of the British Royal Navy and the Royal Air Force. It is artificial because it does not arise from an overall appreciation of national strategic needs but rather from factors concerned with tradition and professional prestige. The nation, grateful for past services ungrudgingly given, has grown accustomed to the demands of the Services for men, money and resources and the Services having accrued this immense credit of good-will, tend to continue their growth and develop their strategies without due reference to the tasks peculiar to the others, or for that matter, without an unprejudiced concern for the wider tasks of Allied combined strategy. It will soon be borne in upon us, if it is not already done so, that such an unrealistic approach to strategy is not only uneconomical, but that it is increasingly difficult to formulate good strategy from such conditions.

There are, however, two things we should be quite clear about: it is essential to retain the navy, doubtless much modified and with its accession of air forces, as part of the proper instrument for the implementation of maritime strategy: it is also essential to maintain the air force at instant readiness, with its reconnaissance aircraft, transports, tactical and strategic bombers, as the instrument designed and shaped to implement our air strategy over land and sea. The obvious is occasionally surprising, especially when, as in this case, the strategies of these two forces appear to duplicate and overlap each other. They must be seen as each forming only a part of a wider strategical concept and the very intricacies of their relative functions is an indication of how essential it is to formulate these Service strategies impartially from national strategy. The relationship between the strategies of these

Services is already highly complicated without any further difficulties arising out of factors inherent in the outlook and structure of these forces. If this distinction of strategical development is firmly held the allocation of functions as here visualized will present little difficulty.

The word 'maritime' is chosen to describe the strategy of the sea, in preference to the term 'naval' because 'naval' so readily introduces a notion of naval vessels or of the Senior Service, whereas it is desired to focus attention upon the function rather than on the instruments by which the function is performed. The armed merchant vessel protecting itself or aircraft patrolling a sea route or striking at a naval or merchant ship is as much a maritime force as a warship, but could not well be designated by the word 'naval'.

Fundamentally maritime strategy depends upon the geographical situation and economic circumstances of the belligerents as well as the technical devices of sea power. In the case of a nation which is actually or virtually insular, fully effective interference with its power to use sea transport will render it unable to act against the land forces of an enemy in a country other than its own (except by the use of air power) or even to survive if it is not self-contained. If, in addition, a country is wholly or largely dependent on the movement of goods by sea for its power to wage war such interference may well be sufficient to achieve victory except for a short and decisive war. This type of war, however, though ever-present to the minds of the British people because they themselves exemplify it, is in reality an exception. In all operations of war other than the defence of a wholly or virtually island state, or group of states, the gaining of command of the sea cannot be decisive but must be preceded or followed by the operations of land or air forces.

Although an enemy's maritime forces may be superior, it may nevertheless, in certain circumstances, be possible to transport forces, food and materials successfully by sea. This can occur where the area of sea available for use is extensive in comparison with the size and radius of action of the naval and air forces available for interference. Nevertheless, for most purposes a fairly general and continuous use of sea transport is requisite and this can only be secured by the neutralization of an adversary's naval and air force in the areas concerned. For example, while it is probable that at most times in the summer and autumn of 1805 Napoleon could have completed the movement of his army from France to England before the British fleet effectively intervened, he did not feel able to accept the severing of his sea communications which must have followed immediately afterwards. Therefore he considered it necessary to delay invasion until he could destroy or seriously reduce the British battlefleet and so secure a longer period of safety for his sea communications in the Channel. Similarly Hitler could have launched an invasion against the United Kingdom during the months following Dunkirk in 1940 except for his fear of the severance or interference of his sea communications across the Channel by naval and air forces.

Throughout the years of history the primary function of maritime forces was by battle to destroy or neutralize the maritime forces of the enemy and only secondarily to operate if necessary against his sea transportation itself. However, a fleet could not always be brought to battle against its will by an enemy fleet but could remain in the shelter of its bases. In such a case the maritime forces were neutralized by threat of battle instead of actually being destroyed in battle: but, for the time being at least, command of the sea was equally secured. It was through this history that the structure of modern navies evolved from a variety of factors and considerations such as the race for superiority in gun-power which brought bigger and bigger battleships and fleets to challenge, destroy and neutralize the enemy fleets and so give protection to smaller naval craft and to merchant shipping. The submarine menace brought drastic changes to naval problems which had to be adjusted by the adoption of convoys for merchant shipping and the provision of adequate escorts. Mines also brought a new menace to the movement of ships at sea and in harbour and in their turn called for new methods and techniques. Again, air power brought numerous changes and the requirement for aircraft carriers. These factors have resulted in a profound change in the structure of fleets in modern times and today their defensive power rests on aircraft carriers, unsupported by battleships, so that naval aviation is the primary offensive and defensive component of the navy.

The new weapons will affect naval aviation in very similar ways to those outlined for the air force and we need not repeat them. In addition, there will be many naval problems such as the provision of ballistic rocket or guided weapon ships to supplement aircraft-carries, for the carrying and launching of offensive and defensive missiles, and guided weapons to supplement or replace artillery. Other naval problems will be brought about by guided bombs, homing and guided torpedoes and mines far more deadly than hitherto. Nuclear motive power will create numerous further problems.

II

There can be no question that the new weapons of this era seriously concern the navy and will bring many consequential changes to this Service. In particular, these new weapons will have outstanding effects on the navy meeting its primary role of controlling the seas, because at the present stage of technical development, nuclear weapons render such targets as fleets, concentrations of merchant ships in convoy or assembly areas, ports and naval bases and even individual major ships themselves, far more vulnerable than hitherto. The large nuclear powered submarine will also have a profound influence on maritime warfare. Until now, submarines have only really been submersibles, i.e. they fight submerged but have to surface for various reasons at frequent intervals during which time they are very vulnerable to attack of every description; even snort fitted submarines come in this category. On the other hand, nuclear powered submarines can stay submerged at great depth for so long as the crew can endure. They can travel fast, can have a great radius of action and can be large and so carry a large number of torpedoes, ballistic rockets, mines and other weapons. This greatly increased offensive power makes the naval task the more difficult because Russia, for instance, does not have to rely on merchant shipping in the same way as do the NATO countries, and particularly the United Kingdom.

On the other hand, our maritime targets lend themselves admirably to guided missile defence although it is true that today the great unknown in regard to our maritime problems is the resultant balance between the offensive value of the future guided bombs, missiles and torpedoes against naval targets, and the defensive value of our future guided missiles and electronic devices to counter them. Also tactical air superiority will certainly play a dominating part in naval warfare and the new weapons will influence this immensely. It is important that an alert mind is kept in deciding development priorities in the future shape of our naval forces because they are most critical.

Compared with the air force, modern weapons should not have such a critically adverse effect on our naval forces with regard to the secondary roles. In particular, local and cold war and the peacetime chores should not be made much if any more difficult for our navies; the ability of the navy to bring power to bear where required and without delay should not be greatly impaired. On the other hand, the new weapons will probably increase very considerably the value and importance of three secondary naval roles in respect of total war. First, the provision of mobile bases for launching nuclear bombs, ballistic rockets and guided missiles, against remote and important enemy war-potential targets, or in support of combined and joint operations. Secondly, the provision of mobile bases for reconnaissance and location of targets, and also for the guidance and control of long range air striking forces, bomber and ballistic rockets. Thirdly, there will be a greatly increased need for naval assistance in the working of our ports and the emergency unloading of cargoes under nuclear attack.

Strategically, the creation of our naval bases and the deployment of our naval forces has developed from the needs and results of past sea power. This strategy has always been liable to change as a result of political and technical developments, but today the new weapons call for a thorough review of the situation. Essentially, the British navy depends on a number of bases in the United Kingdom and overseas. Certainly, nuclear weapons bring such a threat to the United Kingdom home bases that every effort must be made to disperse, duplicate and protect the vulnerable areas, and possibly to repair to Canada for some of the required facilities. Likewise, Britain must disperse, duplicate and protect her home port facilities and assembly areas of the merchant fleet, and should have plans and facilities ready for artificial harbours, and for unloading over beaches and also reduce the need of imports to a minimum at the outbreak of war.

The new weapons also bring new considerations into the overseas bases, and much like the fleets themselves, their future vulnerability and usefulness depend very much on the outcome of the relative efficacy of offensive weapons, such as guided bombs and ballistic rockets and

o

defensive guided missiles to counter them. Overseas bases of limited area, as with warships themselves, are especially suited for guided missile defence; such warship defence can have great power against bombers. The implications of all these factors must be taken into account in the review of our naval bases and shipping facilities, and on an Allied rather than a national basis. Our reallocation of naval dispositions will follow accordingly.

Britain has in the past and continues at present to be well provided with maritime bases across the world — Gibraltar, Malta, Cyprus, Aden, Ceylon, Singapore and Hong Kong and in addition, the Dominion bases. Today, however, a serious political question has arisen as to how long some of these bases can be retained and relied on. Britain and her friends anxiously await the outcome of this issue. On the other hand, the United States herself has never possessed such a network of maritime bases throughout the world. In consequence, the American navy is shaped as a 'long-legged' force compared with the British navy. America has organized her navy so that it can operate far from her dockyards with the aid of fleet trains of supply and repair ships. These fleet trains are of course expensive as they involve a substantial addition of ships and men to do the equivalent work of a 'short-legged' navy. In short, bases economize in ships and men. In any event, even with her long-range fleet, the United States has been forced to depend in some substantial measure on the bases of her NATO Allies and of Spain.

Conventional naval tactics evolved within the framework of conventional naval strategy and the then contemporary weapons. Up to the beginning of the Second World War, the battleship dominated fleet tactics, and the submarine threat to merchant shipping dominated convoy tactics. Today, the aircraft-carrier dominates current naval battle tactics with still the submarine and mining attrition threats a primary menace to merchant shipping. The new weapons of this era will have a powerful influence on current naval tactics because until defensive guided missiles can guarantee the security of concentrated maritime targets, every measure will have to be taken to avoid targets worth while for nuclear attack. We must adjust our concepts of tactics so that every single ship presents a separate target for air attack rather than the fleet of convoys and concentration of ships as formerly. The development of vertical take-off and landing aircraft and helicopters should assist in this, but great thought, study and imagination will be required by the naval authorites to appreciate and determine future naval tactics. This study should be made on an inter-Allied basis taking the advice from all the scientific genius available.

As with all the Services, nuclear warfare will bring to the navy a new concept of war readiness. The Senior Service has always been in sufficient readiness to deal with political incidents and emergencies, and as more recently, in local and cold war problems. In future, however, the peacetime navy must be capable of combating effectively and immediately air, submarine and mining attack, both offensively and in the defence of shipping, ports and harbours. Against the possible use of nuclear weapons and modern mines this will be a major naval task in the early days of a future war. In addition to assistance in defending our ports, assistance to the working of our ports, and the improvisation of facilities at minor ports and even the emergency landing of cargoes over beaches is a task which may reach considerable dimensions in vulnerable countries such as the United Kingdom. Such port assistance is a role which may well be undertaken by the naval reserve and many preparations made in peacetime. This would of course necessitate new or extended relations between the Admiralty and other non-military Ministries.

III

The new national strategy has also a profound effect on maritime forces strategy. Like the army, maritime forces at present have to give first place to air forces in the deterrent to total war. Also, as with the army, the new conditions make it necessary that our peacetime maritime forces must be ready to fulfil their various roles at the outbreak of war without having to wait a period of mobilization.

Maritime forces have long had the secondary role of bombarding enemy coastlines and shore stations. The great destructive power of the new weapons, however, changes this secondary role into a primary role of great importance. Indeed, for the first time, maritime forces in the form of aircraft carriers with nuclear weapons, together with ballistic rocket and guided missile carriers, could play a leading part in a direct offensive against land forces and the home front. Our nuclear powered submarines can also be given an offensive power which could revolutionize their primary role from safeguarding sea communications to one of contributing directly to the offensive against the enemy home front.

Vertical take-off aircraft will enable the future carriers to be much smaller and so less vulnerable to general attacks than the present large ones. The mobility of these carriers will be greatly increased and may well prove them less vulnerable than shore bases to attack by ballistic rockets, and they could make a nation less dependent on foreign bases which is specially important in the Middle East. As it is, they can contribute in deterring an enemy from attacking a belligerent's home front so long as there is at sea a powerful carrier force ready to retaliate. Such a force would doubtless help to deter an enemy from beginning hostilities with nuclear weapons. On the other hand, the degree of offensive potential represented by the aircraft carrier is likely to draw attack by an enemy who see their destruction as of the first importance. The vulnerability of the aircraft carrier to air and sub-marine attack is really a measure of how much such vessels could mean to the final result in any future conflict. It has been suggested, therefore, that aircraft carriers will necessarily be among the first casualties of attack by aircraft, ballistic rockets and submarines of revolutionary design, greater range and mobility and capacity for evasion, together with their homing weapons. The present Russian submarine fleets, alone, are something like five times as great as those possessed by Germany in 1939; we have already seen that no final answer can be given to the vulnerability of the future aircraft carrier with their guided weapon and other new defences: or for that matter, the future vulner-ability of the submarine. It seems, at least, that some very promising weapons to protect the aircraft carrier are under development. It also is reasonable to suppose that those very qualities which give the aircraft carrier its deterrent and offensive character, dispersal, mobility and evasion, will contribute in no little measure to its own defence. The framers of maritime strategy must bear in mind all these changing factors.

The mobility of aircraft carriers enables air bases to be moved against the enemy from an unforeseen direction and to exploit air routes over the least defended territories and against the weak points of his defence. Indeed, the sea-borne air bases of the navy are the counterpart to the bases of our bomber forces and provide great mobility and offensive power at critical places. The importance of aircraft carriers as bases for operation in cold or local war cannot be overestimated. If we were unfortunate enough to have our bases whittled away, let us say, in the Middle East, they could form, in certain conditions, a suitable base or bases in emergency. Aircraft carriers are also of great importance in the sphere of cold and local wars because they can provide mobile air bases round the periphery of the Sino-Soviet land-mass where these forms of war are likely to occur. Such mobility, and even flexibility, of naval and air power is an important counter-balance to the overwhelming manpower of Communist China.

Our maritime forces and their strategy must be shaped to give first place to aircraft carriers and ballistic rocket carriers, stocked with nuclear weapons to add to the power of the deterrent. Secondly, they must continue to be able to provide effective support and chores to our armed forces in cold and local wars. Thirdly, should the deterrent fail and a total war occur, the foregoing requirements which provide for the deterrent against global war would be more appropriate for waging a total war with nuclear weapons than a maritime force shaped to meet a long war of attrition against our merchant shipping.

Doubtless ballistic rockets and guided missiles, accurate at ranges of 2000 miles and over, will be introduced into the Services some time in the future. Nevertheless, meanwhile and probably for many years to come, there will often be advantages in using naval vessels, both surface and submarine, to reduce the operational requirements of these missiles from over 2000 miles to say ranges of 500 miles and under.

With the submarine menace of the First and Second World War and the increase of air power during the latter our navies found them-selves, at least until the invasion of Normandy, thrown back largely on a defensive and protective role. On the other hand, in the Second World War, the American navy in the Pacific showed the way to a new maritime offensive strategy. With the new weapons and the emphasis on the maritime use of air power our navies have recovered the offensive thrust. In cold and local wars, particularly against the Soviet communist powers, our navies will assume more than ever their traditional offensive power and will carry the war to the enemy in a variety of senses.

In common with our other surface forces which provide the thrust against the enemy and the depth for defence on land, the navy will provide an increasingly important thrust on the seas thus stretching the enemy war potential to the utmost. In the First World War, for example, the British naval blockade was in a sense equivalent to the strategic bombing of the Second World War, and was in fact a war-winning factor of the First World War. The blockade of the Second World War which tightened the German economy and put a strain on the German home front and war potential increased greatly the effectiveness of Allied strategic bombing, and also resulted in an important diversion of German war potential which was directed to her naval strategy. In like manner the United States naval strategy in the Pacific was the handmaiden and counterpart of air strategy.

It is clear that air power has become the primary feature of maritime power, not only in its new offensive role but also in its traditional role of safeguarding the sea. Indeed, in many respects naval vessels are now ancillaries, being the carriers of air power. It is true that naval vessels always have been carriers of weapons of one sort or another — guns, torpedoes, mines, etc. — but aircraft and ballistic rockets, particularly for attack deep into enemy territory, bring with them a whole new range of problems in which air strategy and naval strategy merge and coalesce. The artificial division of Service responsibilities in British maritime strategy is manifold: army guns for the anti-aircraft defence of our ports and coastwise shipping: air force fighters for intercepting aircraft laying mines in British ports and coastal waters and the navy for locating and destroying them: air force shore-based aircraft for maritime reconnaissance; and both naval carriers and air force shore-based aircraft for repelling attack on our ocean convoys.

Since the advent of air power, the British Admiralty has fought a rear-guard action in the naval claims of ships versus aircraft, and in their anticipation of the march of invention the Air Ministry made exaggerated claims. Whatever the respective desires of the two Services, events resulted in a closer and closer affiliation of maritime and air strategies so that today there is a vital inter-dependence of naval and air forces. Clearly, however, the time has come for the complementary functions of the two strategies to be fused more closely, both in respect of the traditional role of securing the sea communications and especially in the new role of offensive action.

Although there would seem to be far reaching advantages in amalgamating the sea and air forces, it would require a most careful Ministerial examination before any changes are made in any amalgamation of the two Service responsibilities. Combining the navy and the air force in their entirety might well not be the right solution at this time, but it would be wrong to take the attitude that such a combination is an impossible idea and should not be examined. Nevertheless, meanwhile there seems little doubt that there is a strong case for integrating the high direction of maritime and air strategies into something more positive than the present co-ordination of the two partisan attitudes at Chiefs of Staff level. Such integration would involve such matters as intelligence, planning, operations, technical policy and operational requirements, if not the financial branches.

A national strategy conceived and formulated merely from the highest common denominator of Admiralty and Air Ministry partisan sea-borne and shore-base approaches to the problem cannot be satisfactory. Clearly, national strategy must be the master and maritime and air strategy its servants.

Many in authority have a genuine difficulty in readjusting their minds and training from their own Service strategy to that of a national concept. Perhaps the strategy of the Mediterranean is an easier instance than others in which a clear idea may be had of how sea-borne and land-based aircraft and rocket carriers could be dovetailed into one whole to provide maximum economy and at the same time maximum efficacy. Here separate maritime and shore-based concepts clearly result in the need for more forces and bases than would a national concept. Furthermore, this example shows how our national forces should be fashioned from an Allied strategy and not simply from separate United Kingdom or United States national strategies. Similarly in the Far East and Pacific, a much sounder and more economical strategy would result from a truly collective and impartial approach to the Allied problems in these regions.

CHAPTER XIII

Air Strategy

I

THE long vistas of military history do not make it easy to give due credit to the originators of naval and army strategies. This is especially so since present day naval and army strategies are the fruit of centuries of development and experience. With the short history of air power and air strategy it must seem comparatively easy to pick out the figures who may be said to have formulated the basic concepts of air strategy. Here, however, there is some national rivalry.

Italian and some American air force enthusiasts uphold the claim of Guilio Douhet who in his book *The Command of the Air*, first published in 1921, expounded the original concepts of air strategy which are largely accepted in practice today. Some British air force enthusiasts, however, accredit Marshal of the Royal Air Force Viscount Trenchard with the original formulation of air strategy. This is too large a claim inasmuch that at the outset, and even when he was in charge of the Independent Air Force in 1918, Lord Trenchard was much more inclined to favour air strategy in support of the Army than in attacking the enemy home front.

There seems little doubt that the originator of air strategy was General Smuts in 1917. Inspired by the German air attacks on London in June and July of that year, and aided and encouraged by General Henderson, he produced the historic memoranda of August 1917. This document formed the basis of the creation of the Royal Air Force and reads:

> As far as can at present be foreseen there is absolutely no limit to the scale of its [air] future independent war use. And the day may not be far off when aerial operations with their devastation of enemy lands and destruction of industrial and populous areas on a vast scale may become the principal operations of war, to

which the older forms of military and naval operations may become secondary and subordinate.

That the Royal Air Force should emerge after the First World War as a separate service, with a strategical concept and importance of its own and peculiar to itself, is a tribute to its leaders of that time and to the vision of statesmen like Field Marshal Smuts. This was not simply a privilege granted to a fighting force whose members had paid heavily in the war. It was an acknowledgment of the vast extent and influence of air power which was to develop later, particularly during the Second World War and subsequently. Air forces as mere tactical extensions of our surface forces were not enough. It was seen that in the air we should need a force of very great striking power, the equal if not superior to those of other European nations. A strategy commensurate with the manifold changes brought about by air power could only be developed from a force conceived and shaped with some idea of the gigantic tasks ahead of it. Regrettably both the British War Office and the Admiralty resisted this new formation, less from a real appraisal of its possibilities than from an innate conservatism which continued to see in surface forces the only battle forces which would decide the issue in war. As observed elsewhere both parties in this dispute overstated their claims with regard to the effectiveness or ineffectiveness of air force strategy. The Second World War, which was to teach us forcibly so many lessons, also demonstrated the validity of the claims for support to surface forces and that of strategic bombing.

While our army and navy have largely self-determined their strategies within their own features rather than within any overall purview of national strategy, air force strategy has acquired this weakness of self-determination, not from tradition and primacy in the affections of the nation, but rather because the possibilities of air power are in a sense even yet undetermined and experimental. With so young, and yet so powerful a service the opportunity to impose on it a strategy conceived in national and international terms, is an important challenge to the wisdom of the Political Direction in Whitehall or Washington.

When the implications of war in the air are considered it will appear that air forces have different functions and operate upon different factors from the two older services, while these in turn react upon the role of the land and maritime forces. In consequence, the old concept of the aim in war being the destruction of the enemy's 'war-will' through the disorganization of his armed forces in battle, requires complete re-examination. It must now be replaced by a new one based upon an understanding of the true nature of air warfare.

The first use of air power was in conjunction with the operations of the maritime and the land forces, viz. to support these forces in the furtherance of their aims or in the prevention or anticipation of the operations of the hostile surface forces. The characteristic of flexibility which results from the speed and range of aircraft and from their relative superiority to natural obstacles has a special value in the support role. As air power grew, its support to maritime and land forces developed from the primary to a secondary role.

The new place of air strategy did not, however, go unchallenged. Right up to the Second World War few reputable army strategists acknowledged that air forces had any role other than supporting the land and the maritime forces. They asserted that the defeat of the enemy surface forces was a pre-requisite to victory and an air strategy which was conceived to by-pass the enemy surface forces and attack his home front direct was discredited.

Although the Admiralty had added aircraft carriers to our maritime forces during the First World War these were to provide sea-borne aircraft for a supporting but not primary role with our naval forces. We have traced elsewhere the great controversy which ranged around the relative merits of battleships and aircraft as the primary component of sea power and around coastal artillery and aircraft as the primary component of shore defence. It was only by learning the hard way in the Second World War that it became clear to the two older services that air strategy could be a strategy distinct from naval and army strategy. It was only then that the primary role of air power was accepted: that is, the capacity to bring to bear the offensive upon military and non-military targets of all descriptions at great distances and in all directions from the base of operations. All projectiles, admittedly except the torpedo, travel to their targets through the medium of the air; but the quite different order of range resulting from air power has been so great as to introduce entirely new aspects into warfare. These consist essentially in the exposure to direct enemy action of constituent elements in a belligerent's war power other than his armed forces — including the heart of his war potential.

These British controversies together with partisan Service prejudice have resulted in the air force being left responsible for providing air support for the army, though this sphere of support remains still very much of a cinderella. In the maritime sphere, we have seen that the controversy over the respective spheres of sea and air power has resulted in a most artificial and uneconomical division of duties between the Admiralty and the Air Ministry: the responsibilities of the former include all carrier-borne aircraft and of the latter all operational shore-based aircraft.

II

Should total war occur, the Allied peacetime deterrent air forces are the ideal weapons with which to prosecute it because the more effective they are as a deterrent the better should they be able to perform their war task. The most difficult and critical problem and one which must be studied and prepared in peacetime is, however, the selection of the target systems and targets against which the strategic bombers and ballistic rockets are to be directed.

There are two broad categories of target systems which present themselves right from the opening and critical phases of total war. They are 'war winning targets' whose destruction leads directly or indirectly to the enemy's defeat, and 'security targets' whose destruction will lessen the enemy's assault against ourselves and thus improve our ability to strike at the former targets. Determining this balance between hitting the enemy harder than he can stand, and of securing our bases from which we strike, is one of the most difficult strategic decisions: it is the balance between what we should like to do and what we have to do.

In making decisions with regard to the selection of target systems, great detail must be known about them. For example, in considering targets within Russia, details must be known about the broadly based system of her industry with its duplications, reserves and organization in great depth which leaves few, if any, vital target systems: details of the thin and highly sensitive railway system, specially in such focal points as Moscow, Kiev, Smolensk and Kharkov, and on the other hand, knowledge of the great capacity of the Russians to excel in makeshift and camouflage: details of the concentration of political power and policy making which in peacetime is focused in Moscow and the concomitant decentralization of the administration of the country to Territories and Regions: details of the number of strategic bomber bases, the number of satellite bases, the number of bombers and reserves, particulars of the aircraft industry and details of the organization and strength of the Russian air defence system.

Subsequent to the opening phases of war, and perhaps even concurrently with them, strategic air forces may be required to support the maritime or the land forces, before and during their critical operations, either by attacking the enemy surface forces directly or by isolating their spheres of operation from outside reinforcement and help. Air strategy must be sufficiently flexible to be able to attack 'war winning' or 'security targets', or to support the surface forces according to the situation.

The respective geographical factors are important in comparing, for example, the strategies of the United Kingdom and Russia. In the former there is a great concentration of vital targets of which the destruction of a limited number would be mortal to the country. On the other hand, the United Kingdom is compact and lends itself to the deployment and highly efficient control of fighter and guided missile defence. In contrast, Russian industry both west and east of the Urals is widely scattered so that there are no comparable concentrations of vital targets. This in turn necessitates that any air defence with fighters and guided missiles is a far vaster problem than for the United Kingdom.

The cold and local war roles of air forces, where the main offensive mass-destruction weapons are normally not applicable, are generally confined to establishing air superiority over and adjoining the theatre for the land forces, the provision of air transport, support for the army and attacking the communications and bases which serve the enemy forces. Although modern aircraft have not only retained but greatly improved their suitability for the two former roles, unfortunately operational aircraft are today less suited for the support role. Such is the price of progress in air power, but developments have already found other support devices, such as, for example, tactical atomic weapons and guided missiles.

The new weapons will increase enormously the importance of the primary roles of the air force: on the one hand with mass-destruction weapons and long range bombers, and ballistic rockets, the deterrent value and destructive power of the offensive, and on the other with defensive guided missiles, the protective power of the defence.

From the tactical point of view the bomber force will require aircraft of the maximum performance in speed, range and ceiling. This increased performance means aircraft of greater power and complexity and thus inevitably their cost must be greater. Indeed, the cost of our next generation of bombers is already so high that the number we can afford to have and operate is strictly limited. Thus, so far as technical changes are concerned, our future bomber force must be of high performance aircraft though in far fewer numbers than we had in the past with conventional weapons. Fortunately the vast improvement in the striking power of the air force calls for a much smaller force for its task. For example, the destruction achieved by one primitive atomic bomb at Hiroshima is equivalent to that achieved by a thousand bombers using conventional bombs at Hamburg. Moreover, fewer numbers will be offset by more accurate bombing, probably in some form of guided bombs. There is a further new development of offensive weapons resulting from the urge for increased performance of which the V1s and V2s of the last war were very primitive forms. These future pilotless bombers and ballistic rockets will become an important complement to our bombers and will in turn necessitate yet further radical changes in the structure of the striking air forces.

Whatever the manned and unmanned weapons of our bomber force, a substantial and highly efficient reconnaissance and pathfinder component will be essential; perhaps even more for the latter than the former weapons. The last war illustrates this clearly because then the composition of British Bomber Command was of the order of one reconnaissance or pathfinder for every ten main force bombers. To maintain an equable percentage of reconnaissance to the destructive potential of nuclear weapons would call for a composition of one for one. On the other hand, it must be remembered that we could accept inferior reconnaissance for a limited policy of attacking only targets of large and known built-up areas. The Bomber Command counter-measure component which was developed during the Second World War to assist our bombers in operating against the enemy defences is a further need which will assume a prior importance with the new developments. This component will be needed not only to assist the operation of our manned bombers, but even more to prevent the un-manned bombers and long range ground-to-ground missiles from being interfered with by the enemy.

Our fighter force will also undergo radical changes as a result of the new weapons. We have seen that the old concept of wearing down the enemy bomber force by an attrition rate of say, five or ten per cent, is totally inadequate against attack by atomic or hydrogen weapons. Something nearer annihilation rate is essential for our survival in future warfare and fortunately the development of defensive guided missiles gives some prospect of this. To attack the modern high performance bomber, supersonic fighters, manned or unmanned, and guided missiles will be essential; and these in turn will be costly both to purchase and to operate, and their numbers limited. These defensive weapons must, therefore, possess great accuracy and destructive power which in the main will be determined by their war weapons. No gun or cannon is likely to be sufficiently adequate under modern conditions in range, accuracy or hitting power, so that air-to-air guided missiles will be essential for fighters. It should, however, be remembered that air-to-air guided missiles will probably bring high and low altitude limitations for some years to come, and everything possible must be done to reduce these limitations.

Ground-to-air guided missiles as a most superior replacement to medium and heavy anti-aircraft artillery, if not low level artillery, will affect our present fighter force substantially with many new operational concepts. These new weapons will be highly lethal though they too will have their limitations, one of the biggest of which will be the cost of stockpiling multiple centres. The shorter their range the greater the number of centres which will have to be stockpiled, each with sufficient missiles to deal with the largest air attack which might pass within their range. On the other hand, the greater their range, the fewer the number of stockpiling centres required; the higher their minimum effective altitude, the more complicated and costly the missiles and their guidance. The confined geographical features of the United Kingdom compared with the other Great Powers, however, probably favour us for ground-to-air missile defence.

The new weapons bring a further defence problem which gives cause for the greatest concern. As the ballistic rocket is developed in range, accuracy and hitting power, it will present a more and more formidable defence problem because, whatever the defence problems against high performance bombers, those against ballistic rockets will be greater by several orders of magnitude. Perhaps the best short-term defence against these missiles is hitting back at target systems on which the enemy depend for their supply and launching. Nevertheless, defence against ballistic rockets is a matter which must be tackled by our scientists most earnestly. Another air defence requirement is an efficient counter-measure force to prevent the enemy interfering with our defences and to hinder him from using any of our resources as navigational or bombing aids.

The modern fighter and the new air defence guided missile will bring a need for many changes in the organization of our defence forces. For example, in the United Kingdom certainly the pros and cons will have to be decided on the question whether the air defence should consist of two separate divisions, one of fighters and the other of ground-to-air guided missiles both directly under the Air Defence Commander, or alternatively, whether each Sector should have a complement of each of these weapons. In any event, the integration of the new missile type with the older fighter type of weapon and the increasing approach speed of the attack will necessitate changes in the Control and Reporting System, which has always been difficult, to gain adequate identification, warning and co-ordination for those who are to control and command our defence weapons.

The strategy of defensive guided missiles promises to be simpler than that of fighter defences. The dominating factors will be the range and effective height of the missile and an adequate early warning system. Perhaps, however, the most difficult problem in the strategy of guided missile defence is the technical development; in deciding the characteristics of the weapons which will prove them superior, at not too great a cost, to the enemy offensive weapons. At present it would seem that the greater the range the higher will be the minimum effective height below which anti-aircraft guns or some other form of weapon will be required.

The operational problems of the strategy will be no more than deciding where to site the missile centres and the size of the stockpiles. Guided missile centres with adequate peacetime stockpiles will of course be expensive and not mobile, so that, for some time at least, there is likely to be a mixture of guided missile and fighter aircraft in our defence systems, and this will call for good and positive tactical control.

The strategy of ballistic rockets promises to be even simpler than that of defensive guided missiles. Subject to adequate knowledge of the target without resort to reconnaissance, the range of the rocket and its guidance accuracy are the factors which will dominate the strategy comprising of no more than locating the launching sites and determining the size of the stockpiles. Maritime rocket-carriers are likely to play an important role, at least until satisfactory long range rockets are produced. If and when air defences are forthcoming which can counter the ballistic rocket, then the direction of attack and reduction in range of operation will become further factors in the strategy. Like the defensive guided missiles, the biggest problem in the strategy of ballistic rockets is technical development in deciding the characteristics of the weapon. It would be too late if it was not until the outbreak of hostilities that it was found that the enemy had greatly superior weapons.

In many ways it would seem that the new weapons will make the air force secondary roles more and more difficult. The weapons best suited for the primary role in total war are becoming less and less suited for cold and local war: indeed, in these forms of war the real power of modern air forces cannot be applied. Similarly, the new weapons render the air support role to the navy and the army more rather than less difficult and complex: inevitably high performance atomic bombers, ballistic rockets and high performance fighters are not so suited as former air power weapons for the air support role. On the other hand, if tactical atomic bombs are used, the power of air support would be increased greatly. Moreover, modern weapons will play a decisive part in gaining air superiority which will be a dominating factor in local war, particularly in the air support role. A secondary role of growing importance, certainly so far as the new weapons affect armies in the field, is air transport.

It is important that the air force secondary roles are reviewed in the light of modern conditions to ascertain what, if any, transfers of responsibilities should be made to the other two Services. A most careful assessment is required as to how far the air force should provide special secondary role equipments, and how far the older Services should provide their own. Under present conditions, it would seem uneconomical for the navy to provide its own shore-based air support and for the army to provide its own air support, but these are essential requirements of these Services and must be provided somehow. In the previous chapter, however, we have mentioned a new relation between maritime and air power.

Finding the right balance between the components of our air force under modern conditions will be more important and more difficult than ever before because of the increased serious consequences of being proved wrong in the event; because of the rate of progress of modern science and the astonishing technical developments; and because of the critical period of years and the cost involved in changing modern weapons. Moreover, today the balance is most critical between the bomber and the ballistic rocket in the striking force, and between the fighter and defensive guided missile in air defence, and between these various equipments in the secondary roles. The solution of these problems to meet the needs of the national strategies will differ for each Great Power. The British Commonwealth as a whole, in particular, has its own and exacting problem in reconciling the needs of its overseas members with those of the United Kingdom and her commitments in Western Europe.

It is too early to assess the relation between the bomber and the ballistic rocket for much will depend on development and technical progress. In air defence, it is likely in the future that the defensive ground-to-air guided missile will play a primary role in the inner defence of vital centres, and the fighter, supplemented by the longer range guided missile, for outer defence. Moreover, the new weapons might make it possible to simplify and thus cheapen our fighter aircraft so that we can have more of them, delegating operations in the extreme top height band to ground-to-air guided missiles. So far as our overseas main bases with their limited areas are concerned, the ground-to-air guided missile might well be able to take over the major role in air defence and so reduce the fighter commitments.

The circumstances of today also call for a strategical review of the deployment of the Royal Air Force. The limited number of costly and complex bombers and fighters and guided weapons, and the requirements of highly skilled maintenance, and the present day great mobility of air forces might well result in a new deployment concept, basing all high performance equipments in the United Kingdom and arranging for them unit tours of duty overseas as required: a concept much nearer to that of the navy and the flexibility requirements of strategy. The air force Commanders-in-Chief and their headquarters must be organized on a basis of functional responsibilities rather than on the present rigid command system for a permanently allocated component force. They must be in close liaison with the national Home air force commands — Fighter, Bomber, Coastal and Transport — so that they can control the training and operations of any air force unit which might be allocated for training or operations in their theatre. Similarly they must be organized and in proper liaison for controlling any Allied air forces allocated to their theatre.

Conventional air force tactics evolved as a result of a number of factors such as the optimum size and carrying capacity of our bombers using conventional weapons: the performance of our bombers: their vulnerability and defensive strength in relation to air-to-air and ground-to-air defences; and the standards of our past navigational, bombing and reconnaissance aids. It was the combination of such factors as these which led to the air offensive operational requirement of substantial numbers of bombers attacking in formation by day and in a stream by night, and the air defence requirement of substantial numbers of fighters flying in close formation for day operations. Future technical developments of bombers, fighters, reconnaissance and support aircraft, together with the accuracies achieved by guided missiles in offensive and defensive roles and the introduction of guided bombs, will probably reduce the tactical numbers of aircraft required both in offensive and defensive operations. This reduction is especially likely because with nuclear weapons, one or two bombers will have the carrying capacity to destroy a primary target. Also a fighter using air-to-air guided missiles will be far more lethal than our conventional ones. Certainly it would seem that tactical air superiority might well be won in a week or two by atomic attack on airfields rather than in months as in the last war. To conform to these new conditions new and vital air force tactics will have to be evolved.

As already mentioned modern weapons present new problems in crew training. Manned bombers and fighters with requisite performance will be so costly, complex and so limited in numbers that only crews of the highest standard will be acceptable. Indeed, it would seem that a future high performance bomber carrying an hydrogen bomb representing a substantial part of the national armoury will need a captain, if not a whole crew, of much greater experience and responsibility than is currently accepted in the Royal Air Force. In fact, the very great cost and scarcity of our future aircraft call for a general review of the structure and standard of our present-day aircrews. Wholly new concepts will be required for training in guided missiles. Some missiles are already recovered by parachute after trials and training practice, and doubtless development of the camera gun, electronics, and other synthetic training devices will help to eliminate some of the need of expending missiles in peacetime, but a minimum live practice will always be required for air-to-air and ground-to-air missiles. For example, Britain may find some of these practice ranges in or around the United Kingdom for all three Services, but it is probable that the air force in particular will need more extensive range facilities of the scope provided at the Australian rocket range. This will entail long distance visits which in turn will bring other problems with them.

III

There are six factors in strategic air power which illustrate the variation from the traditional so-called Principles of War. Air power has so affected these principles that a review of them is not mere iconoclasm but is, in our day, a necessity. Here, in brief, are outlined those factors which in some instances may appear to partake of something of the nature of the Principles of War, though reflection reveals a different emphasis and a new angle.

Security of the base. With the threat of nuclear bombs security of the base will be quite a different problem from that of the Second World War. To illustrate from that war the emphasis on security: Germany in 1940 had over a thousand fighters and nearly two thousand bombers, but in 1944, as a result of our bomber offensive, she altered the whole balance of her air force and had over two thousand fighters and only some two hundred bombers. Today we must secure our bases by a powerful striking force at immediate readiness; and an adequate defence of fighters and guided missiles together with a bold plan of duplication and dispersal. The first principle of air warfare used to be the attainment of air superiority by attrition but today it is not simply the pre-requisite to victory but the key to our survival. The fashions of decisive battles of the Second World War are now outmoded and we must achieve air superiority over enemy territory and over our own defence area by the use of fighters, defence missiles, ballistic rockets and attack on bases, operating in concert one with the other.

The selection of the Target. This is intimately linked with intelligence reconnaissance and a knowledge of the structure of the enemy reserves and potential. The Second World War had many examples of conflict between the various political, civilian and service authorities on the target systems and targets which should be attacked. There was conflict regarding the various key targets comprising some critical element in the enemy economy which required precision bombing, and area bombing aimed at the general destruction of towns and the like. A particular controversy arose over the value of area bombing primarily to create a general dislocation and destruction amongst the centres of population, and precision bombing of focal targets in the enemy transportation system. As a general assessment a medium strength bomber raid during the Second World War could damage heavily (*a*) one large factory and put it out of action for from three to four months: (*b*) one large railway centre which if attacked in isolation could be repaired in a few weeks, but if it were attacked in conjunction with related centres the effect was cumulative: (*c*) one industrial residential district where the effect was short-lived but cumulative:

(*d*) one air base where the effect was short-lived but justified tactically. Air forces then were inadequate to force a quick decision on major industrial countries such as Germany or the United Kingdom where many cities survived the heaviest of sustained attacks. A city could recuperate with surprising rapidity from a series of heavy raids and its manufacturing capacity be mainly restored. As a measure of Bomber Command effectiveness in the Second World War, analysis shows that because of an inadequate standard of navigation almost fifty per cent of the bombs dropped on south-west Germany between May 1940 and May 1941 fell in open country, while of a hundred bomber raids made in September 1941 over the Ruhr, only one bomb in ten fell within five miles of the target. Britain began the Second World War with her largest bomb weighing only five hundred pounds, which was no greater than that employed during the First World War. Strategic needs, however, called for the development later of the twenty-two thousand pound bomb. The development of nuclear weapons has revolutionized the strategy of air attack. Today, it seems clear that a very small number of bombers could possess the power to destroy an enemy's war potential and indeed his means of life.

Certainly we must have the ability to find the target and deliver weapons effectively against the target: a factor intimately linked with navigational and bombing aids and the development of ballistic rockets and guided bombs. Already, great progress has been made on the methods and devices used in the Second World War.

Effective range. This is most important and among other things it illustrates the interrelation with the strategies of the other Services. During the Second World War the full effect of air power had to await army and naval operations to provide the necessary bases and reduce the depth of enemy defence. Eastern Germany was beyond effective range until southern Italy was captured, and great amphibious operations were necessary before Japan itself could be reached. This is still a consideration in terms of cold war and local war, though today, bomber forces can reach any part of the world without previous land or sea operations. Modern air power can carry mass-destruction weapons thousands of miles which could destroy a city completely, or indeed devastate a whole country.

The time factor. The belligerent nations in the Second World War survived air attack because it was applied gradually. It took us over four years to build up our bomber offensive while now we must be ready at the outbreak of war to strike what must be mortal blows. When the atom bomb appeared the threat gave priority back to the offensive and placed the dependence of Western security on deterrent. As already emphasized the potential enemy has the initiative and our plans must be constantly ready as well as sensitive to every political, military and scientific change. This flexibility at the planning and actual operations stage is essential to counter any surprise plan which may be launched by the enemy. The United States make no secret of their might and strength and readiness: and it is most important that the potential enemy should really appreciate the extent of this preparedness. A most trying problem, however, is how far such a force can be kept at immediate readiness which is something new and difficult to the free countries. It is clear that profound changes are necessary in our own air force war-readiness because the necessity in an Armageddon will be annihilation of enemy aircraft rather than attrition, and issues will be settled by front line forces and peacetime stockpiles rather than war-time production as in the Second World War. Germany, it should be remembered, stockpiled for the Second World War and adopted a blitzkrieg strategy. Such a policy then was only possible by an aggressor nation, but it did result in the overthrow of France and Poland in a few weeks. As a future war may be won in the first round, we cannot ignore this lesson. Moreover, atom bombs of the Nagasaki type are now rapidly being relegated to the status of tactical weapons. Whereas the earlier atomic bombs did their damage chiefly by blast and fire, now other effects of hydrogen bombs may transcend its blast and fire effects. A five megaton bomb will destroy a circular area of three hundred square miles to lethal radiation. In addition, 'fall out' would be fatal to both sides in town or country whoever should launch the weapons.

Strategic bombers are now the chosen instruments of Allied strategy and clearly our first aim should be to destroy or neutralize the Russian, Chinese and their satellite strategic bombers and guided missile sites. The actual plan, however, will depend on intelligence, the enemy front line strength, his reserves, his stockpiles of nuclear weapons, the number of alternative bases and his defences.

The ability to apply air power depends upon the degree of air superiority possessed and this has the same twofold aspect as the command of the sea which comprehends power to interfere with the enemy's use of the sea (offensive) and power to prevent his interference with our own use of it (defensive). The difference is that before the advent of air power, defensive and offensive command of the sea was obtained, for all practical purposes, by the same means — the defeat or overawing of the hostile forces — and could scarcely be conceived separately. On the other hand, defensive air superiority can well exist without offensive air superiority, as the one may be attained largely by different means from the other.

In the sphere of strategic bombing it is of immense importance to realize that, with the possession of ballistic rockets, air superiority can be achieved theoretically at least without using a single aircraft. If we assume that the passive counter-measures depend entirely on the use of defensive guided missiles and other ground weapons, we see how defensive air superiority may exist without the possession of aircraft.

In practice, of course, no belligerent would deliberately neglect any economical means of securing the air superiority which he needs. However, the strict analysis of air superiority into its two components, and of these again into their basic constituents, may well lead to a sounder order of priority in the provision of the various weapons and the build-up of the necessary types of force. A belligerent strategically on the defensive will normally seek to obtain the maximum degree of defensive air superiority at the outset of hostilities, deferring, if necessary, the development of offensive air superiority in the full sense of the term to a later stage, dependent on the course of the war and his prospects of a general change-over to the strategic offensive.

Air superiority, either defensive or offensive, is rarely absolute. The success of the various measures and counter-measures may vary through an immense range of kind and of degree. In particular, air superiority can vary in respect of place and of time; it may be local and it may be temporary: alternatively it may tend towards universality and permanence. Generally speaking, a high degree of air superiority can, nearly always, be achieved temporarily or locally by concentration either in defence of a particular target or system of targets at a particular time, or offensively in support of a specific operation. It is, however, only as a belligerent gradually gains general ascendancy over his opponent that temporary and local superiority are converted into a superiority more widespread and lasting, which in the end secures practical immunity for his own targets and full power to operate against those of the enemy almost without interference. An apt example of this is the air superiority which was achieved over the United Kingdom and over the Normandy beaches and subsequently over the Allied armies for the invasion of France in 1944.

Notwithstanding the foregoing, it is important to realize that the development of high speed and high altitude aircraft, nuclear weapons, electronics and computors, guided missiles, guided bombs, and ballistic rockets, has a profound effect on giving different emphasis to the different aspects of defensive and offensive air superiority. Not least is the problem of establishing superiority between an attacker using a single or at least a small number of high performance bombers each carrying a weapon capable of destroying a whole city, and a defender using defensive guided missiles together with a small force of fighters armed with lethal guided missiles. The problem is greatly different from the old methods of gaining superiority over a belligerent's large bomber force by attrition by a large fighter force. The problem is also greatly different from the use of a large bomber force to make an air base impotent, and even then only for a short period, compared with the great and long term effect of a single nuclear bomb which would be used today. With ballistic rockets armed with nuclear war heads, the problem is still more critical and seems still more difficult to solve. Arising out of all these new problems is one certain factor and that is that technical developments will play an even greater part than hitherto, though personal military direction will still be paramount even if it is only in the sphere of intelligence.

It is interesting to note how the development of air strategy has duplicated the course of naval strategy, and how in so many of its aspects it has assumed roles which were traditionally those of the navy. It has assumed, throughout its history, the role of bombardment, of support to the army in the suppression of unruly states by show of force or actual bombardment. It has grown steadily into an arm of great offensive power and stands now where naval power stood in the nineteenth century as the prime deterrent to aggressive action on the part of others. The old concept of 'the fleet in being', that is, a fleet shut up in its home harbours but still necessitating a large force to ensure that it did not escape to engage in blockade or pursue an offensive role elsewhere, has found a parallel in air strategy. An air force ready and equipped with nuclear weapons could in a similar, though much vaster fashion, hold the attention and air forces of an enemy for an undetermined period, since the capabilities of such a force in being are of such very great magnitude, and cannot be ignored.

This simple parallel of past and present needs does illustrate the strategic tasks ahead of our own national and Allied air forces. The new developments have revolutionized the concept and doctrine of national strategy primarily because of the profound effect they have had on air strategy. No great nation can, in these days at any rate, succeed in forwarding its policy by an all out war because both victor and vanquished would be destroyed by the multifarious effects of nuclear attack. Our best means of survival are therefore to maintain in peacetime a deterrent force of powerful stockpiles of hydrogen and atomic weapons. Bomber forces, ballistic rockets and fleets at immediate readiness to deliver these weapons and the knowledge that all aggressors are aware of their strength and of our determination to resist aggression, together with an air defence and home defence which will make any potential enemy pause and doubt his ability to strike an effective surprise blow, are our best means of defence.

It is vital that there should be a radical and non-partisan review of air power based on a national strategy formulated within the framework of an Allied strategy. For example, it is quite unrealistic to consider our bomber or air striking force in terms of total war except as one unit of the Allied forces. Again, it is unrealistic to conceive an air defence of the United Kingdom against an all-out Soviet communist attack, in isolation, there could be nothing adequate under such a concept. We can only make sense of our defence by considering the whole geographical extent of the Allies, all their territories and bases throughout the world, with the multiplications and varying distance and time factors which would make simultaneous attack impossible, together with the whole Allied defence and striking forces available for counter measures.

Thus, under existing conditions and in terms of total war no British deterrent force could be adequate alone. In this sphere more than any other our National joint strategy must be integrated with a combined Allied strategy based on the power of a strong deterrent of the might of the Allies. It is singularly apt that in discussing the strategy of air forces we should find ourselves intimately concerned with those wider problems of Allied and combined strategy. Such considerations lie deep in the very essence of air power.

CHAPTER XIV

Home Defence

As in any future total war the home front will be involved as much, if not more, than the armed forces fighting at sea, in the field and in the air, a separate chapter is given to home defence. Home Defence is a comprehensive term which includes both the military and civil defence aspects of securing the home front and which never before have had the same emphasis and urgency that they have today.

With continental nations, throughout history, the home country has been defended by armies deployed, often in association with fortifications, to prevent enemy armies from over-running the frontier, and if this failed, to prevent the capture of key centres and areas upon which the continuance of hostilities depended. This home defence was essentially one for armed forces. The histories of France, Germany, Russia and the other continental countries, up to and including the two World Wars, is studded with examples of this strategy. On the other hand, with island nations, the home country depended on naval forces to secure the sea communications together with land forces deployed along fortifications to prevent the landing of invading forces. Again, citizens as civilians were not used in any organized form in this role. This aspect of strategy is aptly illustrated by the history of the United Kingdom through the centuries up to and including the two World Wars.

The ease with which the United Kingdom has been defended in the past in comparison with the common frontiers in Europe, particularly against invasion, makes it difficult for many to appreciate the effect of the threat of attack or of direct enemy action in former times on the continent. Whereas, then, the British navy succeeded in securing the United Kingdom, armies on the continent often failed to secure the defence of their countries or their peoples. Theirs was a strategy of Home Defence in the strictest sense, since the areas behind the land defences were those which kept the war in being; and in ideal circumstances they could be said to be securing the homeland even if certain parts of the country were over-run, provided that such areas were not key areas containing perhaps the capital city which generally housed the seat of power and continued resistance. To assert this is not to say that the peeople of a continental country were unaffected by an invasion so long as the army remained intact. Then the issue for an aggressor was not how vulnerable were the people behind the lines but how strong were the opposing armed forces wherever they might be. The question today for the non-aggressor is the effective defence of a whole country and its resources as well as its people against direct, and unless countered, heavily destructive air attack.

Thus, the advent of air power has superimposed a further and most difficult problem on home defence, because no longer can naval or land forces defend the continental or the island home countries from direct enemy attack. This new factor was not suddenly revolutionary but evolved gradually with the development of the power of air forces. The first attack on England, on Christmas Eve 1914, by a single German aeroplane which dropped a bomb near Dover Castle did no damage. This was followed by air attacks on London, the Midlands and other towns, by airships and by aeroplanes. In one instance, these early attacks caused a riot which required troops to restore order. The attacks became increasingly effective and even though the casualties and material damage was not great during the First World War, generally there was much public nervousness and the output of work was reduced substantially.

As the air attacks increased, more and more units of fighter aircraft and anti-aircraft artillery, hitherto allocated for the defence of the British naval and army forces, were reallocated and deployed to counter the new threat at home. The general arrangements for the home defence of the United Kingdom which had been vested in the Admiralty since September 1914 were, in consequence of the German air attacks, transferred to the army. In addition, the place of Civil Defence was established as a component part of the home defence of Great Britain.

It is worthy of note that these air raids made by Germany on London in June and July in 1917, had an indirect effect disproportionate to the damage and casualties then caused. They led ultimately to the formation of the Smuts Committee which eventually transformed the Royal Flying Corps and the Royal Naval Air Service into the Royal Air Force.

Lighting restrictions was the first home defence measure to be introduced in the United Kingdom. Initially, these restrictions were controlled by the Admiralty, War Office and Home Office, each in its own sphere and each trying to enforce the regulations with different interpretations and emphasis, but this led to confusion and control was subsequently centralized in the Home Office. The first lesson in home defence problems had been learned.

The second measure which followed on the heels of lighting restrictions was local air raid warnings. Control, first entrusted to Chief Constables, was subsequently transferred to the Commander-in-Chief Home Forces; the military being responsible for initiating the warnings which were then disseminated by civilian telephone operators to places listed by the police. Already the complications of home defence were becoming clear because the warnings and false reports were resulting in serious stoppages of work. As the air attacks increased and the German Gotha raids began, public demand, in some instances in panic form, grew for general warnings. First maroons, or sound bombs, were introduced, followed by police on bicycles and in motor cars carrying 'Take cover' placards and blowing whistles, ringing bells and sounding horns. The demand for air raid warnings was followed by an equal demand for public shelters, particularly in the East End and places where people lived crowded in flimsy dwellings. The main lesson from the First World War was that direct air attack on the people caused great loss of morale out of all proportion to casualties and material damage. We shall see later that this loss of morale can, to some extent, be reduced by effective home defence.

Although properly, 'blockade' belongs to the chapters on military strategy, in order to get a proper perspective of home defence, it is as well to mention here the serious threat which the submarine and mines brought to this country in the First World War. This new menace to our merchant shipping came close to starving us out and was perhaps the first pointer to the shift which was to come in the balance between our security by overseas military operations and by direct threat to the home country.

II

By the time of the Second World War, the air threat to the United Kingdom had grown very greatly and Britain had accordingly developed home defence forces on a large scale. The greater part of her fighter forces and indeed of her whole air force was devoted to home defence and Fighter Command had been created to command these forces. This force was composed of both regular and auxiliary units. Moreover, first priority in the whole war effort during the early part of the campaign was given to increasing the size and effectiveness of these fighter forces. Anti-Aircraft Command had also been formed largely from Territorial units. Britain began the Second World War with a considerable force of anti-aircraft artillery which was increased greatly during the campaign. She also had a very considerable barrage balloon force whose units were deployed round important centres to deter the enemy from making low attacks.

These military forces engaged in home defence created many new problems in the formulation of policy and plans, and in command. Fighter Command and Anti-Aircraft Command belonged to different Services and so the post of Air Defence Commander was created and given to the Air Officer Commanding Fighter Command who thus held two appointments: one Service and one inter-Service. Nevertheless, there was always the complication of co-ordinating not only the requirements of the three military Services, but also of co-ordinating those of the military with the several Civil departments concerned. For example, co-ordinating the military problems and the siting of A.A. guns and balloon barrages with the civil assessment and priorities of the various targets and target systems in the country; the divergent military and civil requirements with regard to warning, blackout, dispersal, evacuation, transport, coastal shipping, etc. The policy and high direction of these affairs was in fact done by committees and in the circumstances worked reasonably well. It is, however, important, to remember that the success of this form of direction depended largely on Britain having the strength of Mr. Churchill as her Prime Minister and Minister of Defence.

Britain also started the Second World War with a wide and comprehensive civil component of home defence. From the time of the

Munich crisis the government and the people had appreciated the part which had to be played by civil defence and great efforts and resources were geared to the problem. After the outbreak of war these efforts were developed into a Civil Defence of great importance and great complexity. Large numbers of ordinary citizens were involved in these activities. Actually the peak strength of whole-time people was at the end of December 1941 when there were nearly half-a-million employed, and the peak strength of part-time people was in March 1944 when there were over one and a half million employed. Certainly Britain could not have continued the war without this civil defence.

As a result of the lessons of the First World War the Civil Defence organizations during the preparatory period were centralized under the Home Office and at the outbreak of war they were transferred to the Ministry of Home Security: a new ministry which was formed because of the great importance of civil defence. The Service departments and the numerous Civil departments concerned were all controlled and co-ordinated by this new ministry and the Civil Defence of the various local authorities were operated through Regional Commissioners who were given far reaching powers for use when communications broke down or in an emergency.

The organization of Civil Defence was developed from that used in the First World War, was wide spread, and embodied every service necessary to maintain the daily life under air attack; these can be grouped under the categories prevention, reduction and restoration of damage. These services comprised: fire fighting, air raid warning, air raid wardens, first aid, ambulance, salvage, rescue, decontamination, hospital, burial, black-out, air raid shelters, evacuation, dispersal of industry, supply of gas respirators and other special equipments, care of the homeless, housing repair, emergency welfare and feeding and emergency transport.

In all, the enemy launched on the United Kingdom a scale attack of the order of 65,000 tons of bombs, 6000 flying bombs and 1000 V2 rockets. The home front battle was, indeed, a campaign of its own and at times victory and defeat were in the balance. It was only the home defence, with the Civil Defence manned by citizens and on the alert during the long years of war, which saved Great Britain from collapse and defeat.

Apart from bombardment, the advent of air power had introduced a further and critical military problem to the home defence of Great Britain. For the first time in modern history the country was exposed to a serious threat of invasion by both sea- and airborne forces. The German air force had become a serious challenge to British sea power, and it also had the means of dropping significant numbers of troops throughout the country. A Commander-in-Chief Home Forces was appointed, military forces and citizens were organized and very extensive preparations were made to defend the coast and the whole country against this threat of invasion.

In the event, it was air bombardment which threatened the country and the United Kingdom was subjected to heavy and sustained air attack on her towns and key centres throughout the land over several years of war. These attacks were made primarily by aircraft but fly bombs and V rockets were also used. The Battle of Britain not only ended any threat of invasion to our country, but it was also the critical air battle which brought the Civil Defence task within the scope of the resources available and which was the turning point in any doubts there might have been in the British people maintaining the will to continue fighting under grim and exacting conditions. After this battle German superiority of air power began to wane and eventually air superiority began to turn overwhelmingly in Allied favour.

III

In the final event, as it affects the citadel of a nation, Home Defence has always been the essence of all defence, but we have seen how strikingly home defence in the direct sense grew out of the two World Wars and became so important in total war that vast effort and resources were devoted to this intimate aspect of national defence. The whole perspective of war and of strategy changed as the result of these two wars, and if any doubts remained, subsequent developments made this change crystal clear. The development of atomic, hydrogen, chemical and biological weapons together with ballistic rockets have transformed military problems from a single concept of conventional military operations to a dual concept of two distinct and quite different vital conflicts going on at once – battle on the home front which certainly could be swift and mortal and battle between armed forces away from the home front which, whether long or short, eventually has a decisive even if indirect bearing on the home front. In total war the direct threat to the home front has become the biggest problem in our security and even to our very existence. The home defence must be able to keep the country going if the ordinary structure of civil life collapses under air attack.

Thus, it is clear that home defence is required on a large scale today both to maintain the will of the people to fight and our ability to continue hostilities. In the First World War, the direct threat to the British home front was one of morale rather than material damage while, in the Second World War, the national damage was on a greatly increased scale but not sufficient to be decisive so long as morale could be maintained. Today, the threat is not only one of morale but that the very means of our daily life could be destroyed almost overnight.

IV

It is more than ever important to be clear as to the respective military and civil contributions in home defence. The military force must deter or reduce the scale and precision of attack as much as possible and they must also be the backbone on which civil defence can operate. Around this backbone, the Civil Defence must be capable of maintaining our daily life in every essential sphere not only during hostilities but during any subsequent period of re-establishing order in the country. In this respect it should be remembered that although civil defence can never win a war, the lack of an adequate civil defence could well lose it.

We must ensure that neither the overall concept of home defence nor the individual military and civil components become outmoded with the march of time. Thus, the individual tasks of all the various facets should be kept under review in the light of the changing conditions of war. This is especially necessary because weapons have been revolutionized since even our own very limited history and expansion of this new aspect of war began.

Today, the readiness required of our home defence is such that the peacetime preparations not only of military but also of the Civil

Q

Defence organizations must be ready to defend the country at very short notice against intended mortal blows. As with all other aspects of defence, we dare not base our plans on any initial period in which to mobilize and gather our strength or to train once hostilities begin.

It is not surprising that many difficulties arise in the direction and command of Home Defence because the whole civil life of the country will have to be co-ordinated with military affairs. All the lessons of the two World Wars emphasize the need for direction to be centralized at the top and for the military and civil authorities to be phased in at the several levels. In the United Kingdom, the Commander-in-Chief, Home Forces, who is responsible to the Defence Committee through the Chiefs of Staff Committee, should initiate, plan, co-ordinate and direct policy, strategy, training and administrative policy for both military and civil forces in home defence affairs. In war he will be the fortress commander. His link with the military forces is through the various Commanders-in-Chief of the three Services at home and with the civil forces through the Director General of Civil Defence who deals with the local civil authorities through his Regional Directors. Clearly there will have to be a genuine desire to co-operate by both Service and Civil authorities or friction will arise with the numerous Civil departments concerned, which could only be resolved at Defence Committee level.

The organization at present adapted in the United Kingdom is that the first line of Civil Defence is provided by the local authorities; the tactical reserve to these local defence forces is the Mobile Defence Corps which is under the Director General; these civil forces are backed by the Territorials and Regulars of the Army and if necessary forces of the Air Force; special naval requirements in home defence, such as might be needed at our ports, are provided by the Reservists and Regulars of the Navy. Should communications break down, or in grave emergency where the centralized controls cannot operate effectively, far reaching powers are given to the Regional Directors. The foregoing outlines the form of home defence devised in the United Kingdom, but naturally, the various nations each have their own form of home defence organization according to their political organization and the expected degree of attack.

Before home defence plans can proceed very far, the political leaders must first give some precise and clear decisions: they must give both long- and short-term decisions on the balance between the civil and the military resources. For example, in this nuclear era, is the United Kingdom in war to be a war production base or merely a platform from which the Allied forces would operate with equipment and arms supplied from America and other bases overseas? Important issues in the United Kingdom home defence policy depend on these decisions, in particular, which centres should be given priority in close defence against an attack; the stockpiling policy; the war industrial policy; the provision and security of ports in war; and the general allocation of man-power in the civil, military and industrial spheres.

As in any military affair, it is important that home defence is not taken by surprise since there is no nation whose people could withstand large scale surprise air attacks if sustained over any considerable period. On the other hand, the more prepared the military and civil components of home defence are for their role and the more prepared the people themselves for the nature of the attack with which they would have to contend, the better will our home defence be able to sustain the daily life in time of war.

Flexibility of plans and preparations is another important aspect of home defence because it is so necessary that adjustment can be made to meet the nature and conditions of attack adopted by the enemy. Whether the attack is widespread or concentrated, whether by hydrogen, atomic, chemical, biological or conventional type of weapons, and whether directed against target systems such as towns, the transport system, docks or power supply will call for the greatest tenacity of purpose supported by an adaptability of method. Each of these variations brings its own problems to the home defence organization.

Another problem which requires the most careful consideration and assessment in terms of past experience is air raid warning. The requirements for attack against supersonic bombers are quite different from the bombers of the past. Against ballistic rockets it is something still more different. The reduction in the period of warning and the arrival of attack repercusses throughout the whole range of home defence problems.

The greatest destruction resulting from air attack in the Second World War was caused by fire and so fire fighting was perhaps the most important Civil Defence service at that time. Indeed, it is clear that without the elaborate and efficient fire fighting organization the home front would have collapsed. It is certain that the new weapons of war will require even more extensive fire fighting arrangements but, nevertheless, our future measures to save life and casualties will have to be extended to cover other aspects such as the deadly radioactivity after effect of nuclear weapons and the new chemical and biological weapons, as well as still further measures to deal with material destruction on a greatly increased scale.

Reporting the results of air attack will become much more complicated because of the widespread damage. In particular, it will be difficult to obtain information of damage caused by hydrogen or even atomic weapons for the very reason that they will destroy all communications in the neighbourhood and for a considerable extent beyond it. Public facilities would be completely disrupted and reconnaissance from the ground would be prohibited for some considerable time. There are technical aids which give the approximate position of strikes of nuclear weapons but aircraft, probably helicopters, would be required to obtain the extent and details of the damage done.

Thus, the new and greatly increased threat to the life and material on the home front will require home defence measures to be stepped-up several orders of magnitude. The task of maintaining the daily life under nuclear attack is so great that the Civil Defence would require extensive help from military forces. Certainly, as far as the United Kingdom is concerned, assistance to the Civil Defence has become a primary role for the military forces. The Home Guard was created during the Second World War primarily to assist the military forces to counter a German invasion of the United Kingdom. The Civil Defence was then created primarily to assist the Civil departments and the police in reducing casualties and damage from air attack and in maintaining the daily life of the country. Now, however, invasion on a serious scale could not occur at the outbreak of a war and in consequence, during peacetime, Civil Defence has been given priority over the training of a Home Guard. There can be no doubt that military forces will have to take a large part in home defence but most exacting demands will also be made on the resources and personal efforts of the civilian population.

As noticed elsewhere democracy brings with it responsibility as well as privileges to a people. A nation which did not either prepare for or continue in its own defence might do so for a variety of reasons: it might not consider the price worth-while: it may think that its rulers or Government were corrupt and better swept away in any case: or the Government itself might in fact be a weak one and discontinue hostilities. Such a nation may not necessarily be merely effete but may be suffering from a disease liable to attack democracies where values may become devalued over the years and where the judgments of the despotic few may gain extraordinary currency. It is therefore more than ever important that public opinion should be preserved in a healthy condition rather than be allowed to suffer from either indifference or an ebullience not consonant with the political and military assessment of the international situation in peace or war.

Propaganda and the distribution of information were further factors of very great importance in home defence during the Second World War. The Ministry of Information did fine work in helping to maintain public and military morale by feeding the right kind of facts in the right way and at the right time to the public. Although it is impossible to evaluate this aspect of home defence in any measured terms, undoubtedly the distribution of information and propaganda would play a vital part in any future war.

v

While the civil aspect of home defence will be greatly increased, the importance of the various roles of the armed forces in home defence also grows. The armed forces must keep the enemy attack in manageable dimensions or the Civil Defence would not be able to begin to deal with their role of maintaining the daily life in one way or another. The armed forces must also be available as a reserve to help the Civil Defence in their duties.

Apart from keeping the enemy armed forces at arms length, the army, and especially the Territorial army, must be organized, equipped, trained and available as a reserve to assist the Civil Defence in any situation and measure in which they might become overwhelmed. They must also be available to support the police, and in the event of martial law, to control the country. It is important for the Government to face up to the full implications of a future war because in the event of serious attack by nuclear weapons, it seems inevitable that we would have to live, work and fight under martial law in which event the role of Civil Defence would be to support the military, a reversal from the commonly accepted situation of the army supporting the Civil Defence in normal times.

Likewise, the navy and again the naval reserve in particular, must be organized, equipped, trained and available to assist in working ports and in unloading ships. Primarily, the air force role in home defence is to reduce the scale of attack, by both offensive and defensive action.

As we will have both civil and military forces each playing dominant roles in home defence in consequence there is a vital need to have them properly co-ordinated. In future total war every agency of Government, national and local, would be engaged in the struggle for survival The peacetime planning for wartime exigency must be done by the Government departments who would be responsible for the efficient working of their part in the total war effort. Thus neither peacetime planning nor wartime control could be centralized under one man or department. In the United Kingdom, the organization of food supplies is the concern of the Ministry of Agriculture, and billeting, evacuation and water supplies the domain of the Minister of Housing. Nevertheless the very variety and complexity of the problems involved calls for a high degree of balanced co-ordination and consultation. The first task of the Ministry of Defence in peacetime, in connection with Home Defence, is to ensure that Service preparations for their wartime tasks are put in hand. Secondly, as Deputy Chairman of the Defence Committee, he must ensure that there is effective consultation between the various responsible civil Ministers, and in particular, to assist the Defence Committee and the Cabinet in deciding how to apportion expenditure.

This task of co-ordination is one of grave consequence in view of the fact that Civil Defence itself involves a great many civil departments which are not easily geared to any military authority in peacetime. It seems certain that a future total war would necessitate some form of martial law in the United Kingdom with the civil authorities conforming to the requirements of the military. In consequence, the peacetime planning for Home Defence should be co-ordinated by the Minister of Defence. The key to the situation is that there should be no question of the military chiefs being able to dictate to the political leaders in peace or in war. The Civil Defence authorities should also have as easy an access to the Minister of Defence as do the Military authorities.

CHAPTER XV

Conclusions

IT is proper to pause now and review our position in regard to war and strategy. Wars have always been considered very great evils which interrupt the otherwise even flow and development of political and sociological progress. The causes of war and the aftermath of war have been closely studied by historians in all their varying aspects but usually study of the actual course of war has been left to military writers. What many professional historians have overlooked is the fact that war is an inseparable part of political and social phenomena, and is itself yet another phase of human existence. Two important points stem from this truth.

First, Clausewitz may indeed have established the maintenance of aim as a primary factor; and in so doing have made concrete many other features of war which in his own day could become manifest and recognizable. But take his most famous pronouncement that 'war is the continuation of policy by other means', viz. by force, and consider it in the light of present-day conditions. Nothing would seem further from the truth in the event of nuclear warfare. Such a war, if wholly unleashed, would be the end of all policies and an utter mutual annihilation. This does not mean, with a turn of events apparently favourable to an aggressor, that nuclear war will not begin, though it throws the emphasis on cold, local and limited wars which may be properly regarded as a continuation of policy by other means. How then are we to meet either contingency?

Secondly, the paucity of non-partisan history of wars and the part played in them of all formations whether Allied, national or Service, materially affects the strategies which we can now formulate; a condition which in turn most materially affects the problem of how to meet both total and limited wars. If we have absorbed nothing from past lessons then our ability and our strategy to cover these two possibilities will remain antiquated and out-dated. History in all its aspects throughout war, political and military, holds some of the solutions, and suggests others, of our current difficulties.

The writing of history is often concerned with a purpose additional to recording the lessons of leadership, strategy, tactics and the administration of war. It also focuses and brings out in relief the glorious battles and deeds which inspire the pride, tradition and the heritage of nations and their armed forces. This aspect of history is concerned essentially with valour and depends to some extent on how the imagination of the people was stirred at the time of the event, and how the historian, literature and art deal with the subject. The fact that the direction of the action was good or bad, or whether the battle was won or lost is only incidental; indeed, not infrequently it is the hopeless odds of the action, such as in the 'Charge of the Light Brigade' which are most prominent amongst the glorious annals of the history.

The truths which history holds (in the military sense), are extremely difficult to determine owing to the vast interplay of factors of all kinds and the inevitable obscurity which enshrouds so much of the detail of war. But these are no warrant for abandoning the attempt to secure whatever guidance we can, since, as I have here tried to illustrate, so much depends on a clear view of the past and an unbiased approach to the future. The prime difficulty in the study of wars and military history is that every war is a new war. Every war has two tendencies of remarkable strength, one towards the past with its customs and usages and the other towards the future with its possibilities; and all problems in war from logistics to overall strategy are complicated by this polarity.

The development of strategy depends primarily on two factors: political and diplomatic considerations and the continued progress of science and technology. It should be noted that the latter factor while it is not controlled by political direction is exploited by it, and since in this context at least it affects military preparedness and military forces, it should be more aptly considered and more adequately dealt with separately.

From the first factor, political and diplomatic considerations, flow the various national aims and readiness, if need be, to exploit policy by war, and the alignments of the nations in their relationships of friend, foe or neutral in the international pattern. This involves too, the size and nature of the effort and resources given to military affairs and national preparedness, as well as to the geographical features with which the prospective belligerents have to contend, and the pattern of their home front and way of life in relation to war. It is conceivable for example, that the present picture of national alignments, of Soviet Russia and her satellites on the one hand and on the other of the Western free countries could be changed by political developments and thus necessitate a complete re-orientation of our respective strategies.

Nevertheless, there seems little change in the Russian policy of ultimate world domination, though there are tactical changes which wax and wane from time to time. Strategically, however, there can be no doubt of the influence on Russian policy created by the existence of NATO and the deterrent of nuclear weapons. Western unity in the military as well as the political sense has ensured a pause in the Russian pursuit of her policy. Yet we cannot be unaware that this may be, not a change of policy, but simply a prelude to a change of direction and the development of a new technique designed to achieve the same or similar end. It is particularly ominous that, at a time of dramatic increases in Russian military power, this switch was followed by a series of brilliant executive Soviet political, diplomatic and economic manœuvres. Already the European free countries are being tempted to lower the NATO guard whilst at the same time the United States, more remote and therefore more realistic, are becoming more and more disturbed as to how to continue to keep world peace against the greatly increasing Soviet threat. One of the biggest dangers to the security of the free countries is the inherent tendency to tire of defence preparations over long periods of peace, and to drop their guard too readily when potential aggressors make gestures of peace, however insincere. In this respect the religious conflicts of history hold a very practical lesson for our age: repeatedly and after long years of relaxation fanaticism has revived and scored easy victories over opponents whose memories of aggression and aggressors have proved too short.

The alignment of nations into alliances and opponents certainly has much to do with setting the pattern of strategy. In this regard, a most important factor in keeping our strategy and concepts of war abreast of developments is the use of political and military intelligence. Indeed, the need for good intelligence in modern war is even greater than ever before. Modern armed forces, of immense strength — though not necessarily numerical — compared with former times, which require a very considerable part of the national potential to produce, may be decisive or wasted, depending as they do on intelligence. This will be more than ever true in the future. The last war found our High Command still geared to a concept that the primary requirement was information concerning battle in the field or at sea. Today, the first requirement from intelligence is the peacetime size of the enemy's atomic and hydrogen stockpiles and of his basic war potential. It is no longer sufficient to know the orders of battle and the current output of the army war potential. We must know, not only his peacetime reserves and expansion capacity of modern weapons, but also his progress in science. We must know as much as possible about the enemy's plans, intentions and decision to make war, and we must have a warning system which gives us the maximum notice and information about the imminence of attack. This is critically important for the strategic air forces, for NATO and for our air and maritime defences in general. It is important to develop the Western early warning system from the North Cape to the Bosphorus and North Africa, to enable SHAPE and the United Kingdom to obtain the earliest possible warning of impending attack for the strategic bombers and air and civil defences. Likewise, America must have an efficient warning system. Great value will also be obtained by linking the European early warning system with that of northern America, particularly so that the several hours difference in flying times from the Russian bases to the various Allied bases in these two regions would help to defeat any attempt to make simultaneous attacks throughout the vital strategic areas of the Allies. Much has been done since the last war to tidy up our intelligence services, though there is still too much of the separate naval, army and air force approach to suit the case of each Service. Inter-Service rivalry in intelligence and competition in scientific research still continues.

In previous times wars fought between governments by professional armies were deliberate acts of policy and within limits their extent and strategy were kept within control. Since 1914, owing to the rise of nationalism and the vast development of technical ability and then later of ideological fanaticism, wars have become more and more struggles between peoples whose countries have been caught up in a chain of reaction which drives them deeper and deeper into events which they cannot control. Wars have indeed become conflicts whose devastation affects the whole peoples of both victor and vanquished and extends even to the rest of the world, and reaches beyond the policy of any government. Today technological advance seems to have gone so far that it is now beginning to turn the conduct and nature of war full circle so that fear of the hydrogen weapon is putting a brake on the chain reaction of aggression and strategy and the peoples themselves are forcing their governments to get war and its strategy into a proper perspective.

In the past the non-aggressor made the deliberate choice to submit or go to war in order to avoid what was considered a greater evil than war itself. In the future the decision to submit or resist is of greater complexity, so vast are the consequences of total war. Herein lies scope for the aggressor to bluff or blackmail the non-aggressor to limits unthought of in previous generations. What then is our own position in relation to the possibilities of this kind of blackmail? Today we have announced ourselves as non-aggressors and have provided a bulwark or deterrent against aggression in the forms of NATO, SHAPE and SEATO and the ultimate sanction of the strategic employment of nuclear weapons. We have also announced that we are prepared to use these strategic assets and to further all means to ensure that they are completely effective against aggression. This means that no doubt must exist in the minds of our political and military leaders as to the point where we call the aggressor's bluff — or where he intentionally or otherwise calls ours.

The political changes over the last three centuries, like the military and strategic changes, have drawn the interest and concern of all the people in nations, as distinct perhaps from a ruling caste, into an active participation in their own and the national fate. Democracy has imposed on us responsibility as well as advantage: an inescapable truth. A people's loyalty to their soveriegn state and their preparedness for war and to defend their state springs from many sources, some of which are deep down in human nature. The strength of loyalty is drawn not only from the consequence of external conditioning, recent traditions and daily environment, but also from a fear of a loss of identity through submission in a standardized society, nameless, immense, impersonal and unfriendly.

It has been suggested that an alternative to the eternal conflict between aggressors and non-aggressors would be a world authority in which is vested absolute control of all instruments of war. All individual nations would have to give up their respective armed forces as separate identities and thus no single nation, or group of nations, would be able either to abet or defy the decrees of the world authority. Obviously, such an organization would be radically different from that of the United Nations which itself has no military forces other than those allocations of contingents made by the various nations. From such a paramount military power all other power would flow: including the power to level national standards of living and the power to move whole populations, or the power to change the way of life or even the religion of any nation.

Apart altogether from the immense ethnological, ideological and religious difficulties which such an idea presents immediately to the mind, the real crux of such a world authority is who would be its leaders because there would be no going back once the sovereign nations had surrendered military power. It is highly unlikely that we could ensure that it would be democratic (by consent) and not a totalitarian (by compulsion) authority.

As a corollary to the great activity often manifested at home, international political policy is handled by a diplomatic machinery which is designed to guard jealously national interests and long term aspects, and is actuated by extreme caution and a care to dot every *i* and cross every *t*. In consequence, throughout history it has been difficult to adjust the tempo of this machinery to the international demands of war.

The interpretation of the *will* of the people to accept and prosecute war and the platform from which it is inspired to greater heights must reside with the political leaders of a nation. The Military leaders are the agents of the Political leaders in directing the military forces they make available for the fulfilment of their object or requirements. Although this allocation of responsibility has always been true, sometimes in the past the Political and Military leadership have merged into one. It is difficult, however, to visualize such a coalescence within the great democratic countries of today where in modern total war, for example, even greater problems lie in the Home front than in any purely military operations. Moreover the Political leaders must direct the national economy and counter the enemy national economy upon which the very strengths of the armed forces depend.

The distinction is no longer clear where the responsibility of Political Direction ceases and that of the Military High Command begins: a division of responsibility sought after by Moltke. This, like the transformation of the Home front into a battle front, particularly in the case of the United Kingdom, illustrates how far we have travelled from conventional concepts. In regard to Britain's national strategy it is well to realize that compartments and divisions of responsibility are artificial and created for convenience and expediency. But the current error is that so many people confuse the relative importance of the parts with the paramount importance of the whole, the sense of 'oneness' among the Service Ministries and the Ministry of Defence is seriously lacking. Unless an improvement in this sphere comes about our national strategy is likely to suffer and the strategies of the three separate Services remain hidebound and stale however well-meaning they may be.

The partisan Service opinions and views vary from agreement, or near agreement, through varying shades and angles to violent opposition. As often as not there is no real national or Services justification for these differences; they are often on minor or even personal matters. The individual point of view arises from a complex of factors such as upbringing, traditions and customs, associations, patriotism, intelligence, character, self-interest, and the desire for a leisurely life or the lure of thrust and ambition. The Service point of view is especially strong. The usages and traditions within each Service are so strong that often they permanently mould the individual point of view. Perhaps this is not surprising since the individual's whole outlook and career depend all too much on the acceptance of this kind of dogma. Thus the undercurrent of the personal point of view, which in turn works and permeates the whole Service structure, is influenced by the special tenets of each Service. Too often an original point of view is condemned or rejected because it is an innovation which does not conform to current Service interest. Advancement depends very largely on the individual being credited with the point of view fashionable to the promoting and appointing authority of his Service at the time. Apart from exceptional cases, ability at the inter-Service level does not influence promotion in the same way as ability at the Service level. This factor is even more pronounced when it comes to an inter-Allied level, for we have not yet reached the stage where much advancement comes to individuals who depart from their own partisan national concepts and Service dogma; views which, as we have seen, are too often determined by vested interests. Certainly, the United States' points of view are often difficult to resolve in Allied strategy because they are more apt than the British to allow their pressure groups and their Service loyalties to over-ride the merits of the case. It is important for the United Kingdom to recognize that the Americans are so handicapped.

In the United Kingdom, recent changes have been made in the Ministry of Defence to give the Minister greater power over the Service Ministries in allocating the national resources to the military departments and to civil defence in accordance with Defence Committee policy. A whole-time chairman has also been appointed as a fourth and non-partisan party to the Chiefs of Staff Committee, similar to the organization in the United States. To make these changes successful, it is important that this fourth person is not only non-partisan but also an effective chairman and not one who merely accepts the briefs of the three Chiefs of Staff who in turn get their briefs from their own Ministries based on their own Service interests. We have yet to see how effective this new arrangement will be.

So far as High Command in the field is concerned the Second World War raised the international joint operational problems to a level never known before and no longer to be evaded by arrangements dependent on liaison. To meet these operations to which vast Allied and inter-Allied forces of all Services contributed, and into which difficult personalities with diverse views and methods had to be fitted, numerous different High Command organizations resulted according to the particular circumstances and the influence of the individual commanders concerned. None of these organizations was a model of perfection, but we must be careful not to overlook the special needs of the time. Nevertheless, one lesson which cannot be questioned is the need to study beforehand the difficulties and complications of High Command organizations concerned in joint operations; particularly in Allied joint operations.

II

From the second factor influencing strategy, the technical one, on which the development of strategy depends, flow the weapons of war. For example, the whole range of weapon development over the years such as the invention of gunpowder, breech-loading weapons, machine-guns, tanks, iron and steamships, submarines, aircraft and electronics, is the result of the progress in science and technology; and their effects on strategy are indisputable. It seems certain that future developments will bring even bigger changes than in the past. It is helpful in getting a perspective of these advances to consider that only fifty years ago few people believed in the practicability of human flight; and certainly no one dared to predict supersonic speeds or that aviation would come to dominate military affairs to the extent that it has done. Only a century-and-a-half ago people could not have believed the effect steam power would have on our prosperity and our way of life, still less its very great influence on strategy and war. Today these scientific and technological changes lie behind us.

National strategy and the requirements of our armed forces are greatly complicated in that they have to be able to deal with cold, local and limited war as well as total war. The actual basic priorities between the military requirements for total war and for cold, local and limited war may vary with changing international and political situations. Because of the complications there is more than one opinion as to what the priorities should be today. So far as the three British military Services are concerned, the analysis of national strategy given in this work, indicates that their size and shape should be planned: (a) first and foremost, as a deterrent to total war; (b) secondly, to meet our NATO obligations and so stabilize politically and militarily the free countries of Western Europe against any cold war threat or encroachment; (c) thirdly, to meet cold and local war threats to the free countries throughout the other parts of the world; (*d*) fourthly, to prosecute total war at short notice should the deterrent fail; (*e*) lastly, to prosecute a limited war.

A further important and outstanding change required in the structures of the three Services results from the need of a new concept of war readiness, not only for total war but for cold and local war also. It is evident that nowadays our safety must stand or fall by the strength and efficacy of our peacetime forces, and as already noticed changes are needed in the relationship and roles of the regular and non-regular forces; in the relationship of front line, second line and reserve forces and equipments; and in peace and war production, and training organizations as well as changes in our old ideas of mobilization.

Changes will also have to be made in the procedure and to some extent in the structure of the Political Direction for it is responsible for the use of nuclear weapons which would have devastating results, but which could have great repercussions on our Allies and on public and world opinion. Furthermore, with limited resources for stockpiles of guided missiles, together with very extensive home defence problems including food, fuel, transport, public utilities, production, public morale and indeed our very existence, there will be the need for the closest co-ordination of the High Command policy, plans and operations, not only with our own Ministries, but also with our Allies. In the United Kingdom, Whitehall will certainly require and demand more control over the direction of military plans and operations than in the past. Because of their impact on the national life and the war potential, the present new weapons will result in the Political Direction seeking more control than previously on strategy and over the military chiefs; and this in turn will mean that the Chiefs of Staff will have a closer link with Allied Chiefs and a more stringent grip on their own Commanders-in-Chief. On the other hand, the new weapons bring new scope for commanders to develop and apply tactics which can overwhelm the enemy.

A general awareness of the common problems of the three Services should come from the grave necessity of having and developing these new weapons and the possibility of going to war with them. Intelligence, early warning, identification of enemy attackers and reconnaissance in its broadest sense relating to both strategy and tactics, are

R

all of the first importance. So too, the three Services must develop counter-measures to hinder the enemy offensive and defensive to the maximum extent. Indeed the efficacy of our new weapons might well depend on such counter-measures. Lastly, the High Command must ensure that they co-ordinate the three Services with the scientific advisors at every level because any future war will be increasingly scientific and major decisions to re-equip our forces far more critical than ever before.

It is only a matter of time before the new unconventional weapons of today become the conventional armaments of tomorrow, and the distinction between conventional and atomic tactical weapons is already becoming blurred. The Western nations must take the cost of armaments seriously. Otherwise, not only is there an endless vista of crippling expenditure ahead, and the Western public opinion will not sustain such a policy indefinitely. A reduction of expenditure on conventional weapons, as the hydrogen stockpile grows, may be forced on us.

Great progress still remains ahead in aeronautics; nuclear physics are only at the fringe of discovery and application; chemical and biological weapons, though seldom mentioned publicly, hold tremendous potentialities and are probably more suited for war with countries of the geographical nature of China than nuclear weapons. Our knowledge of gravity and its control is still largely unexplored; and the tremendous development of astronautics will most probably be closely analogous to what in fact has happened in aeronautics, each step leading to numerous further steps so that today's fantastic forecasts will become actual achievements. Who knows, inter-stellar rockets have so many possibilities that they may bring all nations on earth into alliance against some outer common enemy. At this stage it would be futile to try and predict the influence of this inter-stellar communication on our strategy. Certainly, the Great Powers would be very disturbed if a potential aggressor was first to succeed with space satellites carrying devices which could be monitored from the earth.

III

The basis of Allied strategy must surely lie first in a unity of interest and purpose arising from a consciousness that the common danger is so strong, so imminent and diverse, that none may stand alone. From this basis national differences and jealousies have to be smoothed out with a sensitive concern for the strength to be derived from national sovereignties and a true assessment of more narrow nationalities. Any aspect of nationality from which strength, rather than weakness, can be drawn must be utilized. The forces at the disposal of such Allied strategy may not be integrated in so simple a manner as lumping them together: their best use should be thought out in terms of their function. It is most important to avoid overlapping and duplication of effort, and a good example of this is the complementary nature of the United States Strategic Air Command, the British Bomber Command and the Allied navies. There are many problems the solutions of which do not present themselves so readily; and the first requisite to their solution is a certain resilience of mind in the Political and Military leaders as well as a spirit of adaptability in the individual Services and commands.

We have mentioned that there is divided opinion as to the basic priorities of our national strategy. Clearly it is much more difficult to reconcile opinion among the Allied countries on Allied strategy, not only in formulating the basic priorities but also in implementing them. For example, the United States' contribution to the deterrent force so far outweighs our own that we can rely on the United States to provide the overall deterrent, our own contribution being confined to some national aspect of the deterrent. On the other hand, NATO strategy and the air defence of the United Kingdom is so much more intimate and critical that we are liable to give it greater emphasis than the United States; certainly in the shorter term policy. Again, the British Commonwealth has so many more overseas interests and possessions than the United States that we might well find ourselves in a critical situation without allies, and so it would be understandable if we gave more emphasis to some of these areas. With the problems of prosecuting total war should the deterrent fail, we must expect wide differences between British and American strategic opinion, if for no other reason than the striking variation in the vulnerability of the United Kingdom and America to modern attack; there are even critical Allied differences about the degree of vulnerability of the respective countries.

Many national interests therefore have to be submerged in the formulation of Allied combined strategy. The following live issue is one apt illustration. There is at present strong pressure on the continent and in the United States for the air defences of the United Kingdom to be pooled in one organization with those of the continental NATO countries. The argument is that the air defence of Western Europe is one problem and greater effectiveness would be achieved by having a single air defence under one central command. The British, however, challenge this argument; for one thing they have the illustration of the Battle of Britain clearly in mind. In this instance, had the Allied air defences been pooled for the Second World War, it is certain that they would have been expended, critically, during the fall of France and the overthrow of our Expeditionary Force and thus the Battle of Britain, which led to final victory, would have been lost.

In assessing lessons from the past, it is important to apply any new factors which have appeared; in this instance, the effect on the problem of nuclear weapons. There is still a strong case even under modern conditions to treat the air defence of the United Kingdom separately from the Continent of Western Europe. In contrast to our continental air bases, those in Great Britain, for many years to come at least, will have an important significance in the strategy of the United States Strategic Air Command, both in respect of a deterrent and in the actual fighting of any total war. Thus, the special importance of the security of Great Britain is emphasized.

Clearly, our Allied strategy cannot yet be formulated without prejudice and compromise because that would require agreed Allied political policies in all affairs that impinge on international strategy. Nevertheless, it is to be hoped that, more and more, we may reach the ideal in the course of time and perhaps one day even reach the realization of a united or federated supreme government for the free world.

What has been described here as strategic priorities is really another way of stating those factors which take the place of those so-called principles which were used to indicate where advantage lay in war. Enough has been said to suggest how far the so-called Principles of War are inadequate to describe current needs and what are present-day advantages. But if the only thing to emerge from this study was the principle of change that in itself would justify, not only a review of our present strategic resources, but a much-needed resilience in our approach to strategy itself. The effect of this truism, the principle of change, is all too apt to be lost on us because it is universal, affecting all things and therefore holding no particular lesson, or alternatively, holding as many lessons as there are people; a condition equally nugatory.

In the light of this principle of change, what emerges that is permanent? What unchanging feature in the swirling fog of war can strategy use? In general, strategical concepts have fallen behind the growth of war during times of peace, awaiting the beginning of a new war for a fresh impetus. At the end of each war ideas of strategic advantage have lapsed or eased with the occupation of enemy territory, to be followed at some later date by a peace treaty and withdrawal. This is consistent with a suggestion in an earlier chapter of this book that war and strategy have a parallel but not a simultaneous development. From the end of one war to the beginning of another, nations have always sought the strategic advantage, but they have sought it, up to the present at least, in terms of what has gone before and rarely in terms of current war-possibilities as exemplified for example in new weapons. The events of the two decades before 1939 amply illustrate this and the subsequent six years of war showed the rapid strides strategy was compelled to take. But some of the most interesting developments have taken place in the post-war decade.

In many countries, our own included, economies have approached a wartime footing and international events have given the search for strategical advantage an unprecedented boost. This on the face of it must give rise to a certain optimism, and indeed many do suggest that we have, strategically, over-reached total war. A certain amount of justification for this view lies in the deterrent power of nuclear weapons, and in the possibility that the Russians may have missed the tide of strategic development and have arrived on the scene just too late to conquer the world by conventional force before the advent of the hydrogen weapon made a general world conflict apparently so impracticable. The new and essential point about Allied strategy is that, for the first time in modern history, the defending powers are virtually as strong, and as ready, as the potential aggressors; a great and overwhelming factor in the principle of the deterrent.

It is, however, this spur of Russian expansion, the most potent threat of world domination in history, which is forcing further and further scientific discoveries, particularly in the field of nuclear weapons and ballistic rockets. Paradoxically, the Western obsession with all-out nuclear war may result in paralysing the power of the West to deal with local situations of peril where we may have the sledgehammer but all too few genuine nut-crackers for small though dangerous conflicts. Nevertheless the new concept and threat of cold war and subversion has initiated unparalleled expenditure of money and resources hitherto confined to periods of actual war. The fact that this spur is likely to continue is not the only thing which will upset any complacency into which we may be tempted to fall. Throughout history the development of weapons has invariably resulted in wars leaving behind them more and more problems seemingly as intractable as those they were fought to resolve; and today, the aftermath problems of war threaten to be disastrous to all concerned. Herein lies the challenge to present-day strategy; and the adage that winning a war is not just forcing the enemy to lay down his arms, but in creating world conditions more favourable to oneself than could have been brought about if there had not been a war, has today a renewed and demanding significance. The changes in war which have overtaken us call for continual adjustment and constant vigilance, and not least in the realm of strategy. Nuclear weapons, the alignment of communist and non-communist, nationalist and internationalist forces, the new forms of cold and local war and the possible form of total war, the treatment of prisoners, the trials of war criminals, all these make for a great review of the whole range of international laws, codes and customs.

But changes are of many kinds, some are voluntary, others are compulsory; and the process of events which has brought us to where we are at present was a mixture of voluntary and compulsory change; a mixture which has extended throughout all fields of political, social and economic as well as military activity. The most impressive thing about present day strategic assets is of course the deterrent power of the hydrogen weapon which by its very determinateness has created an entirely new concept, or at least modified an old one, that the line of maximum penetration is no longer a geographical contour but a line in events. It is conceivable that this deterrent power could change or its use be abandoned but it does not comprise the whole of the deterrent. The Political and Military powers of NATO also make part of the deterrent and this organization is itself a startling innovation from a strategic point of view.

In no sense is this essay an appeal for change for its own sake but rather an appeal for the awareness of change, in war, in weapons, in strategy and the motives for and in war. All this involves a change in ideas of strategy at all levels; and the changes we have experienced in the last ten years are to some extent the measure of expediency. NATO for example is an expedient, a good one it should be noted, and one which is serving its purpose remarkably well. But only when the principle of NATO is wholly accepted, not only in Western Europe, but in other vulnerable areas of the globe, and Political and Military organization evolves capable of meeting the prime threat anywhere on the globe, can we feel that a great step forward has been made in global strategy with the establishment of an Allied strategy.

Our history is filled with examples of advantageous expedient but now we may not 'muddle along' taking whatever fortune chooses to give us. The political changes in the East, and especially in the Middle East, which have altered the British strategic position in that region, are a good illustration of this point. While the deterrent concept demands the resolution of Allied strategy it in turn demands of each nation within its influence, ourselves included, a strong national strategy. This last will take a long time to resolve unless the Services take a large view, not merely submitting to necessary change but endorsing it with strategical concepts which subserve the national interest. The strategy of the home front as a possible battle front is another essential which will demand very great resilience, not only from the nation as a whole, but from the Services in whatever function they have to perform in respect of its security.

Thus, the Services also can no longer rely on the brilliant expedient; there is no time. Forces and weapons cannot be easily adapted for roles which are no longer traditional; these new roles and their difficulties must be thought out and resolved as far as possible. It is the function and not the Service which matters today; and this essential emerges most clearly of all considerations. Nothing therefore should be allowed to stand in the way of a complete understanding of the jobs to be done, how they are to be done and who are to do them; this should form the basis of a sound Service strategy.

The somewhat ominous pause which the deterrent has given to world war should itself free us of the illusion that man has at last got war in hand. It is precisely at moments like this in history when a strong strategic vision is most needed, because so much is involved. We must certainly develop this new approach to strategy if we are not to be, in a few years perhaps, either annihilated or trying vainly to adjust a strategic rationale to a fresh cataclysmic situation called total war.

INDEX

INDEX